WILLIAM N. YEOMANS, an MBA from Cornell, has over twenty-five years of
corporate management experience, including twelve years as corporate director of human resource development at JC Penney, where his leadership
in developing managers played a major role in Penney's repositioning. For
the past ten years he has headed his own management consulting firm. Mr.
Yeomans is the author of a number of books, including the bestselling
1,000 Things You Never Learned in Business School. His articles have appeared in the *New York Times, Glamour, Cosmopolitan, Mademoiselle,* and
other major publications. He lives with his family in New Jersey.

7 SURVIVAL SKILLS FOR A REENGINEERED WORLD

William N. Yeomans

A PLUME BOOK

PLUME
Published by the Penguin Group
Penguin Putnam Inc., 375 Hudson Street, New York, New York 10014, U.S.A.
Penguin Books Ltd, 27 Wrights Lane, London W8 5TZ, England
Penguin Books Australia Ltd, Ringwood, Victoria, Australia
Penguin Books Canada Ltd, 10 Alcorn Avenue, Toronto, Ontario, Canada M4V 3B2
Penguin Books (N.Z.) Ltd, 182–190 Wairau Road, Auckland 10, New Zealand

Penguin Books Ltd, Registered Offices:
Harmondsworth, Middlesex, England

Published by Plume, an imprint of Dutton NAL,
a member of Penguin Putnam Inc.
Previously published in a Dutton edition.

First Plume Printing, June, 1998
10 9 8 7 6 5 4 3 2 1

℗ REGISTERED TRADEMARK—MARCA REGISTRADA

The Library of Congress Cataloged the Dutton edition as follows:
Yeomans, William N.
    7 survival skills for a reengineered world / William N. Yeomans.
        p.   cm.
    Includes bibliographical references.
    ISBN 0-525-94233-5 (hc.)
         0-452-27490-7 (pbk.)
    1. Vocational guidance. 2. Interpersonal communication. 3. Interpersonal relations.
4. Self-management (Psychology)
I. Title
HF5381.Y468   1996   IN PROCESS (.A2-Z)
650.1'3—dc20   96-19398
                                                        CIP

Original hardcover design by Eve L. Kirch
Printed in the United States of America

To Kay, whose candor and caring make all things possible,

and

To Anne, who began it all and kept me on course.

Contents

PART
I

CAREER
SKILLS

1

INTRODUCTION

Skills for a Reengineered World

"Organizations need fewer and fewer of better and better people." —Michael Hammer, reengineering expert

Alan: *"Hey, Mark, how goes it?"*
Mark: *"Oh, man! I just got laid off. Twenty-two years with the company and I'm out."*
Alan: *"So, how's everything else?"*

Okay, how are things going at work? I can hear the groans from here—and no wonder. You've been downsized, reengineered, outsourced, delayered, right-sized, empowered, TQM'd, one-minute-managed, and customer-focused. What now?

You are smack in the middle of the fastest changing work environment since Henry Ford cranked up the assembly line. Employers that used to welcome you into their family now boot you out the door. Promotional ladders have turned into footstools. Bosses who used to guide your career are working full-time saving their own. That annual increase now comes around with the frequency of Halley's comet, and you're doing the work of two or three people because there's nobody else left to do it.

Welcome to what President Clinton's secretary of labor, Robert Reich, calls the "anxious class"—all of us who can't count on having a job next year and who see our income losing ground to inflation.

You are in a new world of work—rules have changed and answers are not always clear. But you can count on this: You need to be more highly skilled today than ever before if you want to find personal fulfillment in the new workplace.

How This Book Can Help

7 *Survival Skills for a Reengineered World* will help you take charge of your own career and your life. It will assist you in developing the skills you need to survive and to succeed on the job and, if there is no longer a job, to get on with your life.

Back in the 1980s, I wrote a book called *1,000 Things You Never Learned in Business School.* At the time I was working with managers and professionals in a wide variety of companies, and it became apparent to me that many knew finance and marketing, operations and distribution—the business disciplines—but something was lacking: the down-in-the-dirt skills needed to work within an organization, skills like managing your boss, communicating, problem solving, listening, and getting things done in meetings.

I saw people who had mastered one or more of those skills use them wonderfully to their advantage, and I saw other people who had great potential held back because they had not gained command of a few key abilities.

So I wrote the book, sort of an "MBA of everything else"—all those real-world, essential on-the-job skills that were not taught in business schools.

A decade later, I realized that the book needed to be revised to reflect the massive changes and turmoil that have entered the career picture. It contains skill training that is timeless and is as valid now as the day it hit the bookstores. But when it was published, no one had heard of downsizing or reengineering or empowerment, political correctness, or even much about quality. So I began writing what I thought would be an update—and ended up with quite a different book. The world has changed that much.

7 *Survival Skills for a Reengineered World* will help you meet that new world head-on by mastering key skills that are essential to success on the job but are still not taught in most business schools (although many schools are trying hard to catch up). They are skills you could learn through trial and error on the job, but that would take years. Some are skills you could improve by attending seminars, but how many workshops can you go to each year? With this book, you can read about them and then practice them on the job, correcting mistakes as you go, until you perfect them. Here are the seven skills:

1. *Career Skills.* These include taking charge of your career and your life, making the new relationship between you and your employer work for you, and designing career strategies and action plans.
2. *Endurance Skills.* A neat package of skills you can't be without today, including using stress to help you through times of change and turmoil, dealing with the latest management fad, making time work for you, controlling nonwork factors that can make or break your career, and exploring alternative and nontraditional careers.
3. *Communication Skills.* Skills in this area are of high concern to employers today because many people lack them. This section covers using the power of speaking and writing and listening to increase your value to your employer and your marketability in the outside world.
4. *Follower Skills.* You may not have thought much about it, but there are skills to being a subordinate, especially in today's flattened organizations. They include taking 51 percent charge of the relationship with your boss; influencing your boss; building a better relationship with your boss; and communicating with your boss about your goals, your performance, and your career.
5. *Leadership Skills.* These are skills you need to be an effective leader in this age of reduced loyalty and increased anxiety, including training and developing your people, giving feedback, coaching, and motivating—all difficult to do in times of rapid change. These are important skills to know even if you don't supervise other people.
6. *Team Skills.* Teams are the way of life today, and you have to know how to lead them and how to function as a member. Skills include building a great team, getting things done in meetings, and unleashing group creativity to solve problems.
7. *Customer Skills.* The customer is king, in case you haven't heard. Skills covered in this section include influencing customers, building relationships with customers, and collaborating with customers in a spirit of teamwork.

Each of these skill areas will help you get reward and satisfaction out of what you are doing and give you an optimistic outlook on the future. They will enable you to take charge of your own career and your own life. As you develop your skills, you'll increase your value to your employer (and other potential employers), and increase your value to yourself.

How to Use This Book

Here are some things you should know about 7 *Survival Skills for a Reengineered World*:

1. The skills you will read about in this book will give you an edge in today's turbulent world of work, will help you add value. They will not guarantee you a lifetime career with your present employer, because people today are outplaced for many reasons—a lot of which have nothing to do with performance. But the skills will make you more *employable*—and that can be a lifesaver today.
2. If you are looking for an inspirational book, this isn't it. If reading it gets you all fired up, fine, but that's not what it is intended to do. What this book tries to do is help you build practical skills that will help you over time. Many of today's business books attempt to distill the "secrets" of success into a few simple principles that are presented in sweeping grandeur, without much detail. This book is built on actual skill development and the step by step methods you have to use to improve.
3. This is a book about work, but much of what is contained here will help you in your private life as well. Giving a presentation to a town commission? Running a meeting for a church group? Managing a Little League team? Trying to motivate a teenager? All these skills are here, and they will help you.
4. The guidance in this book will work best for you if you stop thinking about what "they" are doing to you or what "they" will allow and concentrate on those things you can control—when you think about it, there are a lot of them. Start with what is possible, what you can do, and don't get discouraged because you can't control the whole company.
5. Each area contains a "Single Best Idea" (SBI). If you don't do anything else, put the SBI to work for you.

Determining Priorities

Now you're ready to begin. But you can't expect to read through this book and be ready to go out and improve all seven skills at once—that would be like trying to find your way around the Internet in one sitting. The Priorities Chart will help you determine where you need the most help and what is most important to your job. Complete the chart—it will take only a few minutes—and decide which areas you need to concentrate on most. As you read through the book, you'll want to spend extra time on those areas.

How to Use the Priorities Chart

The skill areas covered in this book are listed on the left-hand side of the chart, and alongside each is a rating scale, "How Well You Do." As you consider each skill, circle the statement that best describes your level of skill. Go down the list and make your choices now. When you are done, go back and look at where your circles are.

The next column is headed "Importance to Your Career." This will help you determine how much it would help your career if you made major improvements in each of the skills. Rate each High, Medium, or Low.

Next, on the right, is the "Priority" column. Here you are going to have to make some choices. Everything can't be a number-one priority. For each skill, consider how well you do it and its importance to your career. Then start setting priorities. Those skills that you do "Not Well" and that have high importance to your career should be your highest priorities, because these offer the best opportunities for giant leaps and big payoffs. Those that you do "Very Well" and are of low importance to your career should be your lowest priorities.

Since all these skills are essential in some degree or another to your success and survival, you should work your way through all of them, even those of low priority—and even those in which you are expert—because you can always pick up a pointer here or a shortcut there, and help yourself improve.

PRIORITIES CHART

Skill Area		How Well You Do			Importance to Your Career: High, Medium, or Low	Priority
		Very Well	Okay	Not Well		
Career Skills	Setting priorities for skill development (chapter 1)	Know where I need to learn and grow	Have some idea	Not a clue	——	——
	Preparing for change (chapter 2)	I'm ready for anything	Maybe I could get by	Scared to death	——	——
Endurance Skills	Making stress work for you (chapter 3)	Stress energizes me	Sometimes tense and worried	Shake and sweat	——	——
	Dealing with management fads (chapter 4)	They work for me	Somewhat confused	What's empowerment anyhow?	——	——
	Making time work for you (chapter 5)	On top of everything	Have too much to do	Swimming up Niagara	——	——
	Political correctness (chapter 6)	Always discreet	Stumble sometimes	Want to see my etchings?	——	——

	Exploring nontraditional careers (chapter 7)	Know a lot about alternative careers	Have considered	Never thought about it		
Communication Skills	Speaking, writing (chapter 8)	Gifted; the words flow	Get my point across	Struggle and stutter	—	—
	Listening (chapter 9)	Listen like a hawk	Sometimes attention wanders	What did you say?	—	—
Follower Skills	Working with the boss (chapter 10)	Have great relationship	Work well sometimes	Impossible	—	—
	Communicating with the boss (chapter 11)	Open and clear	Get through now and then	Conversations with a pit bull	—	—
Leader Skills	Leading (chapter 12)	Great leader	Pretty good	Autocrat	—	—
	Motivating people (chapter 13)	They are all juiced up	Some are turned on	Comatose	—	—
	Giving feedback (chapter 14)	Clear and effective	Sometimes get understanding	Everybody gets mad	—	—
Team Skills	Building a team (chapter 15)	Ara Parsegian would be impressed	Playing .500 at best	Off in all directions	—	—

(Continued on next page)

Customer Skills				
Getting things done in meetings (chapter 16)	Always get results	Sometimes wander and waste time	Mosh pits	—
Creative problem solving (chapter 17)	We get new ideas that work	Occasionally hit on something new	Kill off ideas as they come up	—
Collaborating with customers (chapter 18)	Mostly win-win	Win some, lose some	At each other's throats	—
Building relationships (chapter 19)	Customers are like family	Good with some, not so good with others	Customers are an annoyance	—

How to Learn and Grow

Maybe at this point you're thinking, "I don't have time to do everything I have to do now, how am I going to learn all this stuff?" Here's how.

1. Have the will to improve. The achievers of this world learn, and if you don't, you are going to be far behind. There are always lots of reasons why you can't do something—and many people who are anxious to remind you of them. But today you have to learn; there is no other option.

2. Make a plan. Reading a book is fine; thinking you are really going to do what the book says is okay, too, but it is no substitute for action.

As you work your way through the Priority Chart and begin to tackle each priority, make a plan of specific actions you will take. "Improve customer service" is a nice thought, but it isn't specific enough to guide you. List actual steps you will take, using action verbs. Put in completion dates. For example:

1. Meet with four customers in the next month to get their views on how to improve service.
2. Practice listening skills with customers. In the next month, get customers to talk for five minutes before making a sales pitch. Paraphrase and repeat back to customers what they say.
3. Meet with your most difficult customer next week and find a common ground of agreement to move toward a cooperative relationship.
4. When customers call with complaints or problems, practice saying, "I'm glad you brought that to my attention."

3. Discipline yourself. Stick to your plan, even when you don't feel like it, which will be most of the time. There are lots of things you do at work you don't like to do, like firing nice people or calling customers who are going to yell at you or cozying up to the boss once in a while. You do them because you know you have to. The same with learning—you have to.

4. Learn by doing. Reading a book like this is one thing—it can be interesting and fun. You say to yourself, "I never thought of that before—that's good stuff," and tomorrow it is gone, flown out beyond cyberspace. Discipline yourself to use what you learn as soon as possible on the job. Practice it, do it as often as possible, critique yourself, and try again.

It helps to perfect a skill if you read about it just before you have a chance to use it. If giving presentations comes up as high priority, but you won't be giving one for six months, you might want to put off reading that section for a while. Then, in a month or two, go back to the chapter and get to work. Using the skill in a live situation is the best way to learn it.

5. Reward yourself for small successes, even if no one else does. When you do something better than you did it the last time, break out a bottle of your favorite designer water and toast your success.

6. Get feedback. Tell people you trust you are trying to improve a skill and ask them to let you know candidly how you are doing.

Now you can get going. I hope you enjoy *7 Survival Skills for a Reengineered World* and that it will help you get more satisfaction out of your career and your life.

> **SBI:** The **Single Best Idea** is this: To survive and succeed today, you need a number of key skills. This book will help you develop them.

2

CAREER PLANNING AND OTHER OXYMORONS

How to Take Charge of Your Career and Your Life

"Where am I going? What am I doing? What is the meaning of life?" —Snoopy, 2/9/75

"Some of them [my subordinates] just want career counseling, which you can do in five or ten minutes."
—Vice president, Kodak, as quoted in *Fortune*, 4/10/89

What does your future look like? Chances are you don't have too much confidence in the years ahead, and no clue as to what will happen to you. Probably you like what you do on the job now. Most people do. But you may not like all the stuff that goes with it. You may not feel the same loyalty to your employer you did years ago, and you may be on the alert for the worst, wary about what is going on around you.

Lifetime employment went out with the Brady Bunch—even the big old paternalistic companies are terminating people by the thousands. Many of those laid off are searching for employment in a labor market where jobs like the ones they had have permanently disappeared. Others, who still have jobs, are waiting for the ax to fall.

Every day there are new reports of downsizings and layoffs. Nearly 7 million people have lost permanent jobs in the last five years. IBM alone has cut its workforce by nearly 200,000 people since 1986, sort of like firing all the people in a city the size of Dayton, Ohio. AT&T, GM, Sears, and the U.S. Postal Service are all vying for second place in the layoff sweepstakes.

At the same time, federal, state, and local governments and public school systems, strapped for funds, are slimming down; and the military, faced with limited budgets and unable to find worthy enemies, is closing bases and mustering out its people. In 1994 and 1995, between 2,000 and 3,000 people were being laid off every working day!

Many companies are continuing to downsize (even though profits may be at an all-time high) because they are under tremendous pressure from investors and analysts to cut costs, and they see getting lean and mean as the smart way to do that.

Undoubtedly, downsizing has helped some companies, but not without a cost. A 1993 Wyatt Company survey of 4,300 workers nationwide found only 57 percent of those in downsized companies were generally satisfied with their jobs versus 72 percent in expanding companies. And in a 1993 survey done by Yankelovich Partners for *Time*, 66 percent of participants said job security was worse than it had been two years before and 54 percent said it would be harder to find a job in the next twelve months than before.

Recently, speaking to a group of 200 young professionals, I mentioned that I had worked for one company for twenty-five years. On a whim, I asked the group how many of them expected to be with their present employers twenty-five years from now. *Not a single hand went up.*

For every person downsized out of a job, nine or ten people have their lives changed. These include spouses, children, the former boss who did the firing, survivors who have to pick up the work, suppliers and customers who now have to deal with new people, and everyone else in the organization who now wonders when the next crunch will come.

A few years ago, if you lost a job, you would just go out and get another. Maybe it paid a little less, but in a year or two merit increases would get you right back to where you had been. No more. Half of those who find new employment today settle for jobs at lower pay and responsibility.

This is a new era of lowered expectations. If you are a younger person, you probably don't expect to do better than your parents—every previous generation has been confident it would do better than the one before.

What's the Bottom Line?

It might surprise you, but *this is not all bad.* Let's look at the pluses as well as the minuses.

Recently, my consulting firm did a study of changes in the workplace, especially changes in boss-subordinate relationships. We surveyed a number of CEOs, senior executives, human resource directors, middle managers, and consultants. The results may not be surprising, but they were impressive in that so many respondents said exactly the same things about what is happening today and its meaning for the future. Based on our findings and other research, I can give you this overview.

1. **Loyalty and trust are in the shredder.** People don't feel strong ties to current employers, and they certainly don't expect employers to take care of them. They know the end may come at any time. And they have been misled enough that they have lost trust. The Council of Communication Management surveyed 705 employees at seventy companies in 1994 and found that 64 percent don't believe what management tells them. Employees feel they have to make up their own minds and take charge of their own careers.

What does this mean to you?

- **You have more options.** People who used to go to work for one employer and stay till retirement sometimes traded security for boredom. Golden handcuffs, inertia, and complacency all kept people from moving around too much, except to similar careers in other companies. Many got through it all right and retired nicely to their condos in Florida, but they had unfulfilled longings . . . to run their own company, open a bed-and-breakfast, write a novel. And some are sitting around right now, watching the seagulls and wondering why they didn't take a chance and do the things they really wanted to.

  Today, you may be forced to do something new even if that's not your dream. I'm sure you know some people who have changed careers, gone with smaller companies, or opened their own businesses—and are delighted with what they are doing, thankful now that they were forced to do what they did.

- **Your loyalty will be first to yourself,** second to a team or project, next to your profession, and last to your place of work. Chances are you will work for several employers, including yourself, over the course of your career. Gene Roche, director of the Career Center at Hamilton College, says that the average liberal arts graduate today can expect to work for ten to twelve employers over a career.

2. Boss-subordinate relationships are changing. Traditionally, the boss had most of the power, but no more.

Now, power is shifting to subordinates. They participate in decision making or make decisions themselves. They take more control over their work, their careers, and their lives. They confront, challenge, and question more. They initiate rather than wait for orders.

Subordinates need to be much more skilled at working with bosses and team leaders. They need to be problem solvers, communicators, team players. Follower skills are becoming as important as leadership skills.

For bosses, the commander style of management is out, and there is more delegation and more teamwork. Top-down just doesn't work very well today (if it ever did). It slows decision making, new product development, and action of all sorts, making it difficult for companies to satisfy customer needs and compete effectively. It kills candor and creativity and weakens commitment. The new relationship is less structured and more collegial. Bosses need new skills to handle this—and have to adapt whether they like it or not.

In some cases, bosses are unnecessary altogether. More and more work is being done outside the normal boss-subordinate hierarchy, in teams.

What does this mean to you?

- **You will have more responsibility.** Your boss has too many people to supervise and can't do it all alone anymore. And gradually bosses are giving in to empowerment and pushing decisions down, allowing you to take charge and act without going upstairs for approval. Chances are, as your company slims down, you not only have more work to do but more say in how it gets done.
- **More of your work will be done as part of a team,** not as an individual.

  Networks and teams are fast becoming the normal organization form. Free access to information, via technology, across a company is eliminating the need for the old organization chart. Companies are replacing management layers with teams and partnerships with customers, competitors, suppliers.

If you aren't already, you'll soon be working in a horizontal organization, designed around teams that lead processes such as new product development, not functions such as engineering or marketing.

- **You may not have a job** as we think of a job today. You may be paid for doing pieces of work, not holding down a job.
- **There will be less distinction between bosses and subordinates.** If you are a boss, you may not get paid much more than the people you lead, because you will be measured by your work and level of expertise, not your title.

3. Traditional rewards will be fewer. Reduced levels of management and tighter budgets are changing the nature of reward systems. Promotions and salary increases are becoming as scarce as chicken molars. It used to be if you worked smarter and harder you could get that bigger job, and then another, and finally that corner office. Today, there are fewer jobs to move up to, and in some companies there's no corner office anyhow, just a work space. Limos, first-class travel, and big expense accounts are disappearing, except for the few executives at the very top.

What does this mean to you?

- **If you are a manager,** you need to find new ways to recognize good work and to motivate people. As a subordinate, you have to learn to reward yourself rather than depend on handouts from your employer.
- **You will find yourself working harder** and longer for fewer rewards (pay, advancement) than your predecessors did. You already put in four weeks more a year on the job than workers did twenty years ago.

4. Career planning is becoming an oxymoron. "Career planning" implies an orderly, predetermined process of advancement. It suggests support and guidance from the employer and some sort of lasting relationship between employer and employee. When you think about the word *career*, you think above moving up. But that is not the way it works today. People are staying in jobs longer because there's no place else to go—most of the jobs above them have been eliminated.

What does this mean to you?

- **You will have new career patterns** as a new compact develops between employers and employees. GE, for instance, says something like, "We may kick you out anytime, but you can stay as long as you are adding value in some way. While you are here, we will give you interesting and important work, resources to perform it, and we will pay you and give you training so that when the time comes, you will be able to find another job in this company or somewhere else."

   AT&T is one of the old-time paternalistic companies that has done a 180-degree turn to the new model. Contrary to its old cradle-to-grave philosophy, it has chopped off more than 100,000 jobs in the last ten years and now grants employment to those who find projects to work on. When work on one project is completed, an engineer, for instance, has a few months to get connected with another, or he or she must leave. AT&T provides training to keep people employable, but many supplement that with outside courses, and continued employment is solely up to the individual.

   Corning Glass provides employees with training to develop skills that are marketable anywhere, inside the company or outside.

   And, more changes may be on the way. Rumblings from Generation X indicate that many young people aren't sitting still for the old tired corporate ways. They are impatient with unchallenging jobs and slow career ladders. They want to be recognized for good performance on the job, not degrees or other outside factors. They want to jump around, not be confined to a career silo or have to operate within a job description. They want praise and recognition and want to get rid of dress codes and other stuffy traditions.

- **You are in charge of you.** You may not want that responsibility, but it is there. And with that comes some liberation. You are not dependent on one employer to look after you for the rest of your life, and therefore you can feel more like an adult than like a kid in day care. You can make decisions about your life in terms of your needs, not just what your employer wants. If you can't be loyal to your employer, you can be loyal to your job and to yourself.

5. Layoffs will continue. Experts tell us that—even with all that has happened—organizations are still fat by a third and that downsizings and reorganizations will be with us till after the turn of the century. Consultant David Rhodes of Towers Perrin predicts that by the year 2000 the typical large corporation will have half the management levels and one third the managers it had in 1990.

There is some sign that the downsizing frenzy is slowing, dropping below a half million a year for the first time in a while. But no matter what happens—even if not one person is fired next year—people will never think of employers in quite the same way.

What does this mean to you?

- **You have more incentive to learn new skills.** When everything is going smoothly, it is easy to put off any concentrated effort to learn something new. But things aren't too smooth today. Your very survival depends on learning and growing, because the methods you use to handle your work and your career are largely based on what was effective twenty years ago—and those aren't the skills needed to survive and succeed in today's world.

  Your energies have to be directed toward adding value to your present employer and upgrading your skills and abilities so that when the string runs out where you are, you can move on to something else. Lifelong learning is your ticket to future success, and you have to take charge of your own development, not sit around and wait for your company to feed it to you.

- **You may be a "one-person organization"** at some time or another, selling your services and expertise to a variety of organizations. You own your mind and your skills, and you are free to market that expertise anywhere you want. A lot of people are doing just that. In 1994, the rate of new incorporations, many of them one-person companies, hit a record high (737,000), and that doesn't include the millions (one quarter of those employed) who were already on a temporary, part-time, or contract basis.

- **You still may lose the job you have.** Layoffs will continue, even though the United States is creating over 2 million jobs per year. You are most vulnerable if you are a middle-aged man, a middle manager, or a high earner. "Almost every one of our clients is pulling out as many middle managers as they can," says Andrew Geller of the Hay Group. (Middle managers made up only 5 percent of the workforce but accounted for 22 percent of the layoffs in the early 1990s.)

To confuse matters, many companies that are firing people are hiring at the same time. They are cutting areas that don't give a competitive advantage and expanding areas that add value. Today, in good times, companies will lay people off. In bad times, they will fire more.

6. Technology is remaking your world. Technology is changing every aspect of work. Manager-subordinate relationships are changing as computers are taking over traditional management responsibilities for passing information down the line. With wide access to information, subordinates are "smarter" and can make more decisions, while managers can concentrate more on supporting rather than directing their efforts. Communications of all kinds are changing. Reports that used to be filled out laboriously by hand (press hard, you are making four copies) are now done in minutes on laptops, and requests for information that used to take days to go through the organization can now be filled instantly on the computer. Working conditions are changing: face-to-face is being replaced by electronic communication, and as that happens, the need for formal offices is decreasing.

What does this mean to you?

- **You can work anywhere.** Technology can connect you with others in your company (or companies) and with customers and suppliers around the world from your desktop. You can work out of a virtual office at home, in your car, in airplanes and hotels, and not go in to a central office—because there is no need to and there may not be an office anyway.

- **You can become a superspecialist.** Technology makes the world a single market and provides opportunities for you if you go out on your own, even if you have a very narrow market. You might not find much demand for your skills as a safety-pin design consultant in a small town in Iowa, but you may in the world market.

- **You must stay technology-literate.** There's no other way today, and with an avalanche of new software and new applications coming down, it is a tough job to keep up. Even old geezers who hate technology and are afraid of it will have to learn.

With that background, we can take a hard look at your career. Do you sometimes feel as though your career is in the swamp and there's nothing you can do to get it out? Well, the truth is there's a lot you can do. You have a fair amount of control over your future—more than you think you do.

Let's look at what you can do to take charge of your career and your life.

What, No Mission Statement?

It's popular today to start career planning by doing a personal mission statement so you can figure out what your purpose is in life. You can develop one if you want to. But grand designs have a way of getting snagged on day-to-day realities. That's why many companies have backed away from traditional strategic planning. Long-range thinking suffers from the following problems:

- It is based on what you know now. It is impossible to predict the future, and there are many unexpected changes along the way.
- What seems like a great career option today may be tomorrow's last-place finisher. How many people have aspired to be middle managers only to find that those jobs are disappearing?
- Long-range plans can make you inflexible. You went to all the trouble of developing them, so you feel you ought to stick to them, even when the world has changed and they don't make sense anymore.
- Just as bad, many plans, when they are completed, aren't used. How may company strategic plans are sitting on the shelf gathering dust?

All this doesn't mean you shouldn't dream or have some exciting plan for your life. What it does mean is while you're deciding on the purpose of your life, and planning how to achieve your highest goals, you'd better start by managing the present. That way, you're much more likely to be ready for the future.

If you're like most people, once you've gotten established in a job or career field, your natural desire is to stay with it. If you get disgusted with your present employer, or your employer decides it can get along without you, you look for a job like the one you had.

There's nothing wrong with that, except that jobs like yours may be disappearing, and you may be limiting yourself by not exploring other options.

Know Your Career Options

To begin with, let's look at what you have now. How well does your present job stack up? Are you secure? Are you satisfied? Do you see opportunity? Or are you struggling to hold on, apprehensive about the future, working harder and harder for less and less?

The Present Situation Analysis will help you see a little more clearly where you stand today. Start with the "Love of Job" section. Take each factor in the left-hand column and scan across till you find something that most closely describes your situation. Circle it and enter the numerical value from the top line. Do this for each of the factors; then add up your total Love of Job score and enter it at the bottom.

Do the same with the "Confidence in the Future" section.

PRESENT SITUATION ANALYSIS

Love of Job

Factor	Super (score 3)	Pretty Good (score 2)	So-so (score 1)	Nowhere (score 0)	Score
The work itself	Stimulating; I can't wait to get to work	More great than not	Ups and downs	Would bore a robot	
Communication and feedback	Always tuned in; open and free up and down	Mostly know what's going on, how I'm doing	More from the grapevine than the boss	There isn't even a watercooler in this place	
Freedom, empowerment	Make important decisions on my own	Make many decisions, not all	Half and half	Need permission to use the john	
Recognition	Plenty of it; satisfying and motivating	Get some, not as often as I'd like	Hear more about the screwups than the good work	Does anyone know I'm here?	
The people	Love them all, even the boss	Like most of them; we have a pretty good time	Some are great, others not	Nightmare creatures	
Pay and benefits	Generous	Pretty good; fair	Could be better	Looking the minimum wage straight in the eye	

Total Love of Job Score: _____

(Continued on next page)

Confidence in the Future

Factor	Super (score 3)	Pretty Good (score 2)	So-so (score 1)	Nowhere (score 0)	Score
Training and development	Learning all the time; company is aggressive about training	Take some courses, have grown in this job	Occasionally learn something	Head full of mush	
Advancement	Good opportunities here; on a fast track	As good as can be expected	Some chance to move higher	Nobody gets promoted here	
Company stability	Stable, solid outfit	Some upheaval, not much	Have been recent management changes, reengineering	Working in a Cuisinart	
Company direction	On target; management knows what it is doing	Seems to be okay	Fair, but too many false starts, not changing fast enough	Lost and wandering	
Company/industry growth	Growth industry; expanding rapidly	Better than most	Barely holding our own	Sinking fast	
Gut feeling	Confident, looking to the future; right place at the right time	Not particularly worried	Concerned about the future	Continual anxiety attack	

Total Confidence in the Future Score: _____

Find where your scores fall on the "Love and Confidence" matrix below.

If you hate your job and have little confidence that it holds any kind of decent future for you (lower left-hand corner), you might as well be doing eight to ten in Leavenworth, and you should be planning your escape.

If you don't like your job, but you feel there could be a relatively decent future with your present company (lower right), you ought to try to change the scope of your job or change jobs within the company. If you love your job but don't think there's a future with the company (upper left), you have to decide. Want to stick it out, have fun, and take your chances, or explore other employers now? If you love your job and have a great future (upper right), you are indeed a lucky dog.

LOVE AND CONFIDENCE

	High	
Score 10–18	Take a chance	Lucky dog
Love of Job		
	Over the wall	Stick it out—change your job
Score 0–9	**Low**	**High**

Confidence in the Future

Score 0–9   Score: 10–18

Three of the four quadrants call for some kind of change. Even if you are in the "Lucky dog" quadrant you should be getting ready—because you never know. Here are your options:

1. Mount a campaign to stay in your present job and survive the next downsizing.
2. Change the nature of your present job—take on new work, additional responsibility, new team assignments, and so on.

3. Change jobs within the organization—move to another department or division.
4. Escape over the wall. Change employers—or go out on your own.

Let's look at each of those options more closely.

The options described are similar to those in my former book, *1,000 Things You Never Learned in Business School*. But much has changed, and what follows reflects the great transformation that has shaped today's workplace.

1. Stay with Your Present Employer

Like a good marriage, staying with your present employer takes work, and you have to take positive steps to increase your value to your employer and improve your chances of being there after the downsizing dust settles.

Whenever you start to tell yourself nothing will happen to you, slam your fingers in the door to wake up and get back to reality. Because there's still a pretty good chance something will—people who had careers of granite in the 1980s saw them change to oatmeal in 1990.

Warning Signs That Change Is Coming

Company situation:

- *We can run anything.* Your company has gone way into debt buying other companies in fields not related to the company's core business. That is, your company has gone into hock to buy businesses it doesn't know how to run.
- *The fad of the month.* In an attempt to make things right again, your company starts implementing programs for reengineering, Total Quality Management (TQM), empowerment, and more. Maybe all at once.
- *Stubbornly low tech.* Your employer is not investing in technology. If you are dazzled at what your competitors can do with technology when you're still doing those things by hand, then you'd better watch out. The costs of trying to catch up all at once are prohibitive, and the catch-up will have to come sometime.
- *Management is committed to 1954.* Management insists on staying with methods and philosophies that worked well forty or fifty years ago. Or even ten years ago. Puffed up with past success, it is determined not to change.

- *We know what's best.* Your company is working hard to sell products and services it produces without finding out what customers want.
- *We know what's best 2.* Nobody listens to anyone below them in the organization. Subordinates are afraid to be critical and have given up trying to convince anyone of new ideas and suggestions.
- *There are persistent rumors* of a major organization change. Or change is actually happening: reengineering, plant or office closing, outsourcing, department elimination.
- *There are hiring freezes* or pay increase freezes for long stretches.
- *Consultants are hovering around.*
- *What are you worth?* You are asked where you and your department added value this past year.

Personal situation:

- You are a middle manager.
- You are a middle-aged middle manager.
- You are a highly paid middle-aged middle manager.
- You are a highly paid middle-aged middle manager in a staff department.
- Your work is being automated or outsourced.
- Your performance appraisals are average or only slightly above.
- Your staff and budget are being cut.
- Your boss looks the other way when you go by.

When the warning signs appear, it may be too late. But maybe not, if you . . .

Tie your work to the business. The more you are seen as adding value to the business, the safer you are. And the best way to do that is to connect your work more closely to getting sales, serving the customer, cutting costs, or advancing technology. Those areas are of the highest value to your employer. Think beyond your prescribed job responsibilities to company goals and direction. What work do you do, or could you do, that would support major company efforts?

This may take some creative thinking, especially if you are in a staff job, but it is worth the effort.

1. Never miss an opportunity to show how your work supports the business—even talking "corporately" gives you the image of someone who is vital to the business.

    Ask "corporate" questions in meetings. Talk with your boss and your peers about corporate issues. If you have an opinion or idea on a strategic issue, write it up and send it around. Show in any way you can that you are interested and involved—at least mentally. You should be thinking on that level anyhow.

2. Get to know the business. At the very least, you should know company sales, profits, earnings per share, return on investment, and other important financial measures. Keep up with company goals and major efforts, competition, and customers. There is plenty of information around on this, and you probably have access to a lot of it on your computer. Even if there is no way you can take on the kind of work described above, you can show a continuing interest in the company's progress.

3. Volunteer for high-impact teams or task forces—even if you just take notes. If you can get attached to one or more of these, you will be associated with important work and you will be noticed by executives on those teams.

    As soon as you get assigned to one team, you should start looking for another so that there are no periods of time in which you are not doing work the company sees as very important.

2. Change the Nature of Your Present Job

"What?" you say. "I sell financial products. I'm on the phone or out with customers ten hours a day. I'm under the gun to make my numbers. What can I change?" Probably more than you think.

If you were the CEO looking down at your job, what would you change? Maybe you would get rid of some of those stupid reports nobody reads, or you might give yourself more authority so you could serve your customers better and faster. Or you might assign yourself to that team working on sales productivity. Or to that task force trying to upgrade antiquated systems.

Make your own list of what you can build into your job that will make it more satisfying to you and you more valuable to the company.

JOB IMPROVEMENT CHART

_____

_____

_____

_____

_____

_____

_____

_____

Now comes the tricky part. You have to keep your boss tuned in to what you are planning to do and make it seem nonthreatening. Bosses don't like change, either.

1. Keep your boss informed. Make the boss a partner in changing your work. Always emphasize the benefits of change—how it will benefit the boss: "Boss, eighty percent of customer adjustments are a thousand dollars or less. If you would trust me to take care of those, you would save hours of time each month to work on bigger issues and customers would get service on the spot instead of waiting till I can get to you for approval."
2. Be patient. Change won't happen overnight, and sometimes it seems nothing is getting better. When you come up with an idea, the boss may say no, then come back two weeks later with a "new idea" that is the same as what you proposed.
3. Start small: "Boss, suppose we try it out for three months with a few customers. If you aren't satisfied with the way it is working, you can always go back to approving all the adjustments yourself."
4. Give it an honest try. If you don't succeed at getting change, you may have to try again, or go to the next alternative, changing jobs within the company.

3. Change Jobs Within the Company

Look around you. Are there other jobs in your organization you would like? Jobs that seem to be more in tune with what you'd like to do than the one you have? Once you identify one or more . . .

Talk with someone you know who works in that area. It could be a person in your own company or someone who works elsewhere. Don't worry about imposing—people love to talk about their jobs. Ask about the minuses as well as the pluses and the skills you will need to succeed.

If you decide you really want that area, go after it. No one will do it for you. And this can get hairy, because it will involve talking with your boss, who may react by saying:

1. "I never realized you wanted to move in that direction, and I'm glad you told me. I'll talk to the head of the department in the morning and see if I can get you over there."
2. "We have a freeze on hiring. If I move you out, I can't replace you, and you know our workload is a killer already. I hope you understand, but right now I need you here."
3. "You Benedict Arnold, I'm going to shoot you dead."

Some thoughts about changing jobs within the company.

- Your boss isn't going to be happy about losing you, especially if you are doing a good job. Be careful to protect the boss's ego. Be as positive as you honestly can be—oh, well, lay it on a little—about your present job and working for the boss. Tell the boss you feel you could serve the company better, and use your own skills and talents better, if you moved to another area.
- Expand your networks. Get to know people in other departments. Volunteer for teams and task forces, or become active in company-sponsored community activities so people outside your department can get to know you and see what you can do.
- Use the company job-posting program if there is one. That is a relatively safe way to look at other jobs without ticking off your boss.
- If your boss is going to shoot you, you have three alternatives, none of them any good. One is to grit your teeth and stay put, if

the boss will let you. It may not be fun. Another is to go over your boss's head to your boss's boss, the human resource department, or the head of the department you'd like to be in. It's a chance, but keep in mind, the first thing any of them will do is call your present boss to talk about your request. The last alternative is to move on and start looking outside the company.

4. Move On

There are many reasons to hang on to the job you have, even though every day isn't especially Eden-like. Crass as it seems, there is always the matter of money. And health insurance. And the established, familiar routine. And your friends at work.

But if the time comes you can't stand it anymore, and you have tried to change within the company with no success, you may be ready to look for another job. This may seem like a virtually impossible task in today's labor market, but there is always a way.

Here are some strategies for changing jobs.

1. Make sure you don't end up out of work. Don't quit before you have another job, unless you want to take a long vacation (which may turn out to be much longer than you want). Keep everything as quiet as possible. There's always the possibility your company will find out about your job search—after all, you'll have résumés out, and someone may hear about that, or a prospective employer may call for references. There's always the chance that your company will see you as a traitor and boot you out before you are ready to go.

2. When you decide, get moving. Start making your contacts, get your résumé updated. Don't wait—it may take six months or even a year to find something close to what you want.

3. When you do leave, leave on good terms. Be positive about your experience with the company, even if it was a horror. Thank everyone, especially your boss. You might get some small satisfaction by trashing everyone in sight, but that would come back to haunt you someday when you need a reference.

Now you have started doing some hard thinking about your career. A little later in the book, chapter 7 will provide guidance on how to prepare for the worst, what to do if it happens, and exploring nontraditional careers.

SBI: Come to terms with the fact that you have to manage your own career and your own life. No one will do it for you today, or even help you very much. That is both challenging and liberating.

ENDURANCE
SKILLS

3

PEACE WITHOUT PROZAC

How to Keep Your Cool in Tough Times

*"Things that stress me out: (1) fear of not having a job;
(2) fear of having a job."*
—Bart Ownes, middle manager, after surviving a
second downsizing at Cincinnati Cyber-Snooze

*"Stress has gotten a bad name. Stress of all kinds is
good—physical, emotional and mental. It's strengthen-
ing. What troubles us is the absence of recovery strategies needed to balance the stress."*
—James Loehr, sports psychologist
(as quoted in *Fortune*, 11/28/94)

Toughing It Out

What are you doing about the stress in your life? The impossible workload, the uncertainties, the difficult people you deal with, the lack of recognition? Maybe you are into all the standard stress-reduction techniques: breathing deeply, meditating, imaging, thinking positive thoughts, chanting mantras, and pruning out in a hot tub.

You are trying to get rid of stress, and no wonder—the symptoms are no fun. You have a headache, no appetite, an upset stomach; you can't concentrate; you're tired and depressed. Maybe you drink too much, take drugs, start smoking again, gobble junk food, fight with your spouse. Meanwhile, you feel sorry for yourself at having been singled out to be put in this tough situation.

But everyone has stress and always has had it. Think how Adam and Eve felt when they got kicked out of the Garden of Eden. The first outplacement. Think of all the wars and plagues and recessions and depressions since then. All the Chapter 11's, company failures, takeovers, and reorganizations that people have suffered through over the years.

What is different today is that global competition, technology, changing demographics, new customer expectations, and a host of other forces are making life more complex and bringing change at a faster rate than ever before. As competition gets tougher, and companies introduce new products and services faster, everyone is struggling to lower costs, get everything done more quickly, improve quality, and become more customer oriented. All that keeps everyone on the edge of their ergonomic chairs. Tension? Stress? Just walk into a meeting, shout "Reengineering," and watch people dive under the table.

With all this going on, even stress itself is changing.

New Rules of Stress

Old Rule: Stress is bad and must be avoided at all costs.

New Rule: Stress can be a powerful force you can use to take positive action.

Along with using those relaxation techniques to get rid of stress, you should find ways to use the power of stress to attack its root causes.

Stress is not always an enemy. In fact, if you could avoid all stress in your life you would be comatose. Stress is normal, and it can be good for you—if it is kept within reasonable limits.

When my former employer, JCPenney, announced it would move its 3,800-person New York corporate office to Dallas, the CEO stated he wanted to make the transition as easy as possible for everyone. Part of an extensive program of assistance offered was a stress-management program. Almost everyone attended it; some went twice! It was run by noted psychologists and stress-management experts, who led people through a whole series of stress-reduction and relaxation techniques. The course was technically very good, but it left many people unsatisfied. "The problem is still there," they said. "Penney's is still going to Dallas."

What they needed to learn was how to use the power of stress to attack the problem, to channel their increased adrenaline flow into attacking the decision of going or not, and getting geared up to find another job. You can reduce stress with relaxation exercises for a while, but the causes won't go away unless you go after them directly.

Old Rule: If you can just get past this tough situation, life will be good again.

New Rule: If you can just get past this tough situation, there is another one waiting for you.

Gilda Radner told us "It's always something," and most of the time it is. An executive I know had a presentation to make to her board of directors. It was her first time in front of the board, and she was—understandably—nervous. She confided to me that she hadn't slept in a week and claimed that without a little makeup, she looked like a ghost. Well, she toughed it out, made her presentation, and pranced back to her desk greatly relieved, color coming back to her face, smiling and happy it was over!

Minutes later, she was pale again. While she was with the board, she had received a fax from a major customer saying it was going with a competitor and would no longer be doing business with her. She immediately booked a flight out that afternoon to see if she could get it back. Meanwhile, she found a message from her husband reminding her that their daughter was playing the lead in the school play that night and to meet him at the school by seven.

Old Rule: There are a few high-stress occupations.

New Rule: Most jobs have high stress.

We used to think air traffic controller, police officer, nurse, performing artist, and a few others stood out as high-stress occupations. Today, because of increased workload after downsizings, uncertainty about the future, and time pressures to get things done, almost every job has high-stress aspects to it.

Even middle management jobs can be highly stressful today. Middle managers, usually seen as secure and unruffled, are today's dinosaurs, waiting for the meteor to hit. They not only face extinction, but while they're still around, they are given more work, tougher goals to meet, and fewer resources to make it all happen.

Where Does All This Stress Come From?

Pick up a book on stress management and you will see a long list of things that cause stress. At home, on the job, on vacation. Even positive things, like marrying the person you love, cause stress! *Everything causes stress!* But there are some things on the job today that really put the pressure on. I'll give you a baker's dozen. You may have some others.

Using the Stress Rating Chart, rate each of the thirteen factors below from 1 to 5 (with 5 being highest) on each of two dimensions: intensity of stress (that is, how much stress the factor causes when it is present); and frequency/duration (how often it occurs and how long it lasts). You may get very nervous giving a speech, but if you do it only once a year, it can't count as a major stressor in your life—unless you spend all year worrying about it.

STRESS RATINGS

Intensity

Rating	Definition
5	Extremely intense stress; debilitating out-of-your-skin panic reaction
4	High stress; makes it difficult to concentrate; shake and sweat, heart pounding, fear
3	Enough to cause headache, fidgeting, anxiety
2	Some stress, distracting
1	Not much stress, everyday stuff

Frequency/Duration

Rating	Definition
5	Ongoing, constant, never lets up
4	Almost every day, all day; occasional letup
3	About half the time
2	Once a month or so
1	Almost never

When you have rated each factor on intensity and frequency/duration, add the scores and enter that number in the "Total" column. Then rank the factors from highest to lowest.

STRESS RATING CHART

Factor	Intensity	Frequency/ Duration	Total	Rank
1. Change, or threat of change: altered responsibilities, reduced budget or staff, new reporting relationship, demotion, transfer, or unemployment				
2. Lack of input: major decisions about your work, your status, your department are made without your ideas and suggestions and handed down from above				
3. Unclear goals (or conflicting goals): not knowing quite what is expected of you				
4. Conflict and difficult personal relationships on the job				
5. Too much work: there's just plain too much to do				
6. Personal habits: things you do to escape from it all (drinking, drugs, sugar highs, smoking, overeating) can come back to actually increase your stress levels later on				
7. Lack of balance between work and home: the work is everything, and anything that goes wrong at work seems much more important than it really is				
8. Being plateaued: you've been there, done that; you are ready to move to bigger responsibilities, but there isn't anything in sight				
9. Lack of recognition: you are working harder than ever before, and you have accomplished some great things for the company; no one ever says "Thanks" or "Good job"				

(Continued on next page)

10. Travel: you spend more time in row 16 seat A than any other single place; week after week on the road, and your kids are growing up without your being around				
11. Giving people bad news, firing someone				
12. Onstage stress: making a stand-up presentation, running a tough meeting, giving a report to the CEO, making a sales pitch to a big account				
13. Money: not enough of it				

Now you know where your major stressors are and you're ready to work your way through them in priority order, taking on the worst areas first. Let's figure out how to deal with them.

A New Way of Viewing Stress

Stress can push you into action and help you perform at your highest level.

Sometimes when you are in the middle of a crisis, you have to work hard to see anything good about it. But there are pluses and minuses in every situation. One friend of mine was deeply upset at being shoved out by a company where he had worked for over twenty years. He had no plans, no goals for his unexpected retirement, and spent his time dwelling on his misfortune. Fifty-six years old, and his life was over. And he was becoming increasingly bitter at his old company—and everything else in life.

One day he came to my office to talk. I suggested he fill out the Stress Analyzer (you will use it in a minute). The minuses were easy for him. He felt he had been mistreated, unappreciated for his years of loyal service. All his plans for his department were cut short and he would never achieve them. The pluses were harder, but finally he started to think of some. He had enough money to get by for a while. He had many years of technical and management experience. He had a good family that was solidly behind him.

Gradually, he began to see a use for himself in the world, and he began to use the energy that anger and frustration gave him to do something positive. One of the problems he'd had before he was downsized was not having enough technical people to get the work done, and although he had budget money, the company would not allow him to add to head count. He suspected other companies had the same problem, and later confirmed that they did. He decided to start a small technical services business to augment the work of in-house staff on a temporary basis, and he worked like a tiger to get his business going.

Today, he laughs about that part of his life. He has a thriving little company, he is making money, and most of all, he has a purpose in life.

That never would have happened if he had continued to concentrate on the minuses and used stress-reduction techniques only to make himself temporarily feel better. Instead, he used the motivation stress created to attack his problems—unemployment and feelings of uselessness.

Stress starts adrenaline flowing, gets your heart rate and blood pressure up. It heightens your alertness and can help you perform better. That is, it prepares you for fight or flight. We inherit this from prehistoric people, who had stress reactions when they peeked around a rock and found themselves face-to-face with a grinning *Tyrannosaurus rex*.

Your tyrannosaurs in the workplace won't do you physical harm, but can hurt you mentally and emotionally. You don't have to choose the flight alternative (avoiding or reducing stress). You can use your increased tension to mount a fight to combat stressors and deal with them in a positive way. The Stress Power Plan below will help. It will show you how to use the power of stress with these four steps:

1. Take stress apart.
2. Deal with the worst-case scenario.
3. Brainstorm specific action.
4. Do something.

Stress Power Plan

1. **Take stress apart.** You have already determined what your top stressors are using the Stress Rating Chart. Take your number-one stressor, or any stress that's eating at you right now, and use the Stress Analyzer below to take it apart and examine why it makes you feel the way you do. Then you can deal with pieces of your stress.

Then, to capture the energies created by stress, describe how you feel. This is an important step in attacking sources of stress because it enables you to determine how those feelings can help you improve the situation.

Are you angry? Apprehensive? Hurt? You can nurse those feelings for weeks, waking up in the middle of the night reviewing them in your mind, or you can use the energy those emotions create to go after the root cause of the problem and deal with it.

STRESS ANALYZER

This is what's causing me stress (describe the situation):

_____

_____

_____

_____

_____

How I feel about this situation (describe your feelings):

_____

_____

_____

Specific aspects of the situation that disturb me	Ways of dealing with it directly

Positive aspects of the situation	Ways of building on positive aspects

Here's an example:

STRESS ANALYZER

This is what's causing me stress (describe the situation):

The company has just had another staff reduction. The boss told me today that we have to "pick up the slack," and now I will have to do Joe's job (Joe is gone) as well as my own. There is no increase in pay. I am swamped just trying to do my own job, much less Joe's.

How I feel about this situation (describe your feelings):

I feel like I have been given an impossible workload, and that is unfair. I have always done my best for the company, and this doesn't seem like a reward. I may be being set up for failure—move over, Joe. I am disappointed and angry. And a little scared.

Specific aspects of the situation that disturb me	Ways of dealing with it directly
It is unfair to expect me to do the impossible.	Determine what is possible by setting priorities. Get agreement from the boss.
I might fail.	I will do the best I can. If that isn't good enough, then so be it.
The company treats people like beasts of burden.	This is my job, not my life. Strengthen off-the-job aspects of my life.

Positive aspects of the situation	Ways of building on positive aspects
There are none! Well, maybe . . .	
Chance to take on additional responsibility.	Organize my work and time to show I can do it.
Joe had some interesting work.	Enjoy those aspects of the job.
Chance to open up better communications with the boss.	Arrange meetings on Joe's work, priorities.
More visibility.	Emphasize aspects of Joe's work that deal with senior management.

2. **Deal with the worst-case scenario.** Instead of living with feelings of doom, spell out the worst thing that can happen and see how awful that is. Maybe it isn't all that bad—or maybe it is. You might as well know.

The worst thing that can happen is . . .

_____

_____

_____

_____

How to deal with that.

_____

_____

_____

_____

Let's continue our example . . .

The worst thing that can happen is . . .

<u>I will work like a demon all year, but because there is more than one</u>
<u>human can do, I will not meet all my goals and I will get a so-so</u>
<u>appraisal rating. A new round of reductions will come along, and I will</u>
<u>be out in the street.</u>

How to deal with that.
<u>I will begin planning now to get myself ready to find another way to</u>
<u>make a living if the worst case should actually happen. Meanwhile, I</u>
<u>will work as closely as possible with my boss to try to keep expectations</u>
<u>reasonable, and get understanding of my situation, and work like hell</u>
<u>to see that it doesn't happen.</u>

3. Brainstorm specific actions you will take. Now you're getting somewhere. It's time to get more specific as to exactly what you will do.

Get someone you trust to work with you in coming up with ideas. Let the ideas flow freely; you can chop them up later.

Specific actions

More of our example:

Specific actions

Clone myself

Sneak Joe in the back door

List responsibilities, set priorities

Estimate time it would take to do each job well

Practice approach to the boss—sell benefits

Anticipate boss's objections and how to overcome

Meet with the boss to get agreement—this week!

Clone myself

---

4. Do something. Enough planning, now it is time to act. Carry out your actions and get it over with. The sooner you act, the sooner you will feel better. Even if you don't eliminate the cause of the stress, you will understand it better and feel happy that you took some direct action to control your life.

But some types of stress are beyond your control. Don't beat yourself up trying to change things you can't. When the executive vice president of sales raises quotas, there's not much you can do to change that. When the Reengineering to Death Consulting firm recommends another staff cut, that's out of your hands. Instead, work on changing those stress factors you can influence, and don't waste your time on the ones you can't.

A Guide for Dealing with Stressors

Change, or Threat of Change

Companies everywhere are busy remaking themselves—into *what* is sometimes not clear, but remaking they are. The fact is, change does not always make things better, especially for people most affected by it.

If change is causing you anxiety—is it change that has already happened or is it something you think will happen? If it is the latter, how certain are you that it will happen?

Decide what parts of the change you can control and determine what actions you can take to get going and attack the problem.

> **Attacking the Source of Stress:** Don't wait for change to happen. Take charge of your own career and prepare for any eventuality. The key is in being ready and knowing what you will do when change happens—take charge of those aspects of the change that you can control.

Lack of Input

Decisions are handed down, and you have no say in any of them. Some of them are okay; some of them are just stupid. But the point is, nobody asks you for your suggestions about how to run your own job! Now, that causes you a lot of stress. If it does, work on your follower skills so you can make your input count.

> **Attacking the Source of Stress:** If no one is asking your opinion, give it anyhow. Let your boss know what your ideas are. Schedule time with the boss to discuss your thoughts. Make your ideas constructive. Go in with answers, not just complaints about things that are happening.

Unclear Goals

At appraisal time, John's boss said, "John, you've accomplished all your goals this year, and your work has been very good, but I have to hold your overall rating down because you didn't bring in four new customers."

"New customers wasn't one of my goals," said John. "Even so, I brought in three. If I had known, I could have gotten another."

"Four new customers is part of every salesperson's job. It always has been, John. You should know that."

"But if you wanted me to get four, why didn't you tell me? A two-minute phone call at the beginning of the year is all I needed."

"But, John, I can't spell out every last detail. You're a professional. You should know your job."

When goals are unclear or nonexistent, stress happens. Why work to accomplish something that is so murky you'll never know when you have achieved it? If the task is unclear, work is frustrating and stressful.

Attacking the Source of Stress: If you don't know what your goals are, write down what you think they are. Make sure you try to connect them with company goals and direction. Meet with your boss to get agreement.

Conflict

Probably, there is at least one person at work who is difficult to deal with and causes you a lot of stress.

Three things you should know right away if you are having problems with someone at work:

1. A problem person for you may be a pussycat for someone else. We all react to people differently, depending on what kind of behavior we are comfortable with.
2. Other people aren't going to change to make you happy, so if you are in a difficult situation, the burden is on you to improve the relationship.
3. Not everyone acts the same way you do, and that is okay. Not everyone makes decisions like you do, or uses time like you do. Some may be more aggressive and competitive, which you might see as scary; or less so, which you might feel is wimpy. Some may show their emotions more, so you easily know what they are feeling; or may control their emotions, so it is hard to get a reaction from them.

When you are working with a person who causes you stress, try moving toward that person's style of behavior a little, for a short period of time, to reduce tension in the relationship. For instance, if your "problem person" talks louder and faster than you do, you might want to up your tempo a little. If the person tends to take more risks and make decisions more quickly than you do, you should move in that direction. If the person takes more time than you do to study a situation, you might accommodate that person by supplying more data and by being more patient.

If you can reduce the tension level in the relationship by adjusting your behavior to make your "problem person" more relaxed with you, you will accomplish more and lessen your own tension.

You can't put your "problem person" on a couch and do a psycho-analysis, but you can think about what motivates that person to act the way he or she does. People do what pays off for them. The payoff may be recognition, money, satisfaction, control, being liked, feelings of well-being, being seen as a professional, or getting things done. If you can show your problem person that what you want will result in a payoff for him or her, it's much more likely you'll get it.

> **Attacking the Source of Stress:** Modify your own behavior for a short time to make the "difficult person" more comfortable with you.

Too Much Work

You are doing two or three jobs instead of one. You are working longer hours than ever before trying to accomplish an overwhelming workload. You wake up in the middle of the night worrying about your work and your career. You need to get control and get some order in all this.

There's no way you can manage an unmanageable workload without involving your boss. Set your goals, priorities, and how you plan to use your time, then discuss it all with your boss.

> **Attacking the Source of Stress:** Decide what your priorities are and where you should be spending your time, then discuss with your boss to get agreement.

Personal Habits

Maybe you overindulge to get away from it all. When occasional overdoing becomes a habit or an addiction, you have a problem.

Physically you feel rotten, and your self-esteem is in the Dumpster. You are actually adding to the stress of work by your own drinking, drug use, smoking, overeating, or other out-of-control behavior.

There are plenty of organizations that can help, and your employer may have an employee assistance referral program. It's up to you.

One way to get through it all, control your stress, and keep ahead of that monster workload is to keep your energy level high. Here are some hints from Lee Smith, writing in *Fortune,* to increase your energy level:

> Do 100 stomach crunches a day. Not sit-ups. Lie on your back, bend your knees. Hands behind your head. Lift partway slowly, pressing your back into the floor. Lower slowly and repeat. Squeeze the stomach muscles as you do this.
>
> Reduce your hours of sleep to six. Take a twenty-minute nap when you get home or on a plane to reenergize yourself. That's all you need.
>
> Eat five ounces of protein at lunch to supplement a carbohydrate diet. Salads for lunch are great over time, but be aware that fruits and veggies raise the level of serotonin in the brain, which is a natural tranquilizer. So if you don't want to be smiling serenely like Jimmy Swaggart at this afternoon's meeting, gnaw on some *red meat* (gasp!) for lunch.

> **Attacking the Source of Stress:** Make sure you aren't adding to the stress you already have with your personal habits. If you are, get help; you may not be able to do this alone.

Lack of Balance

Get a life. If work is everything, your work-related stress will be harder to deal with because there is nothing to balance it against. Stressful situations at work, if you're one-dimensional, seem much more important than they really are. You should have personal goals and interests in your life outside your job. Nothing will energize you more than having a life of your own outside of work.

Remember to put your work in life perspective. Think of this: You are one of nearly 6 billion people on earth, most of whom live in poverty. Our planet is a tiny speck in the universe, which is 8 to 12 billion years old. The nearest star is the sun, which is 93 million miles away. The Hubble Space Telescope has spotted M100, a galaxy in the Virgo cluster, that is 56 *million light-years* away.

How big are your problems anyway?

> **Attacking the Source of Stress:** A compelling interest outside of work can get you through a lot of tough situations.

Being Plateaued

Maybe you won't get to be CEO, but you hope for another promotion or two. That might have been realistic a few years ago, but today you may find yourself peaking at age thirty-five or forty. A lot of people are. Organizations have flattened out, layers of management are gone, and opportunities have disappeared. Even with that, a few people will still get promoted, and whenever that happens, if you're not one of them, it can add stress to your life. And, too, discrimination (or reverse discrimination) still plays a part in some promotional decisions, and this can cause great stress if you are a victim.

Another problem has to do with obsolescence. If you are in a technical field, your knowledge has a half-life of five to eight years. That means half of everything you know today will be obsolete in five years, and someone who is just coming out of school will be more valuable to the company—and cheaper to employ.

Okay, it looks like you are going to be in the same job for a long time, maybe forever. That doesn't mean you have to turn into a root vegetable. You can build challenge into your job, keep learning, and become more valuable to your employer. At one point in my corporate career, I was in the same job for ten years. But I kept on changing it. No one told me I could (or couldn't), so I did. It was a very different job when I left it than when I came in, and I was a different person. I was seldom bored.

Boredom is a very real danger if you are plateaued and can do your job in your sleep. That can be stressful because you will feel you are wasting your life.

Ways to deal with being plateaued:

Change the nature of your job.
Learn new things; acquire new skills.

Enrich your life outside the job: work on community-service projects; start a hobby.

Start your own business part-time.

Train someone new; become a mentor.

Volunteer for committees and task forces.

Build your networks.

Attacking the Source of Stress: If you're bored, don't just sit there. Take positive action to change your job and make it more interesting.

No Recognition

Some bosses aren't good at giving praise or are too busy. Or they feel you ought to know if you are doing a good job—after all, you get paid for doing good work. But you have to have recognition; it's a universal human need. If you aren't getting yours, you are going to have to educate your boss.

Attacking the Source of Stress: Tell your boss it would help you if you got more feedback on performance: praise when you do well, constructive criticism when you need to improve.

Travel

If you're like many people, you love to be places but hate getting there. The whole process of travel is designed to be aggravating, if not outright stressful. Why would you spend good company money to be crammed into a long tin can, turn over control of your life to someone in the cockpit you don't know, eat lousy food, and squint at movies on little screens?

All of this, besides taking enormous amounts of time and boring you to death, takes you away from home, the place you want to be in the first place.

Here are some suggestions from frequent travelers.

Call ahead to the hotel and arrange transportation so you don't have to search around at the airport.

Always get boarding passes before you go to the airport. Get any changes processed beforehand so you can go right to the gate when you get to the airport and don't have to grow old (and stressed) standing in line.

Get there at least a half hour before flight time.

If the waiting area looks crowded, go to the podium even if you have boarding passes—you may get bumped if you don't check in.

Order special meals twenty-four hours in advance.

Take it easy on the booze.

Work on the airplane, but take time for a movie or a novel, too. Use your laptop for games.

Carry on all your baggage if you can.

Ask if there are upgrades available before you get on the plane, and at the hotel.

Don't take a hotel room you don't like, or if something is broken like the TV or the safety latch on the door.

Use room service if you don't want to eat alone in the dining room.

Find alternatives to travel like E-mail and videoconferencing, and save the company money and yourself a lot of grief.

> **Attacking the Source of Stress:** Don't get pushed around; ask for what you want, and arrange what will make you comfortable.

Giving People Bad News

Bosses have unhappy jobs these days, and some are having emotional and other health problems from all the dirty work they have to do. After firing 120 subordinates, or even one, you may begin to wonder why you became a manager in the first place.

The rules in giving bad news are:

Be direct.

Say what you have to say.

Tell the employee you are sorry.

Give the employee some hope (for instance, that the company will provide severance and outplacement).

> **Attacking the Source of Stress:** Remember, this is work. It is not personal. Sometimes you have to do things that are distasteful, and that is part of every manager's job.

Being Onstage

If speaking in front of groups bothers you (and it does everyone), the best way to reduce the stress is to be prepared. When you know your stuff so well you are confident in delivering it, giving a presentation will seem much less threatening.

Usually, when you are under stress, other people can't tell. Build on that, and by showing how cool you are, you will become cool.

> **Attacking the Source of Stress:** Prepare, and know your presentation so well you can do it in your sleep.

Money (Not Enough)

You have more going out than coming in. Credit cards are maxed out. Costs are going up and your income isn't. Your dad had a BMW when he was your age, and you are struggling to keep up the payments on a Geo.

Use the energy this difficult situation creates to attack the problem.

> **Attacking the Source of Stress:** Take positive steps to build income and reduce expenses. Use the strategies outlined in the "Financial Planning" section of chapter 7.

> **SBI:** Use stress-reduction techniques to get temporary relief, but use the power stress gives you to attack root causes of stress.

4

HOLY COW, I'VE
BEEN EMPOWERED!

How to Springboard from the Latest Fad

CEO: "Ned, our market share is going south, and sales are flat. We've got to turn this thing around. We need a real quality program in here, and we need it fast. I want you to spearhead it for us."

Ned: "Great. I know of a couple of consultants who might be able to help us. What's your timetable on this?"

CEO: "I want results by the end of the quarter."

The Program of the Week

Part of being a manager is the continuing search for that magic potion that will bring you and your company greatness. Each generation of managers takes its turn at stirring up witches' brews, and, not wanting to do what their predecessors did, they tweak old processes, give them new names, and introduce them with great fanfare: "Finally, we have found the answer!"

Those of us who have been around a while have lived through Theory X and Theory Y, participative management, flex-time, two-way communication, and the open-door policy. We have tried job enrichment, zero defects, quality circles, and Japanese management. We have been centralized, decentralized, and positively reinforced. And when all else failed, we've put on masks and gone to sensitivity training.

Some of those strategies actually worked well for a few companies, because those companies made them work. They knew how to do things right anyway, and probably if they had employees recite the multiplication tables every morning sales and profits would have gone up and *Fortune* magazine would have done a feature article on the Miracle Multiplication Table Process.

Many panaceas, introduced as the future of management, quickly become jokes around the organization. Not that there is anything wrong with the approaches themselves—who can argue with participative management? The problem is usually in the way they are managed.

Still, the quest continues. The last few years have brought in a whole new crop of potions, nostrums, and elixirs. Many of them make a lot of sense, some are being applied well, and a few have even saved companies from ultimate disaster. But many others have quickly ended up as the chortle of the week.

Nearly 80 percent of medium and large employers have adopted some form of quality circles, TQM, team-based systems, or some other "new" approach. With mixed results. For every employee who has been successfully empowered, for instance, there are a bunch cowering in their work spaces, trying to be invisible till the craze is over and they can get back to work.

And, after all the fuss, a recent survey of several hundred companies found that use of these management tools and techniques doesn't seem to correlate with good financial results.

Why New Programs Fail

Obviously, not all new programs fail. Many are great successes. Toyota, Motorola, Hewlett-Packard, Ford, Honda, L. L. Bean, Xerox, Milliken, and a few others have made TQM work for them. Hallmark, Taco Bell, and Bell Atlantic have done well with reengineering. Nordstrom has truly empowered workers, doing this well before anyone invented the word. Another retailer, JCPenney, has been using participative management—involving salespeople in buying and merchandising decisions—for nearly a hundred years.

But for every one of these success stories, there are hundreds of failures: programs begun with great hope and promise, only to be cut back or abandoned when they didn't prove to be the magic cure.

Here are some reasons programs fail:

Management is impatient. U.S. managers want quick fixes, and if a program doesn't produce change overnight, they want to ax it. Most true change efforts don't work in a day, however—or in a month or a year or two years. "Two years? Good God, we don't have time for that." This is not entirely management's fault. Wall Street analysts and big institutional investors put a lot of pressure on companies. If the numbers aren't good this quarter, management will hear about it. Two quarters in a row, there's hell to pay.

Management doesn't take the time to understand what the concept (quality, for instance) is, and what it takes to make it work, and therefore doesn't support it or fund it properly.

A corollary to that: Management feels "We are better than they are." After learning a little about what other companies have done to make an effort succeed, management says, "We don't need all that, we can do it with half the staff, half the budget, and none of the training. Our managers can make this work." They can't, and they won't. Six months later management declares the program no good and drops it. In trying to streamline or "improve" a process, management sucks the life out of it.

Management tries to impose the process with no involvement of the people who have to make it work. People don't like that, and don't support the process, which is not theirs but management's. "Quality? It's just a way to get more work out of me."

Everything is seen as a program with a beginning and an end that operates separately from the rest of the business. But empowerment, customer service, and self-directed teams are not programs. They are a way of life, as much a part of the organization as marketing, sales, and finance.

Management expects too much. Wanting a 100 percent improvement, it fails to see that 30 percent may be truly remarkable.

How to Pick the Winners and Support Them

So, what does all this mean to you? It means that, ready or not, new things are coming along. Within the next year or two, top management in your organization is going to get very excited about some new approach to greatness. And wanting to leave their mark on corporate history, like Henry Ford's assembly line or Lee Iacocca's miracle turn-around at Chrysler, they will latch on to the new approach, install it with great fanfare, and expect that it will finally be the answer they have been searching for.

It may turn out to be more like Howard Hughes's *Spruce Goose*, which flew once and has been sitting in hangars ever since.

You may be asked to run the implementation of this new process. Or help with it. It may change your responsibilities and the nature of your job. It may increase or decrease the resources (budget and people) you have to work with. It may relieve you of your job altogether and put you out in the street.

The trick is to anticipate how much the new attempt will help or hurt you. If you are asked to be involved in its implementation, you'd better be sure the company is serious about it, otherwise you will be forever associated with a failed program, another company ha-ha.

The new program is headed for trouble if:

- The CEO talks a good game but isn't putting resources behind the program.
- There is no clear picture of where the company wants to go with the program. Instead there are lots of fuzzy slogans.
- Nobody talks about customers.
- The program seems to be for people in the factory or people working with the customers, not for management.
- It will be imposed from above without much input from lower levels in the organization.
- It is a one-shot deal. There are no long-range plans and it is seen as a "program," not a way of life.
- The company is making only a limited investment in training, or no investment.
- The company has a history of implementing programs-of-the-week with great fanfare, then, not getting instant results, pulling out of them.

It is usually an honor to be asked to be involved in any new company direction, but if too many of the above warning signs are there, you may want to try to avoid it. If you can. Sometimes it is not possible and you will have to make the best of it.

If you are asked to go into a situation that doesn't look good to you:

1. Express your gratitude and your concerns. Do that at the outset, not after you are involved. Your best leverage is before you start, before you accept the offer, not after the program is under way.
2. Try to get some firm agreement that your concerns will be addressed.
3. If the response is "Don't worry about it. Everything will be fine," it won't. Find out what the possibilities are that you can opt out. And what the penalties will be: will you be seen as less than a team player? Uncooperative? Negative? Being critical of top management? Probably. But those might be forgotten much sooner than being associated with a large-scale flop.
4. If you do get involved with the program, give it all you've got. Even if it is only in a limited area. I've seen individual managers who have great quality or customer service efforts going in their own departments at the same time the company overall is struggling to get the same effort off the ground. These managers are seen as heroes, and others gather around to learn from them.

Meanwhile, it might help to understand some of the areas that are intriguing companies today.

Reengineering

Reengineering, as we all know by now, is everywhere. Any company that is not reengineering is not worth a nickel of investors' money. Even companies that are having record sales and profits and are gaining share of market are reengineering because they feel it will give them an additional competitive advantage . . . or because it is the thing to do. Other popular terms for reengineering include restructuring, rightsizing, streamlining, downsizing, and "You're fired."

Although a few companies are reengineering without trashing their workforces, a lot of others have gotten rid of people in bunches.

Reengineering, in its purest sense, is not designed to fire people, although that often happens as part of the change. It is primarily meant to do wonderful things for an organization.

> . . . jobs evolve from narrow and task-oriented to multidimensional. People who once did as they were instructed now make choices and decisions on their own instead. Assembly-line work disappears. Functional departments lose their reasons for being. Managers stop acting like supervisors and behave more like coaches. Workers focus more on the customers' need and less on their boss's. Attitudes and values change in response to new incentives. Practically every aspect of the organization is transformed, often beyond recognition.
>
> —from Hammer and Champy,
> *Reengineering the Corporation*

No wonder everybody wants to reengineer. But the road to such a corporate paradise may have more than a few speed bumps. How closely does the above description fit what's happening in your organization?

Reengineering involves examining the processes in an organization and redesigning the business around those processes so the organization can serve its customers faster, more accurately, and more profitably. Most companies today are organized around functions: sales, order department, distribution, credit, and so on, all doing bits and pieces of the overall job of providing products and services to the customer. This creates a lot of paper passing, which is slow, unnecessary, and does a disservice to the customer. Reengineers look at processes instead of functions, and in doing so they often find ways for one person or department to take over all the functions involved in the process, eliminating wasted time and effort.

Sometimes, as work is redesigned this way, it can be done by fewer people than were in the chain before. And that brings layoffs.

But, of course, some companies skip the bother of reengineering and just go right to firing people. When management looks at ways to cut expenses, it runs into salary cost, which is normally the largest expense after raw materials or merchandise, in some cases the largest overall expense. When combined with the cost of benefits, it becomes a real eye-catcher—cuts here will produce dramatic effects on the bottom line. At least in the short term. What happens competitively when there aren't enough people, talent, and expertise to get the job done? We are about to find out in the next few years.

Eighty-three percent of the largest industrial companies have reengineered, and 70 percent say this has increased productivity. But that has not come without a price. Of remaining employees in those firms, 69 percent say reengineering is just an excuse for layoffs, 55 percent feel overworked, and a full 75 percent are afraid they'll lose their own jobs. (Data from Pitney Bowes Management Services Inc.)

Even James Champy himself, co-author of *Reengineering the Corporation*, now has some doubts. He says in his new book, *Reengineering Management,* "Reengineering is in trouble ... [it] has gone only halfway ... half a revolution is not better than none. It may, in fact, be worse."

What Does All This Mean to You?

1. If your organization hasn't reengineered yet, chances are it will. Get ready.
2. Be careful, because now that reengineering is getting a bad name, consultants are coming up with new names to disguise it. Whenever you hear "efficiency," "return to investors," "team management," "improved customer service," or even "take a look at our organization," run for your life.
3. Just because sales and earnings are good—they may even be the best they have ever been and your company may be leading the industry—you can't relax, because management feels investors are insatiable and want the company reengineered to anorexia. In fact, many of the downsizing headlines today are followed by subheads about record earnings.
4. If you get reengineered out of your job, there's one small consolation: chances are your ex-company is going to be a worse place to work—survivors are going to be overworked, stressed out, and angry. It will not be the warm fuzzy place it was when you were there.

Empowerment

"If you empower dummies, you get bad decisions faster."
—Rich Teerlink, CEO, Harley-Davidson

Empowerment involves pushing problem solving and decision making to the lowest possible level, giving those people most involved the authority to make decisions that will serve customers better and faster. It makes a lot of sense. Eliminate levels of approval that slow everything down, and respond to customers quickly with answers right out there on the front line, where people know what to do anyhow.

Empowerment is not new—it has been around for decades, ever since managers discovered that people one or two levels down (where they came from themselves) might have tiny sparks of intelligence and might be able to make decisions without screwing up everything. Management has been trying to make empowerment work, in some form or another, since World War II.

Problems with Empowerment

Empowerment could work wonders if companies could do it right, but there are several roadblocks in the way.

1. Managers feel threatened giving away decisions they usually make. Justifiably so in today's employment market: "If I give my people all the decisions to make, what does the company need me for?" So managers talk empowerment but don't let it happen.
2. Companies have zero tolerance for mistakes. When you start to give people more authority, no matter how well you train them, they will make mistakes. And first thing you know, you are on the carpet for not staying on top of what's happening in your department.

   Many people, deep down, don't trust other people and feel they can do things better themselves.
3. Managers can make a good case for limiting empowerment. Usually they will pick the dumbest, most incompetent person in their department, and say, "Elmo could never handle that." And everyone will agree.
4. Companies will talk empowerment but won't invest in training to give people the skills they need to make empowered decisions. So they screw up because they don't have the skills and then management says, "This empowerment is hooey."
5. It is very difficult to empower people who have spent their whole careers having others make decisions for them. They have grown so dependent they find it very hard to take on the responsibility for themselves.

But, done well, empowerment can be a major competitive advantage. If the standards of performance are clear, if people are trained and qualified to handle the increased authority, and if management can hold back a little on hammering people for mistakes, empowerment can improve performance and build customer loyalty beyond anything known before.

True story: In a Nordstrom's store in Seattle, a customer was looking fondly at a cashmere sweater and said to a salesperson, "My aunt would love this sweater, but she lives in Cleveland and I don't know what size she is."

Without blinking an eye, the salesperson said, "There's a phone, call her."

Now, what do you think would happen if you walked into most department stores and tried to use the phone to make a long-distance call?

But think of what that empowered decision did for Nordstrom's. First, it got them a sale. Cost of the sweater? $250. Cost of the phone call? A few bucks. Second, it was such a surprising turn of events (and such a simple, direct solution to a problem) that the customer will remember it forever—and will tell about five hundred friends. And they all will have very good feelings for Nordstrom's and want to shop there.

Nordstrom's has a real advantage in that it grew up as a company with empowerment. The Nordstrom family has, from the very beginning, told its people, "Do whatever it takes to make the customer happy," and has supported that by trying not to second-guess decisions salespeople make.

If you work for an organization that has mostly a top-down control culture, empowerment will have a more difficult time taking hold.

Here are some special empowerment situations and how you can handle them.

If your boss doesn't want you to be empowered: Maybe, despite the best intentions of the company, your boss doesn't want to get on the program. If that happens to you, do this:

First, make sure you are qualified to be empowered. Maybe your boss is hesitant because you haven't demonstrated you can do it.

If you can honestly say you can take on additional problem solving and decision making, it's time to talk with your boss. But don't just go in beating your chest like Tarzan and saying, "Me want

empowerment." Have a plan first. Fill out a chart like the one below and take it with you as a guide for your discussion.

EMPOWERMENT PLAN

Types of Decisions/ Approvals I Could Make	Benefits to the Boss	Benefits to the Company

If you feel you need training or coaching to do this successfully, make
that part of your discussion list.

Don't eat the whole pie at once. Start with a slice. Suggest to your
boss that you would like to begin with one or two decision areas first to
prove you can do it. If it doesn't work out, he or she can always yank
back your decisions. Stress the benefit to your boss: freeing up his or
her time to work on higher-level issues, to get out of the trenches, and
to take some pressure off. Also it can create happier customers and
make the boss look good.

If your people don't want to be empowered: If you have been making most of the decisions for your people, they probably won't feel comfortable doing it themselves, at least at first. Identify decision areas they
should handle. Better yet, let them identify those decisions, or do it to-

gether. Start with simple ones. Provide training in problem solving and decision making. Then gradually turn them loose. Provide positive recognition, and be tolerant of mistakes, looking at them as learning experiences.

Here's an approach that works for me. You can use it if you supervise only a small group or if you manage hundreds. You can also use it with your team.

Recently, a client company asked me to work with factory foremen to get them to "take charge" and not run to the plant manager with every little decision or problem. The company culture, very conservative and careful, had not supported that in the past, and foremen did not believe the company really meant it.

The first thing I did was get together informally with a number of foremen to talk about their jobs. From these discussions we came up with a list of responsibilities. (You can get these from job descriptions, too, but be careful. Most job descriptions were last updated when unicycles were popular. And, too, there are real benefits in involving the people themselves in this process.)

We came up with sixteen responsibilities, such as:

1. Assure that all materials, equipment, and tools are on hand and in order.
2. Find ways to motivate people doing routine jobs.
3. Keep subordinates fully informed as to what they need to do. Keep your manager or supervisor informed of what is happening in your area, and keep subordinates informed about what management expects of your area.
4. Set high standards of job performance and quality for subordinates, and be sure they understand those standards. Discuss job performance with each subordinate on a regular basis—both strengths and areas for improvement. Discuss problems immediately.
   . . . and so on.

Then, in workshops I ran for the foremen, I had them work in small groups and gave each group four or five responsibilities to work on. I asked them to come up with an action plan for each responsibility covering exactly what they had to do to carry it out and what decisions—now made by the plant manager—they could and should be making.

When they were done, we got the groups back together and called in the plant manager and several people from corporate. Each group reported on its work.

This was followed by discussions, sometimes spirited, and participants hammered out a course of action. It is not working perfectly, but foremen are making a lot more decisions than they did in the past, and productivity in the factories has improved.

If your company is downsizing. Can you empower people while others are being laid off? No.

It is hard to implement anything when there is no job security, no loyalty to the company, or no belief in what management says. All the talk about empowerment, teamwork, and on and on is just that—so much talk.

If you are empowered. Your boss tells you the company wants to empower people to act on behalf of the customer and that from now on, when customers have problems or requests, you should make decisions first and check with him later. "The answer is yes," he tells you. "What is the question?" Oh, boy!

Before you run off and begin deciding, check out these:

Find out what kinds of decisions you can make and what the limits are. "If the customer has a defective $2 part, can I replace it without approval?" "Of course!" "If the customer has a defective $20,000 machine, and needs it to keep his business open, can I replace it without approval?" "Hell, no!" Somewhere in between is your limit. Pin it down.

Find out what will happen if you make a mistake. Not that you intend to, but just in case.

Find out if the company is going to give you problem-solving and decision-making training, and if not, will the company pay for you to attend outside courses.

Do you need other resources to do this? Budget money? (Forget it.) Access to information, files, duplicate keys, a cellular phone? Laptop computer? Whatever it is, now is the time to discuss it with the boss.

If at first you are uncertain about a decision, check with your boss. But don't go in and ask, "What shall I do?" Go in with what you think should be done and say, "What do you think of my approach?"

Go ahead and use your new power, and take over the decision areas you and your boss identified. Don't wait six months; it will all be forgotten.

Quality

Becoming Quality Connected

Quality was supposed to be the answer. Companies worked at it, counted on it, worshiped it. Like many fixes du jour, it has disappointed. Up to two thirds of U.S. managers think total quality management (TQM) has failed in their companies.

Everyone should be doing something about quality these days. Unfortunately, there are lots of deterrents to quality, like trying to make a profit. Someone is always coming up with great ideas for saving money and taking that saving to the bottom line. Like the engineer a few years ago who found a cheaper gasket for a luxury car. Savings: $10 million per year. Result: Oil leaks under every car, angry customers, increased repair costs, and erosion of reputation.

And, too, there is the rush to get product (or service) out the door: "Ship it and we'll fix it in the field."

Quality efforts were a long time coming in the United States, but in the early 1980s, long after the Japanese were building quality into everything, some companies finally started listening to quality gurus W. Edwards Deming and Dr. J. M. Juran. In the next few years, the business community went quality nuts. It began to spend big bucks on statistical measurement, consultants, quality meetings, and filling out mountains of quality award forms. It became obsessed with cost cutting, cycle times, and defect reduction. And many businesses found that as their quality figures went up, their sales and profit figures went down. Wallace Company won the Malcolm Baldrige National Quality Award in 1990 and two years later went Chapter 11.

What these companies succeeded in doing was getting everyone's work efforts focused on quality to the extent they forgot about the customer. Going after new production records, they forgot to return customer phone calls. Rushed to meet deadlines, they had no time to explain anything to the customer. UPS, after years of working feverishly to reduce delivery time, found that customers really wanted to spend more time with drivers and get their advice on shipping methods. What UPS had seen as quality was not what customers saw as quality. The best quality processes in the world, if they don't show up in customer satisfaction, won't show up on the bottom line.

Many quality programs were badly implemented, halfheartedly supported, and surrounded by unrealistic expectations. And when ISO 9000 came along, it gave companies a detailed set of guidelines for quality-related processes—testing products, training employees, keeping records, and fixing defects—but did not address the quality of products or services actually produced! Or whether customers were happy.

But many companies are working to change their cultures, to build quality throughout their organizations. And some have made remarkable progress. Motorola used its Six Sigma Program to eliminate virtually all product defects. General Motors improved the quality of its cars and eliminated many of the problems of the 1980s. Xerox, whose share of market was dropping, launched a major quality training effort, involving everyone in the organization, and turned the company around.

Eastman Chemical, Federal Express, Solectron, Westinghouse, and AT&T, all Baldrige Award winners, outperformed the Standard & Poor's 500 by at least 3 to 1, some by as much as 6.5 to 1.

Now we have a new generation of quality: Return on Quality. This measures the cost of the quality project against how much it is going to improve the bottom line. AT&T has found that when customers feel that quality has improved, it will show up in better financial results three months later.

Quality is a given today. No company can compete without it—both quality of products and services, and quality of support areas in the company to keep expenses down and productivity high. What used to be sensational in the 1980s, and a real competitive advantage, is only a starting place today. It will get your foot in the door, but it won't distinguish you from hundreds of other companies that are working on quality, too.

What does this mean to you?

Make sure you talk about it, and if the company doesn't have a formal program, start one in your area. Everyone loves quality, and you'll be seen as a champion if you are on the leading edge.

If you are asked to participate in a quality program, or if you are going to implement one in your own area, here are some things you should do to make quality work.

Go the whole nine yards. Resist pressures to look for ways to save money. Quality demands an investment of dollars and time. If you "streamline" it, you'll doom it. But don't try to fix everything at once. Start with a few goals, and do them well. You can add others later.

Get a clear picture of what quality looks like. Get all your people and your customers involved in deciding what quality is and don't let them end up with fuzzy slogans. Set specific quality-improvement goals with your people. Don't decide them on your own and try to implement them.

Focus on customer needs, not on company needs or Baldrige Awards. Build quality around customers and what they want. It's the only reason to do it. Consider internal as well as external customers.

Be as much involved in the quality effort as your people are. Don't exempt yourself—that only gives the signal that quality isn't very important.

Give everybody training in quality—what it means and the skills they need to achieve it.

Measure progress and give rewards and recognition to everyone who does well.

Make long-range plans for continuous improvement. Quality isn't a one-shot deal or a "program," it is a way of life. Give it time.

Thriving on Diversity

"Value diversity," a familiar buzz term, is not technically a fad, but it fits in this chapter because it is more talked about than honored.

For instance, women now make up 57.8 percent of the workforce. But, while 15.1 percent of males in the workforce are managers, only 7.5 percent of women hold managerial positions. Blacks and Hispanics make up almost 20 percent of the workforce, but their representation in management is very small.

Current wisdom is that between today and the turn of the century only 15 percent of additions to the workforce in the United States will be white males. The rest will be women, Americans of African-

American, Hispanic, Asian, Native American, and Pacific Islander descent, and immigrants.

Whatever group you are in, as you look around the workplace there are people there whose values, appearance, lifestyles, work habits, and even languages are different from yours. If that bothers you—makes you uncomfortable, suspicious, or apprehensive about "why they act that way"—you are in trouble.

You are also in the majority, because human beings don't naturally accept differences. A recent study of workplace relations financed by fifteen large companies and foundations found that more than half of those surveyed still prefer working with people of the same race, sex, and education level.

But differences are here today, like it or not, and what you must do is look for talents and strengths in people around you, look at how they can contribute rather than how they are different.

In case you haven't thought them through, here are some reasons for supporting diversity:

- It's the law. Equal Employment Opportunity (EEO) programs direct that equal employment opportunities must be given to all kinds of groups. (Affirmative Action, for years the stimulation to actively work on providing opportunities for protected groups, is now under question.)
- The population of the country is diverse and becoming more so. Your customer base is diverse. Why not your workforce?
- Diverse groups, with ideas coming from nonhomogeneous sources, can increase creativity and innovation. Even the tension of dealing with people who don't share the same backgrounds can stimulate creativity.
- One of the major obstacles to diversity programs is resistance of white males, who fear being passed over in favor of women or minorities. So if you are a white male, you have a lot to lose. But white males still dominate at the upper levels of business and will for some time.

    Diversity can complement just about every company program described in this chapter, mainly by bringing in varied viewpoints and enhancing creativity. TQM, teams, reengineering, and empowerment can all be enhanced by the tensions and power of diversity.

What does diversity mean to you?

1. If you have problems working with people who have backgrounds different from yours, you'd better try to become more comfortable with it, because that's the atmosphere you are going to work in for the rest of your career.

   - Make a special effort to get to know people who are different from you. Go to lunch or out for a drink with them once in a while.
   - Listen carefully to others' views. Don't make judgments right away, but try to understand where they are coming from.
   - Tell yourself it is okay for people to be different from you.
   - Try to use divergent and varied viewpoints to come up with better solutions to problems and better ways of operating.
   - Find ways for everyone to make a unique contribution—seek out and build on people's strengths rather than focus on how they are different from you.
   - Remember, this is not just being nice to people or loving all people regardless of race, creed, or color. It is your career that is at stake. This is not optional; you have to make diversity work for you.

2. If it isn't obvious to you, you may want to assess your employer's position on diversity. Take a mental trip around your organization. Are minorities represented in top management or is it all white males? Do you still hear ethnic jokes and slurs? Do the women and men eat lunch at separate tables? Do blacks have tables of their own? Are holidays of all groups recognized, or just those of Christian whites? Are all the men called "Mr." and all the women called by their first names? You can begin to see very quickly how the culture of your company actually feels about diversity.

3. You will have to reconcile your own feelings and beliefs with those of your employer—not the views your employer states, but those it actually practices. If you are working for an organization that does not value diversity and you do . . .

   - You can stay put and do nothing. And suffer because you are discriminated against, or because your conscience is bothering you.

- You can try to change the organization by encouraging the hiring and promotion of people from diverse groups. In some organizations that will not do your reputation any good, and will brand you as a do-gooder—or worse.
- If you are a victim of discrimination, you can file a complaint with the Equal Employment Opportunity Commission. Doing this will effectively end your career with the company, and with the current EEOC backlog, your case may come up in about the year 2056.
- You can leave and go somewhere else.

4. If, on the other hand, you work for a company that values diversity and you don't, you have another kind of problem that I don't have a good answer for. Not in today's world.

Self-Directed Work Teams

Here is a concept that has great potential for organizations, and some are beginning to use it successfully. But for all their virtues, teams are:

- Slow to make decisions and get things done. Just the process of getting people to agree is difficult.
- Costly in terms of time team members have to invest in team activities.
- Not generally built into company appraisal or incentive systems. That is, team members do not get any special reward or recognition for being effective team players.
- Suspect. Managers may not love teams, since their people are off doing things on their own with the team instead of doing their regular jobs.

But teams can move a company ahead. They can come up with creative new directions and can energize a workforce—people love to participate in teams.

What do teams mean to you?
If you are asked to be on a team, make sure you:

Find out what the mission of the team is. "Improve customer service"? That's too vague. Get something more specific that can be measured. How will you know when you are there?

Pin down the parameters. What decisions can the team make? What resources does it have? Where can team members go and who can they talk with?

Find out how much time you will spend on the team. What will happen to your regular work when you are doing team work?

Determine what consideration will be given to your success as a team when it's time for appraisals, merit increases.

Ask your boss how he or she feels about your participating in the team.

Introspection

Today, more and more people are looking inside themselves for answers. That's fine and probably healthy. Now some companies are "helping" by incorporating introspection into training programs or bringing in consultants to facilitate the process. If you fancy spilling your guts in front of your boss and your peers, go to it, but it is not for everyone, especially in this age of competitiveness when nobody wants to be seen having any sort of weakness or self-doubt. Some companies, like Procter & Gamble, have tried introspection programs and canned them.

Introspection is a fancy term for a commonsense idea, as most of the fads in this chapter are. Essentially, when you get in touch with yourself, you will be more self-confident, better able to deal with ambiguity, and more inclined to take action and find balance in life. You should become more creative and more willing to work in support of the goals of the team or the company rather than your own. Not bad for taking a few minutes each day to figure out what is going on inside you.

What introspection means to you.

If you fancy this sort of thing, and your company offers it, by all means go ahead. But there is no reason you can't do it on your own. Here's a simple approach to getting in touch with yourself:

Write down everything you want to accomplish in your life. Everything. Then sort, combine, and narrow down the list to a half-dozen key goals. That's what you are about and what you should devote your energies to. Or, write down what you would like to be remembered for when you go to the great boardroom in the sky—what a friend would say about you, a business associate, your spouse, or a child.

When you are done, you should have a clearer idea of what is important to you in life, and that should give you better direction on where you should go from here.

Alliances

Building alliances with suppliers is a good way to work with them to reduce costs—doing that successfully can help both your company and its suppliers. Sometimes, though, companies start out to make partners of suppliers, then whack them if they don't reduce prices and end up with less trust and a worse relationship than they started with.

If you work with suppliers, you will have to find the right balance between building problem-solving relationships and setting high standards for quality and cost control. Talk with suppliers about alliances and partnering only if your company will support that sort of relationship. If your company's only interest is price, forget trying to make that seem like an alliance.

Here Come the Consultants

If they haven't swarmed over your company and your department yet, they will. Consulting is a $20-billion-a-year business, growing at the rate of 10 percent per year. There are about 80,000 of them out there. Their services run from critically important, organization-saving strategies to promotion of silly fads, buzzwords, and other kinds of management fizz. All of them are expensive.

But consultants hold great power in today's world. Good ones are relied on and respected and have the ear of senior management.

Because consultants, like killer bees, are on the increase today, you ought to know how to deal with them.

Before You Hire a Consultant

- Ask yourself if you can do the work in-house.
- Look around before you sign a contract. Find consultants who have expertise you need, and check with recent clients to see how well they performed. Ask friends in other companies for names of consultants that have helped them.
- Look at all sizes of consultants. Large mega-firms have huge resources and tons of expertise. They will dazzle you with fantastic presentations and parade endless MBAs through your office. Small ones do not have the resources and the wide client experience to draw from but can give you personalized, caring service—and may have just as much expertise to offer.
- Be sure you get a written agreement as to what services are to be performed, by whom, when, and at what expense. Fees quoted by consultants normally are for their time. All other expenses are extra.
- Become part of the consulting team. Make other managers in your area part of the team. When the consulting job is done, you may be able to carry the process on to other parts of the company without going outside.
- Make your own people responsible for implementing and sustaining the changes resulting from the consultant's work. Consultants can't implement very well, and they can't sustain change over time.

When the Consultant Comes Calling

Many consulting jobs involve talking with people in the organization. Remember, the consultant has the big boss's attention, and it is not uncommon for the CEO to ask the consultant, "What did you think of Joe?" (you).

So, when the consultant comes to see you:

- Keep a positive attitude about your job and the company.
- Don't trash co-workers or bosses.

- Be candid, even if critical. You can always hedge by saying, "Look, this is a great company, and this is one way I think it could be even better. . . ." Give the consultant your ideas and suggestions, even ones that have been shot down in the past.
- Remember, not all consultants are there to eliminate your job.
- Don't try to bluff the consultant. Consultants have talked with thousands of people, and they know when you are blowing smoke. A good consultant will dig until he or she gets something out of you—but will think less of you for stonewalling. "Everything is fine, this is a great company, I really don't have any suggestions for improvement." "Oh, sure . . . Let me ask the question this way. . . ."
- Keep away from minor gripes and bitches. Keep your suggestions focused on things that will help the company achieve its goals and/or will improve response to the customer and build business or increase profits.
- Talk in the consultant's language. Consultants love buzzwords because they invented most of them. Talk about empowerment and quality if you want to impress the consultant. Phrases like "Walk the walk," "win-win," "paradigm shift," "market driven," and "know your customer" are music to a consultant's ears.

Employee Counseling

If your company has an employee-assistance program, it could save your life, or at least make it bearable. Before you use the program, however, find out who inside and outside the company will have access to your records. There was a case, for instance, where an employee had been very open with a counselor, only to find later that records were subpoenaed and used against him in a divorce custody suit.

Use the assistance program if you need it, but be aware that it may not be as confidential as you are led to believe.

Mentoring

Mentoring is a sound enough idea—latching on to someone who can teach you something and do your career some good—and it has worked well for many people. Today, however, traditional mentoring is on the way out. That esteemed higher-up, worried about hanging on to his or her own job, has little time or patience for giving others advice. Also, would-be mentors could be worried that they might lose their jobs to the younger and lower-paid people they are supposed to guide.

Forget mentoring? No, today the new approach is to find many mentors, inside and outside the company—senior people, peers, even subordinates. Build constituencies, learn from all of them, and go to them for support. Look around the organization, look at suppliers and customers, even at competitors. Who are the people you admire, the people who have skills and experience you would like to have? Find ways to keep in contact—take a mentor to lunch, get on a team with another, ask to assist another with a project assignment.

There are potential mentors all around you who can help you learn and increase your value to your employer—and help you become more marketable to other employers. But you will have to take the initiative to seek them out, court them, and build relationships.

SBI: As exciting as new programs may be, it takes sustained effort, attention, and big bucks to make them work. Support your company's efforts, but be realistic about what is needed for success.

5

So Much to Do, So Little Time

How to Get the Most Out of Your Time

Boss: "How are you coming on your goals for this year?"
Sam: "Hey, I don't have time to work on stuff like that."

Okay, I know you're working hard. Maybe you are working so hard you're worried about burnout. Burnout is new, but being burned out is not. There were always people who worked hard, were exhausted, and had the hopeless feeling they would never get it all done. I knew plenty of people, even back in the Jurassic era of the 1960s, who put in incredible hours six or seven days a week. Back then it was not wise to phone the boss and say, "I'm dog tired, depressed, and I think I'll stay home today and rest."

Today, you call in, mention burnout, and the company will rush over a half-dozen psychologists and social workers, and put your HMO on alert that there may be big treatment on the way. I'm not demeaning your titanic efforts, I just want you to know that you are not the first person in history to work hard.

You may not want to admit it, but you probably don't mind working hard, putting in those long hours. If you're like most, you enjoy what you do, you like being needed, and you relish that sense of accomplishment. When you finally get home and relax with a double Snapple on the rocks, you can say, "I really earned this." What absolutely destroys you, though, is the fact that you have twice as much to do as you can ever get done, and always feel a sense of failure that you are not finishing it all. And even if you were able to accomplish everything, the company would reward you by giving you more to do, and even if you could do *that*, you probably wouldn't get a raise or a promotion.

There is nothing I can tell you that will solve your workload problems, and don't believe anyone who claims they can. There are only twenty-four hours in any day. You can work effectively maybe seven or eight of them, stumble around and go through the motions for another four, and that's it. If you have sixteen or twenty hours of work to do every day, you aren't going to get all of it done, no matter what I tell you.

But what I can do is this. I can help you think of time differently and approach your work in a way that will help you get the most out of the time you have.

Rules of Time

1. You can't manage time. Like Ol' Man River, it just keeps rolling along. You can't stop it or buy more of it. What you can do is to focus the way you spend the time that's available.
2. Short-term tasks, projects, crises, and day-to-day routine tend to capture your time and prevent you from working on larger goals and priorities that are more important to you.
3. If you want to do more with the time you have, remember this: *You can't do it alone.* The key to effective time use is involving others who matter—especially your boss.
4. Time, by itself, is only part of the work equation. Programs that ask you to keep time logs and calculate time versus goals miss the point. You can invest an hour in a project and waste it completely. You can spend fifteen minutes and make real progress. The difference is how well you focus on work that is important and how much problem-solving ability, creativity, and judgment you apply to getting that work done.

   So what you should be thinking about is not just time, but time in terms of priorities and brainpower applied. If you can find ways to focus your time on those things that have the highest payoff *and* apply concentrated intellect to the time you spend, you will get more done, do it better, and get control of your workload.

What Happens to Your Time?

Over the years, I have kept a record of time killers mentioned by participants in my seminars. Here are the ones most often mentioned:

Killers imposed on you

Interruptions
Shifting priorities
Waiting for answers
Unclear job definition
Unnecessary meetings
Too much work
Poor communication
Equipment failure
Disorganized boss
Red tape
Conflicting priorities
Travel

Killers you impose on yourself

Procrastination
Poor planning
Can't say no
Poor delegation
Untrained staff
Poor attitude
Disorganization, lack of discipline, clutter
Not listening
Indecision
Socializing
Fatigue
Leaving tasks unfinished
Paper shuffling
Outside activities
Unclear personal goals
Perfectionism
Attempting too much

How many of these rob you of time? Maybe all of them—I hear them again and again. But always, people come back to the number-one killer, "Too much work." And they say, "Solve all the others, and that will help, but I'll still have too much work."

Let's see if I can help you deal with the problem of too much work by helping you focus your time and apply brainpower.

DEALING WITH TOO MUCH WORK

Focus Time	Apply Brainpower
Clarify priorities	Use problem-solving skills
Get agreement	Apply creativity
Reconcile time vs. priorities	Use the power of teamwork
Plan	Get support from your boss
Delegate	Use your influencing skills
Wage war on words	Use communication skills
Say no	Motivate your people
Watch the killers	

Focus Your Time

1. Clarify Priorities

Using the Goals and Priorities Chart, list your goals in the right-hand column.

If you are not sure what your goals are, you have discovered the first reason for your time problem. You are working like crazy to get things done without being sure if they matter or not. Or you are knocking yourself out taking care of all that day-to-day stuff without paying attention to the longer-term direction of your job. If you aren't sure what your goals are, use your judgment in filling out the chart the best you can—put down what you think your goals should be. Do you want to produce more? Reduce errors? Stay within budget? Complete a project ahead of time? Involve customers more? Learn a new skill? Get more involvement from your people? Make a stronger contribution to your team? List those goals in the left-hand column.

Of course, you still have to take care of routine tasks. Lump those under "Operating Work."

Look at your goals and ask yourself, "How do my goals help the company build business? How do they serve the customer better? How do they help the organization control expenses?" You may want to go back and revise your goals to show the relationship between what you are doing and the success of the business.

If you have only one or two goals, break them down into major sub-goals. You need six to ten goals to make this work. If you have forty goals, combine them into six to ten.

Now assign priorities. Those goals that are closest to the customer and/or the bottom line should be your highest priorities. Start with number 1, your most important goal; number 2 next; and so on. Do this the best you can. You'll probably start out thinking all the goals should be number 1 or they wouldn't be on the list. Maybe they should be—but try to make some distinction. If you do nothing more, make a group of highest importance goals, a group of next highest, and a group of third highest. You'll need some ranking when you go to talk with your boss.

GOALS AND PRIORITIES CHART

Priorities   Goals

☐ _____

☐ _____

☐ _____

☐ _____

☐ _____

☐ _____

☐ _____

☐ _____

☐ _____

☐ Operating Work: _____
_____
_____

2. Get Agreement: Talk with Your Boss

Go to see your boss after you have filled out the Goals and Priorities Chart. Don't talk about time; talk about goals and priorities. Get the boss to agree to them first. Then you can decide how you should be spending your time.

Never say, "I have too much to do." That is a sign of weakness, and as is the rule for animals in the jungle, weakness could make you easy prey for natural enemies—like the voracious hairy downsizer. Go in with your goals and priorities laid out and ask for the boss's agreement. Tell the boss you want to be absolutely sure you are spending your time where it counts the most in supporting department and company goals.

Another way to do this—and a very revealing approach—is to have your boss fill out the chart for you while you fill out another copy. Then sit down and compare and discuss the differences. I have known people to come out of sessions like that, eyebrows up to the ceiling, saying, "I've worked for the boss for three years, and we didn't agree on one priority!"

The key question here is: "Boss, are these the goals I should be working on, and do I have the priorities right?"

Talking with your boss may well be the most important and revealing step you can take in getting control of your time.

When you and your boss agree, and you are pretty sure of your goals and priorities, put a copy of the chart on your calendar, or punch it into your PC. Look at it first thing every morning so you can plan your day around priority work.

3. Reconcile Time Use versus Priorities

Here's a simple way of finding out how well the work you do every day contributes to accomplishing your goals and where you may have to make some adjustments.

First, forgetting about your goals for a minute, think about what you actually do on the job. Using a normal week or a normal month (if there are such things), list the activities that make up your work time on the Activities Chart below, and the percent of time you spend on each. List activities you *actually do* (not those you plan to do if you ever get time).

ACTIVITIES CHART
(What you do on the job)

Major Activities	Percent of Time Spent in Each Activity
TOTAL	100%

Now compare your activities—where you are spending your time—with your goals and priorities. Fill in the Time Allocation–Brainpower Chart on pages 86–87. In the left-hand column, list your goals, taking them from the Goals and Priorities Chart. Start with your number 1 priority and work down.

Now move to the next column. Working from your Activities Chart, list those activities that are helping you accomplish each goal. Since some activities may contribute to more than one goal, you may have to list them more than once.

As you work your way down the chart, filling in activities alongside each goal, you will begin to see a pattern. Some of your top priorities may look a little hungry for attention. Some of your lower priorities may be getting too much of your time. You will have to judge.

Move to the next columns and decide if you should be spending more or less time on each goal. Then indicate which activities you need to spend more time on, or which activities you need to add; and which activities you should spend less time on, and which you might eliminate. The bottom-line question is: "How well am I focusing on my goals?"

Leave the "Brainpower" portion of the chart blank for now.

Goals (In order of priority)	Activities That Help to Accomplish Each Goal (List what you actually do, from the Activities Chart, not what you *plan* to do)	Time You Should Spend on This Goal	
		More	Less
Operating Work			

4. *Plan*

Take a few minutes to plan every day. Oh, I know you're too busy to plan, but ten or fifteen minutes of planning each day can save you hours later on and can assure you focus your work where there is the most payoff.

Do it on the way to work, when you first get there, or last thing at the end of the day. Make a list of everything you have to do that day and keep your list someplace where you can see it. Before you dive in and start doing tasks on your list, look at it alongside your priorities. Are you spending enough time on your priority work, or are you spending all your time on "other" operating work? Where can you trade off and buy some time for your priorities? Schedule time for your goals and priorities into each day's agenda; otherwise weeks and months fly by and you never get to them.

You won't always be able to follow your plan—chaos will sometimes win out, but it is a place to start.

BRAINPOWER CHART

Activities to Increase/Add; Decrease/Delete	Brainpower Needed (Rate 1 to 5)	Skills Needed to Apply Brainpower

> "Clients tell me, 'Every morning I plan my day. Every evening I wonder what happened.' "
> —Jerrianne Hammock, management consultant

As you plan, remember:

- Many things take longer in actual practice than you think they will when you plan them. Leave some slack for interruptions, tasks that are dropped on you, and unexpected difficulties in getting the work done.
- You tend to work on those things that you like to work on and procrastinate on the others. Work some of both into your plan, especially if they are essential to accomplishing your goals.
- Pay attention to your big priorities. If you are like most people, you spend too much time on low-priority work. The reason for setting priorities in the first place is so that you can concentrate time and brainpower where it will do the most good. All work is not created equal.

- When you are planning a meeting, figure out how long it should take, then see if you can cut the time in half. Most meetings run twice as long as they should. Learn how to run tight meetings, and encourage others you meet with, and especially members of your team, to do the same.
- Planning a trip? Weather delays, equipment problems, traffic, hours of downtime jammed in coach—what a waste!

  Think about alternatives to travel. Some trips are absolutely necessary, of course, but there are at least a few every year that could be done on videoconference, conference call, or even by E-mail. If you feel that trip to Mexico in February is one of the absolute necessaries, and your hotel just happens to be on the beach, go ahead and travel, but don't come back and complain about lack of time.
- Leave room for playtime in your schedule. Really! Not the whole day, but fifteen minutes now and then. It can help you work better when you get back.

5. Delegate

Give away some of your work. Doing part of your job will give your people a challenge, energize them, let them know you respect their abilities, help them learn, and free up some of your time.

Take another look at your Activities Chart, and see what work you could give to someone else. Don't do *any* work someone else can do for you.

If you can't find anything to give away, or if you are reluctant to pass your work down to those semi-incompetents who report to you, it may be because:

You are insecure and have little confidence in your role as a manager.
You are a control freak by nature, and can't stand letting anything go.
You are overly pleased with your own ability, and assume no one else can do it as well.
You haven't coached and trained your people to the point where they can handle higher-level work.

Here are five rules for delegating:

1. Don't try to delegate to everyone the same way. Some of your people are better prepared than others, have more experience,

and have shown more ability to do the job. Others may be newer at their jobs, or have less ability, and may not be able to accept extra work anyhow. Know your people and what they can handle.

2. Make sure each task you delegate is clearly defined. Limits of authority, costs, time, expected outcome—all these can be determined mutually but should be clearly understood ahead of time.

   Also be sure that the degree of delegation is understood—"Check with me at every step of the way" is one extreme; "Go away and come back when it is done" is the other.

3. Be sure employees have the resources they need, and that you provide budget, staff, equipment, and training. This includes information—everything that employee needs to get the job done.

4. Give recognition to people who take on new responsibilities and handle them well. You don't have to wait for some significant milestone. When you see something moving ahead well, let the person in charge know you are pleased.

5. Be careful that when you push work down it doesn't float back up. People who are new to the decision-making game, haven't been trained, or just plain don't have the courage to do it will court you to make decisions for them. Don't do your people's work. Help them, guide them, coach and train them, but get them used to making their own decisions.

   When someone on your team says, "Here's what *you* ought to do," you say, "That's a great idea; why don't you take charge of that and get it done!"

6. Wage War on Words

Technology was supposed to make your life easier and save you lots of time. In some ways it has. But it has also given you instant access to everything. There is just too much information in this world, and more is being generated every nanosecond. It's impossible to deal with it all. What you need is an information strategy so that generating, receiving, and passing on information doesn't gobble up great bunches of time.

1. You don't have to read everything that is sent to you. Decide what is important to your job, what you have to act on, what you are interested in, and focus on those. Let the other stuff slide. When you read a business or trade magazine, for instance, check the contents first and pick the articles to scan. Notice I didn't say

"read," because most times you can get the essence of an article by scanning subheads and bullets.

2. Get rid of stupid reports! Look at the reports you are preparing and those you are getting from others. Look at all of them, whether they are handwritten, word processor–generated, or done on spreadsheets. Try to get rid of those that don't do you any good. Combine and simplify the reports coming to you, and make strong suggestions about those you are preparing for others.

   You could probably cut report work in half and not lose a beat—and gain a lot in terms of time and productivity. Don't accept any report as a given just because it has been around for a long time. See if you can dump it. Look for reports that were created as reactions to a one-time screwup—to insure it will never happen again, even though it won't anyhow.

3. Take the time to organize the stuff you save on your hard disk. Use a system for finding it after you have stored it away. Looking for things can waste a lot of time, as can doing them over when they've disappeared into those mysterious labyrinths inside your computer. The same is true for your paper files. This doesn't mean everything has to be neat and tidy. If you can find what you want, you are using the right system. I'll bet you know at least one person whose work space looks like a landfill, but who can find anything right away in those heaps. That person is using a system that works for him.

   A messy desk is the sign of a cluttered mind. On the other hand, an empty desk must be the sign of—well, you get it. Some people need to have projects piled all over where they can see them.

4. Try to deal with things as few times as possible. You check your E-mail—you have eight messages. Or ten or fifty. Try to do something with each as it comes up. That way you can trash-can it and not have to come back and look at it again. The same goes for voice mail messages (set a time for returning all your calls at once, maybe an hour in the morning and another in the afternoon), and all that paper that comes floating in.

7. Learn to Say No

> "*Saying yes to someone else is usually an automatic no to something you had planned for yourself.*"
> —Ann McGee-Cooper, author of
> *Time Management for Unmanageable People*

I know it's tough, especially when you want to be seen as cooperative and a good team player. But there are times you just know you can't take on anything else and do it well. Face up to that at the outset, when the request comes in, and say, "I'm sorry, I wish I could, but with what I'm committed to right now, I wouldn't be able to do the kind of job on it we both expect."

8. Watch the Killers

Notice I didn't say "eliminate them." Most time-management programs will tell you to avoid interruptions, fight procrastination, and clean up your desk. I'll tell you the same thing, but with the qualifier that interruptions, procrastination, and a little disorganization may not be all bad.

- Hard to get your work done when you have so many interruptions? You don't have to take every phone call right now. You don't have to stop what you are doing to pass the time of day with someone who just wants to goof off for a while. Unless, of course, that person is the company president, your boss, or an important customer. For others, when they pop into your work space and ask, "Got a minute?" say, "I'm on a roll with this report I'm working on. Can I get back to you this afternoon?"

   On the other hand, some interruptions may actually help you. They give your mind a break and you may feel refreshed and have new ideas when you get back to work.

   Sometimes you may interrupt yourself and find yourself daydreaming or leaning into the next cubicle to tell a joke. Despite the scowls you may get from the boss who feels laughter and hanging out are not productive, a little playtime once in a while is healthy.
- Are you guilty of putting stuff off, particularly things you don't want to do? Sure you are. If it's high-priority work, you'd better force yourself to do it. But, otherwise, letting it go for a while may

give you a chance to think of better ways to handle it. Besides, if you wait, you may find someone else is working on it, or it may disappear as a need altogether.

Apply Brainpower

Take another look at your goals and priorities, this time from the point of view of the amount of planning, creative thinking, and problem solving needed. Use the "Brainpower" section of the Time Allocation–Brainpower Chart to do your analysis.

Rate each goal in terms of the amount of brainpower needed to accomplish it.

---

1 Extraordinary amounts of planning, creativity, problem-solving ability, etc.
2 Large amount of all the above
3 Medium amount
4 Some
5 Routine, doesn't require much brainpower (just time and persistence)

In the right-hand column, list the major skills needed to apply the brainpower you have identified. Use that list as a guide for skills you need to develop to the fullest. Each of those skills is covered elsewhere in this book.

If you can concentrate on your top priorities, and then build the skills needed to do your best work on those priorities, you will be using the time you have more productively. You will still have too much to do, and you will still face unexpected problems each day that louse up your best plans. But you will be more focused, and you will know where you should be directing your efforts.

You'll never get it perfect, you'll never get it all done, but you can get it better.

SBI: A big part of using time effectively is talking with your boss to clarify and agree on what the priorities are, then focusing your time and skill on those priorities.

6

IT'S POLITICAL
CORRECTNESS, HONEY

How to Deal with Nonwork Trivialities
That Influence Your Career

*"Let us be careful not to make a world so fine and good
that none of us can enjoy living in it."*
—Garrison Keillor

It may come as no surprise, but things you do at work—other than
work itself—can make a big difference in your career. An offhand re-
mark that offends a member of the opposite sex can ruin you. A messy
work space can be viewed with horror by a finicky boss. Wearing "different" clothes can run you into that glass or tile ceiling way ahead of
time. Because these things are everywhere at once, command so much
attention, and seem to be more important than they really are, I call
them "Nonwork Trivialities," or NWTs.

What may be acceptable or normal in one organization may be dis-
graceful behavior in another, and it is important to understand the culture of your employer to put all this in perspective. If you are a highly
competitive go-getter, you'll be welcomed as one of the family in some
supercharged companies, but you'll have people diving under their
desks in a more laid-back organization. Just look around to determine
what is the correct behavior for your organization. What are the senior
people doing? More important, what are the fast-trackers doing? What
code of behavior do they follow?

Finding the norm for your organization will help you be seen as part
of the team, and while it probably in itself won't get you promoted, it
will keep you from standing out as someone who doesn't quite fit. Most

companies have a subtle way of dealing with people who don't quite fit. It's called outplacement.

Of course, you may not want to compromise your own values and lifestyle to accommodate your employer. Many people are challenging the traditional ways of organizations, particularly the older established blue chips. That may be healthy, and you may want to do it yourself, but be aware of what being your own person may do to your career. It's a tough road to travel (except if you are in the top 1 percent of performers and your contribution to the organization is so great it will put up with anything to keep you).

Here are some NWTs you deal with every day—and suggestions on how to handle them. Some are mandated by law, and you may get fined or busted if you don't comply. Others are set out in company policy, and still others are strictly up to you, working within the unwritten guidelines of your conscience and your company's culture.

Political Correctness

Whatever you do today, chances are you'll annoy somebody. And if that somebody is vocal enough about your transgressions, you may be in big trouble. Use "he" when you mean "he or she"? Make an ethnic joke? Call Native Americans "Indians"? Hang a sexy picture on your wall?

There is no end to it. There's a group that is helping separated and divorced couples sue their ministers for not providing good enough guidance prior to the marriage service. There is a group in the Midwest protesting the harvesting of corn, claiming cornstalks have primitive nervous systems and feel pain when the ears are pulled off. A branch of an animal rights organization now tells us that the term "animal" is degrading, especially to household pets. It puts them in a second-class status and fails to recognize them for the joy they bring. The group suggests the term "furry people" instead.

None of the groups in the paragraph above exist; they were all made up by me. But, as you read about them, I'd bet you were almost ready to believe they were real. Political correctness has come so far today that none of us are surprised at anything, no matter how extreme.

The question is whether we are spending so much energy trying to make things correct for everyone—even those who are happy with things the way they are and aren't looking for help—that we're losing sight of other important things—like serving the customer.

Here are some guidelines for being politically correct:

Treat everyone as equal.

Never use a slang term to refer to any person or group.

Don't refer to any person or group in a way that makes a value judgment. Calling a woman a "lady" can get you in trouble.

Never make jokes or derogatory remarks about anyone who is different from you. If you are a blonde, you can make blonde jokes. If you aren't, you can't.

Don't raise red flags. Wearing a fur coat around animal rights people is asking for it.

Being politically correct may mean you will have to compromise some freedom of expression. Being politically *in*correct will cause people to think less of you and can hurt your career. You will have to decide what is important for you and where to strike the balance.

Work Habits and the Virtual Office

You've worked hard all these years to get that big office, and now that you've arrived, there is no big office—and no other offices, either, not in the traditional sense. You can grab a space with a phone and a PC, or you can work at home, or in a hotel, or in your car. But forget that mahogany wastebasket—it's on the way to the company museum with the quill pen used by the founder. Technology has made it possible for you to function just as well at the counter of the local doughnut shop as in a draperied, wood-paneled office. And that's just fine with some people who like the new freedom, and with many companies that are tearing out offices in order to reduce real estate costs, promote team interaction, and stay flexible to respond to the next change.

What does the virtual office mean to you?

1. You'll have to give up some perks—like a traditional office—and be happy working in new environments. No one at the doughnut

shop will be able to tell your rank by the size of your space at the counter.

2. You'll lose out on some of the fun of being with people. While working at home or out of the car is a nice fantasy, the truth is you probably enjoy being with the people in the office. But chances are you won't be in the office as much as you used to be, and when you are there, you may not be in the same work space all the time.

3. Virtual offices demand a new work discipline. If you oversleep and arrive at the traditional office late, someone is bound to notice. If you roll out twenty seconds before starting time at home, just in time to turn on your computer, no one will know you still have sleepies in your eyes and are sitting there in your underwear. But the demands for you to produce are greater than ever before. Virtual office does not mean virtual work.

4. Technology has eliminated free time as we know it. Beepers, E-mail, car phones, faxes, and modems make you accessible twenty-four hours a day, every day. Even when you "get away" you aren't away. How many days can you last on vacation before you check your voice mail?

5. You should try to balance this new total accessibility with time for yourself. You want to be there when someone needs you, but you also need time for play. With technology, you can do both. You can call in from the golf course, answer E-mail on weekends, and check voice mail at night. Any one of those may take only a few minutes, but they show you are accessible and on the job.

Your Work Space

Some offices are set up so that no one has a permanent space and you just grab any work space available, plug in, and get to work. Others have "open space planning," low walls that afford you the rich experience of hearing conversations on all four sides of you all day long.

Whatever your situation, you must think about the impression your housekeeping creates in others.

Here's a guide.

If Your Work Space Looks Like . . .	It Gives the Impression That . . .
Somebody's attic (papers, boxes, folders, pictures, books, magazines, and other junk piled everywhere)	You have a big workload. You are very creative. You are sloppy and careless. You won't be able to find anything. You have no consideration for the next person to use the space.
A museum (clean and organized, no clutter, everything in its place; nothing on top of your desk)	You are neat and organized. You are very efficient. You don't have much to do. You are compulsive and have other emotional problems.

Probably, you want to be somewhere in between hopelessly sloppy and neurotically neat. As in so many other things, it is best to think of your work space in terms of the impression it gives of you, especially to your boss, your team members, and your customers. Keep them comfortable, so they are not wondering about your psyche. In most organizations it's best to leave your personal expressions and flights of decorating fantasy at home.

Dress

Dress is gradually becoming more casual, but again it depends on the culture of the company or industry you are in. When I run a seminar for bankers and suggest casual dress, they show up looking as though they're going to a board meeting. Pushing money around is formal stuff. People at another client, in high tech, think business attire is clean blue jeans.

Many companies now have dress-down days; even some of the big, stuffy accounting firms have them. But not without concerns. No sooner have some companies gone to dress-down days than they have begun producing videos, booklets, and E-mail messages on what business casual looks like and what is acceptable.

The best rule on dress today is not dress for success, but dress for your customers—whomever it is you serve, inside or outside the company. What you want to do is dress in a way they admire and that makes them comfortable. One rule is this: Even if your company has dress-down days, and even if others show up looking like they've just been fertilizing the lawn, be a little classy. There are great-looking casual clothes. Wear them.

Vacations and Time Off

There is a lot of pressure on you to cut back on vacation time or to not take it at all. Or to check in and do at least some work every day you are away. You have to do what you have to do, but think what it would cost you in credibility at work to tell everyone (including putting it on voice mail), "I'm going to be on the beach in Maui next week and will be hard to reach. If there's an emergency, contact Bob. If not, leave a message and I will get back to you next Monday." You decide, but I will tell you this. If you get away from work completely and take a true vacation, you will be more productive and of more value to your employer when you get back.

Even if you love what you do and can't stand to be away from it for a minute, or are scared to death that if you go away something awful will happen and you will be on unemployment when you get back, you should take your vacation. It puts everything else in perspective. A few days of skiing big mountains, splashing in the tropical surf, or touring ancient ruins can help you understand that, in the total scheme of things, what you do at work is not the beginning or the end of the world.

Conferences and Conventions

Maybe you belong to a professional society or a trade association, and need to take time off once in a while to attend a conference. Your boss, meanwhile, thinks that conferences are just excuses for having a party, which of course they are, and lets you know that going to a conference is pretty close to taking vacation time.

But, frivolities aside, being active in one of these groups is a great way to keep up-to-date on what is happening in your field and to broaden your networks. Always come back with a report of the highlights for your boss (and for others in your area). Be sure to show the connection between what you learned and what your organization needs.

What else can you do?

When I was elected national president of the American Society for Training and Development, I knew this would mean extra time off the job, and I had to sell the benefits of what I was doing. I invited my boss to attend the national conference. Nothing I could have said or shown him back at the office could have matched this experience—there were six thousand people from all over the world there, hundreds of seminars and workshops, and Tom Peters spoke at the opening session. My boss and I never had another discussion about the value of my involvement with this organization.

Budgets, Expense Accounts, and Company Money

Like all NWTs, how organizations want—or don't want—you to spend their money varies widely. Some keep tight control, insisting on frequent budget reviews and allotting stingy per diems for food and lodging, while others see budgets as guidelines and expense accounts as perks.

The thing to remember about company money is this: Whatever your organization's philosophy in this age of lean and mean, it will respect expense control. You will always send the right message if you operate somewhere between restraint and downright cheap. Stay within budget, keep your travel expenses within reason, and show that you are concerned about protecting the bottom line.

Messing Around

You spend seventy hours a week at work, you get to know those you work with very well, and you see them at their most attractive. They are usually pretty well scrubbed and groomed, and act with restraint and politeness. No wonder you become attracted to people on the job. A recent survey by *Men's Health* magazine showed that 68 percent of the 1,400 responding had had sex with a co-worker. People who read *Men's Health* may not be representative of the general population, but still, we're not talking going out to lunch or having a drink after work. We are talking about 68 percent having sex. Some of them even did it right in the office. Favorite place? On top of a supervisor's desk.

All right, so there are lots of appealing people at work, and maybe there's someone special who *really* appeals to you. Now comes the tricky part, because relationships at work have some danger attached. Maybe that's why they are so popular. Here are some things to think about:

1. You never look at each other at work. You meet far from the office where no one else ever goes. You communicate carefully and in code. You are completely businesslike in meetings or other business situations. With that kind of caution and restraint, you can be 100 percent confident that everyone in the office knows you are messing around, and they are yakking like magpies about it. Office affairs are much more fun to talk about than company strategic plans, and people will go to great lengths to find out about them so they have something more exciting than cafeteria food to pick over at lunch.

2. So, everybody knows. That may not be so bad, if you don't flaunt it (and if neither one of you is otherwise committed—like married— which adds another dimension to the situation). Most CEOs, according to a survey done for *Fortune*, feel it's okay for office romances to happen, even if they sometimes cause upset. Some believe the passions of romance can increase productivity. Boss-subordinate romances may not be such a good idea, though.

   A note on productivity: My own completely unscientific observations are that seminars, meetings, and problem-solving sessions composed of men and women are more energetic, more fun, and more creative than those of same-sex groups. I think this is because people show off for the opposite sex and work harder to impress them. It brings a tension and an energy that adds to group productivity.

3. The best advice is to tell yourself you are never, ever, going to get involved with anyone at the office under any circumstances. But if you do, try to follow these guidelines I have gotten from veterans of office hearts and flowers:

   • Don't grope each other in the office.
   • Don't have lunch together every day, at least not in the company cafeteria.

- Remember, you can be attracted to someone without getting involved. There may be good reasons for not starting something that will become very complicated.
- Think through what is going to happen when it is over. It's likely to end at some point, especially if one of you is married. The real problems start when the breakup comes. One or both of you will be hurt, and it will be tough working together every day afterward. Breaking up is hard to imagine when things first start heating up, but remember, the eternal flame burns out in about six months.
- In this age of sexual harassment, with accusations flying around (by both men and women) at the least sideways glance—how do you get a romance started safely? Who makes the first advance, and how? How far can you go, and how fast? Most companies do not have step-by-step sign-offs as Antioch College does, so you are on your own.
- Be sure that job security, promotions, career moves, pay, or other job factors play no role in any invitations. You saw Demi Moore in the movie *Disclosure*—you know this applies to women as well as men.

Sexual Harassment

Sexual harassment is no triviality, but it is so central to the whole subject of attraction in the workplace, we should talk about it: what constitutes harassment, and what is just an annoyance. True harassment is a very ugly thing, and there is no doubt that a lot of it has gone on over the years, mostly men exercising power over women. And nothing should diminish its seriousness. In the purest sense, harassment is the boss offering or demanding the trade of sex for promotions, salary increases, or job security. Today, though, courts have interpreted harassment so broadly that it covers almost any type of discomfort. If someone doesn't like those off-color jokes or that sexy centerfold on the wall, that can be deemed a "hostile environment" and fall under the definition of harassment.

The problem is, if you offend someone, no matter how innocently and how slightly—and even if the offense has nothing to do with sex—that person may accuse you of harassment, and once accused, you are guilty. And you will never be looked on the same way, no matter how good your work and how great your potential.

The best way to avoid trouble is to think of things you say and do in terms of how others may perceive them. Here are some things to consider:

What about that little joke you are about to make? Could it be offensive?

That compliment you want to give? Will it seem too personal?

How about that encouraging pat on the back? Is touching appropriate?

The friendly question you want to ask? Will you be digging too far into someone's personal life?

Inviting someone, especially a subordinate, to have a drink after work? Can that seem like a condition of employment—that if he or she doesn't go, the next raise or promotion will be in danger?

Does all this caution take some of the spontaneity and fun out of the workplace? You bet. But it is a small price to pay for showing that you respect others' sensibilities and are ethical about the use of power.

Tolerance for Boredom

Take a look at people you consider successful at work. One thing most of them are able to do is sit through the dullest, most god-awful meetings and look interested, hour after miserable hour. How do they do that?

Then, when the meeting has gone hours past its scheduled time, but there seems to be a ray of hope that it is ending, one of those boredom-tolerant people will—of all things—ask a question or introduce another topic, thus adding another half hour to the ordeal.

Certainly, a lot of what goes on at work is not of peak interest, and people tend to get into detailed discussions about trivial things. But until everyone learns how to run meetings and how to participate in them, there will be dull meetings, and part of your job will be to sit through them. And look interested. Because however tiresome the subject being discussed, somebody there is interested in it and will be disappointed in you if you don't appear to be, too.

Part of the problem is that you think a lot faster than people talk. Once Sarah has said half a sentence, you know pretty much where she is going, and you finish it instantly in your mind while she takes another eight minutes to get through it all.

Things to do when you are bored:

1. Listen to what's being said with the following questions in mind: "What can I get out of this? How can this help me?" Set yourself a goal of finding one useful thing every five minutes. Even if it is a real stretch.
2. Bounce off words or phrases to get ideas. Meetings can be rich sources of ideas that have nothing to do with the content of the meeting. Being in a meeting, especially during parts of it that don't interest you, is a little like being in jail—sentenced to two hours of monotony. But being there, without any way out, can be a break that will allow you to think about larger issues, to explore the outer limits, and to think of ridiculous things that might translate into usable ideas.
3. When you are thinking ahead of the speaker and know where he or she is going, it is okay to drop out momentarily—this is a great time to connect for new ideas as described in point 2 above. Then slip back in and check on what's being said before dropping back out again.

First Impressions

People tend to form impressions of you quickly, and those impressions are hard to change later on, even if there is strong evidence that they are wrong. There are plenty of opportunities for creating good first impressions at work, even with people who know you pretty well. Every time you go into a team meeting, on a customer call, or into a discussion with your boss, you have an opportunity to start off on a good note and set the tone for the rest of the time you have together. When you get up to make a presentation or go into an interview or a performance-appraisal discussion, how you behave in the first few seconds can make a big difference in how well the session goes.

Behavior that creates good first impressions:

High energy and interest
Opening grabber—something that gets the other's attention and shows you have done your homework and are prepared
Asking questions about the other's needs
Bringing something new to the table—a fact, an example, something you found out, saw, or heard

Confidence
Good dress and grooming

Behavior that creates bad first impressions:

Low energy, apparent lack of interest
Confusion about what is about to happen
Being unprepared
Concentrating on your own needs, not on others' needs
Rehashing old, stale stuff
Apologizing for your lack of ability
Messy appearance

Your best hope is to be prepared.

1. Plan your opening. Think through what will happen. Review background information so you can talk intelligently about the topics to be discussed—whether they are team goals or your own performance in the last appraisal period.
2. Relate to the big picture early. Know how the organization is doing beyond your own area. Be ready to talk about sales, profits, competition. Get up-to-date on what is happening in other departments that will be represented at the meeting.
3. Anticipate the positions others will take and recognize various viewpoints at the start. That will help head off confrontations later on and cause others to see you in a leadership role.

Tobacco, Alcohol, and Drugs

Back in the mid-1970s I was part of an executive group of about ten people. We met regularly in a small conference room, and every one of us smoked—cigars, cigarettes, pipes. In fifteen minutes the air in that room was blue. By the late 1980s I was in a similar-sized group, and only one of us smoked. But not in the meeting room—because he was considerate he went out into the hall. Today he couldn't smoke in the conference room even if he wanted to, nor could he smoke in the hall or in his office or in a rest room. He could smoke only out in the street, or in a room reserved for smokers that looks like an opium den, with people sitting around staring at the walls, the vapors of hell blowing around them.

I know people who have quit smoking just because it was so difficult to do at work and made them seem different, at odds with the culture of their company. Like all other NWTs, you will have to decide—if you smoke—how others perceive that behavior and whether it is hurting your image.

There used to be an unwritten rule that said if you had too much to drink for lunch, you shouldn't go back to the office. You were supposed to go home and sleep it off. Better to explain an afternoon's absence than why you were doing the Chivas Regal Reel around the office. Now it seems that more people are drinking designer water at lunch, but alcohol and drug abuse are still big problems in the workplace. Many employers have employee-assistance programs to help abusers, and if you or someone you know has a problem, this is the way to go. If your employer doesn't have a program, your personal physician will know local agencies that can help.

The point is that it is very difficult to break a long-standing habit or cure an addiction without help. And chances are slim that you will help a fellow employee by bringing up his "drinking problem." Get help from medical care professionals or organizations that specialize in treatment.

Excuses

"**I** was only following orders." "My alcoholism made me do it." "The marketing department screwed up." "We've had a lot of bad weather." "That's what the consultant recommended." "The banks loaned us more than we could repay."

For many people today, thinking of an excuse is not hard—even those who haven't had a new idea in ten years show remarkable creativity when they have to distance themselves from a problem—particularly one they created themselves.

We live in the blameless society, and we are all used to making excuses and hearing them. An excuse may get you off the hook for a while, but it might lower the esteem others have for you—particularly if you deny being part of a mess-up everybody knows you were in the middle of, or if you pass the blame to someone else—particularly a subordinate, which is cowardly.

How you handle excuses probably depends on the demands of the culture in which you work. Many organizations are not forgiving of errors and punish any type of mistake severely. But in this world, where everyone is dodging around playing CYA, how much respect could you gain and how disarming would it be if you said, "I loused up on that one. It was my mistake. I wish I could do it over, but I can't. I'm sorry."

Attitude

I'm not going to give you an inspirational lecture here, but I will say this. You are free to adopt any attitude you like and view things the way you like, but if you are consistently negative and defensive, or if you withhold information or kill off ideas, if you stick to your own agenda and don't care about the other person's, or if you won't compromise and can't work well on a team, you will not be thought of very kindly by your boss, your co-workers, your subordinates, your team members, or your customers.

You are already thinking, "That's not me, nothing to worry about here." But before you skip ahead, do this. Listen to yourself. Next time you are talking one-on-one or in a group, in a meeting, in the hall, in an airport, or at lunch, listen to the attitude you are projecting to others. You may not like it too much, and if you don't, make a conscious effort to be more positive.

Your Plan for NWT Management

How can you be sure your NWTs aren't damaging your otherwise good work? Well, you could ask co-workers to rate you, but they might be polite and evasive or think you are insecure. Another way is to take a brutally hard look at yourself, especially in light of what you have read above, and figure out where you have to improve.

Look at how others handle political correctness, or dress, or work space, and pick out the best examples for your own use. Whatever, don't dismiss NWTs as unimportant.

Make some notes on the chart below and get to work.

NWT MANAGEMENT CHART

NWT	What I Need to Do to Improve
Political correctness	
Dress	
Time off	
Money	
Messing around	
Boredom	
First impression	
Smoking/ drinking, drugs	
Excuses	
Attitude	

SBI: Use the behavior of the fast-trackers in your company as a model for handling NWTs.

7

STUMBLING DOWN THE PATH LESS TRAVELED
Preparing for Unexpected Change

Employer: "If you come with our company, you'll have a great future. If your work is good, in about three years you'll get a lateral move. Then, if you continue to do well, in another two years you'll get another lateral move. And then in another couple of years . . ."

Get Ready

Jack Martin is—or was—an upper middle manager for a big paternalistic company. When I first met him in the 1980s he was doing just fine. He managed a big region, had twenty-five years with the company, lived in a nice house with his family, and was coasting toward a comfortable retirement. He said his company was a great place to be, and indeed many people felt it was. A good part of his retirement income was based on company stock, which was at about $75 a share and on the way up.

But a funny thing happened on the way to the promised land. Jack's company forgot to change with its customers and persisted in selling a product line that had peaked several years earlier. Its bloated bureaucracy, which grew during the gravy years, pretty well assured that the company couldn't come out with new products in time to keep up with the competition. And it didn't. Subject to endless reviews, approvals, and alterations, products came out well after the competition had grabbed large shares of market—and they weren't as good as the competition's anyhow.

By the early 1990s, the company's stock had dropped into the $30 range and twenty thousand people had been laid off. Including Jack. He was given a generous severance package, but at fifty-four and at a high salary, his prospects for finding another job comparable to the one he'd had were slim. White, middle-aged, a middle-management male, once untouchable, he was now the most vulnerable of all.

The toughest part about it was that Jack was completely unprepared to move on. Despite all the signs and not-so-subtle warnings, he had refused to believe anything could happen to him right up until the day he was told—and *even then* he had trouble believing it.

The devastating effects of job loss go way beyond the financial. You have grown up thinking of your self-worth in terms of your job. When people ask you what you do, you do not say, "I'm a parent of three children" or "I'm an avid gardener." No, you say, "I'm director of marketing for Placebo Pharmaceuticals" or "I'm a reporter for the *Binghamton Bugle*" or "I'm a senior sales consultant for preowned cars." You define yourself by your job. The loftier-sounding the title, the better you feel about telling people what it is and the better you feel about yourself.

Job loss means loss of identity and self-image. But it will be a lot less debilitating if you face up to the possibility that it will happen and prepare for it. In school, you knew there would be exams, so you studied. When you get in your car, you know there might be an accident, so you put on your seat belt. Chances are one in three that your job will disappear in the next few years, and the odds go up the higher up you are. So why not be prepared?

Jack Martin would have been better able to survive the jolt in his career if he had done some planning beforehand. And you will, too.

Steps for Preparing

1. Start now.
   Make copies of documents you will need.
   Update your résumé.
   Make a list of what you will ask about.
2. Tend to your networks.
3. Learn something new.
4. Stock up for winter. Take a hard look at your finances.

1. Start Now

Things to do this week:

- Make copies of important personal stuff to keep at home—
appraisals, letters of commendation, employee handbooks, benefits booklets, phone numbers, reports, and anything that will help
you later that the company may not let you take with you if you
are terminated.
- Tailor your résumé. You've got it sitting in the drawer, but it is
geared for the type of company you are in now, and that may not
be where you are headed. Repackage your résumé so that you can
tailor it easily to specific employers later on. Put it in your word
processor, ready to be changed and produced. Don't spend six
months polishing your résumé, or use writing it as a way to procrastinate from beginning the job search.

  Your résumé should:

  - Target specific employment areas. Tailor the presentation of
  your objectives, accomplishments, and employment history
  so that it will have the highest appeal to specific employers.
  For instance, if you are a product manager in a large company, your objective if you are applying to a smaller firm
  might be to obtain a marketing director position. If you are
  applying to another large firm and know you can't land the
  top job, your objective might be to manage the marketing of
  a major product line.

    Your accomplishments should also be tailored to spe-
  cific employers. An accomplishment like "Led a paperwork-
  reduction team" might have high appeal to a prospective
  employer that is streamlining its operation, and you might
  want to put that near the top of your accomplishments list.
  "Won the company sales contest in 1996" would appeal to
  another company that is introducing new products.

    Once you get started, you may end up with ten different
  résumés.

    Your résumé should also:

  - Show how you are unique. Emphasize those accomplishments, skills, and strengths that make you stand out from the
  pack.

- Show you are in touch. With quality, teamwork, diversity, and the global marketplace.
- Be short, two pages max.
- Be clean, simple, and easy to read.
- Be honest. Sell yourself, but never misrepresent facts on a résumé.

- Another thing you should do now is list the questions you want to ask if you are fired. Put them down on paper, because you will forget to ask them in the heat of the execution interview. How much severance pay will I get? Any extra because of the circumstances? Length of service? What about benefits? Do I take any with me? What about COBRA? What about my retirement plan? What about outplacement—will I get help finding other employment? How long, what kind of help? What about letters of recommendation?

Find the answers to as many of these questions as you can ahead of time so you can be sure you get what you are entitled to—or more. Most companies have personnel manuals and benefits booklets that cover at least some of them.

Make note of items you will want to negotiate, such as longer benefits coverage, more help with finding another job, or a larger severance package. Don't accept the employer's first offer but come back with a counteroffer you feel is reasonable. Your employer wants to get rid of you as quickly and cleanly as possible, and may give you more rather than get into drawn-out disagreements with you.

2. Tend to Your Networks

Your best hope for moving on, or recovering from a career meltdown, is to turn to others. Personal referrals are powerful and are by far the best way to get yourself reestablished. Your employer may offer an outplacement service, give you counseling, and help with your résumé. But at some point you will have to go out on your own and begin making contacts. It helps if you have established networks of people to call on.

Update your contact list. Think of all the people you know who have good jobs and enter them in your database. They can include your family, friends, neighbors, business associates, customers, suppliers—anyone you know who might be able to help in time of trouble. Keep going until you have about a hundred names.

But don't stop there—expand your networks. You can meet people by becoming active in trade and professional societies, charity work, community activities, church work, clubs, and sports. That's not the only reason for belonging, of course, but it can be an important by-product. Besides personal growth and doing good work, these activities build relationships, and the more people you know, the better chance you will have to keep that wolf away from the door.

3. Learn Something New

You must keep up with your profession. Whatever field of work you are in, it keeps changing, and you have to stay on top of that. You have to know your company and your industry. You'd better know something about total quality management, working in a diverse workforce, and gaining a global perspective. Beyond that, there are a number of skills you should have that will increase your value to your employer. Go back and review the Priorities Chart in Chapter 1. What skills do you need to improve?

4. Stock Up for Winter

What would happen if you got caught in a downsizing tomorrow? How long would it take you to find new sources of income, and how much time would you waste just deciding what to do? What if you decided to start your own business? How much could you invest in it? How long could you sustain yourself until some money comes in again?

Using Financial Planning Chart 1, you can do a simple financial plan.

(1.) List your expenses, from your checkbook or tax records, as they are today. Include rental or mortgage payments, car expense, other transportation, loans, food, clothing, taxes, home maintenance, utilities, recreation, and so on. You may have to estimate some expenses, but you will probably come close.

(2.) Mark those that are fixed and those that could be reduced.

(3.) List sources of income: wages, rental income, dividends and interest, self-employment income, other income.

(4.) Mark those sources of income that are in jeopardy, those that might be eliminated or reduced.

FINANCIAL PLANNING CHART 1

(1)		(2)	(3)		(4)
Annual Expenses			Annual Income		
Items	Amount	Fixed?	Sources	Amount	In Jeopardy?

TOTALS:

Using the Financial Planning Chart 2 on the next page:

(5.) List fixed expenses; then reduce your discretionary expenses as far as you can and list them also. Total these expenses to find what it would take for *minimum survival*.

(6.) Eliminate income that could disappear. Reduce income that could decline, and enter the smaller amount on the chart. List income that would continue at its present level if employment ended.

(7.) Determine the gap between your income and minimum survival expenses.

FINANCIAL PLANNING CHART 2

(5) Minimum Survival Expenses		(6) Annual Reduced Income	
Items	Amount	Sources	Amount

TOTALS: _____   _____

(7) GAP:_____

Look at the gap. "Pretty scary," you say. "If I lose my job, I'm broke." That's why you have to find some way to keep yourself going before change happens.

But probably, even if the worst happens, it will be some time before you face the largest gap. Outplacement, severance pay, and unemployment insurance will fill part of the gap for a time. How long will you need to depend on those? As a rule of thumb, figure you will need a month for every $10,000 you make now to get yourself reestablished—less if you do your planning now.

What's the best way to handle loss of salary? The answer is pretty obvious: Try to build income and reduce expenses.

Using the Gap Chart, list what you could do to fill the gap. Where would you get money? What kinds of things could you do? How could you cut expenses?

Ways to get income

Apply for Unemployment Compensation.

Get temporary work—use a temp agency that places managers and professionals.

Do some consulting.

Find a part-time job, work that will provide a little income but will leave you time to get reestablished.

Start taking income out of those dividend reinvestment plans.

Start your own business now, even if you are employed. Work a few hours a week to get it going.

GAP CHART

Ideas for Building Income (List as many as you can)	Ideas for Cutting Expenses (List as many as you can)

Where to cut expenses

Cut down on eating out.

Cut out vacations.

Cut back on long-distance phone calls.

Cut up your credit cards. Putting off credit card payments is an option, too, but it will cost you in the long run.

Postpone expensive presents and gifts.

Hold off on special classes for kids.

Refinance your mortgage.

Set up a budget and stay with it.

Every once in a while, say, "The hell with it" and go out and have a good time.

For the future: If you should lose your job, you may want to roll your company 401 K funds into an IRA (separate from your personal IRA); you may be able to put these funds back into a 401 K at your next employer, if you should want to do that. Talk with your accountant or tax adviser about the best strategy.

When It Happens

The day comes: The boss calls you in and gives you the news. Sorry, but that's the way it is. It's unfair, you don't deserve it. You are scared, you are angry, you are history.

By the time you clean out your work space and get home, you are already thinking of how to get another job, knowing you will not rest until you get reemployed. And as noble as that is, remember, unemployment is only 40 percent about finding new work. The other 60 percent is keeping yourself together—active, alert, productive, and positive.

Here are the realities of unemployment:

- Your layoff probably wasn't directed at you personally or your job performance. It's just a part of having a job today.
- If you do get the ax, no matter how well prepared you are, you will feel betrayed. The older you are and the longer you have worked for the company, the greater your sense of loss will be.

- You will have too much time to think about yourself and dwell on what happened. And you'll probably torture yourself with things you should have said or done to make the situation better. Even though you can't go back and change it, you will keep thinking about it. Expect this; it is normal. It is just your psyche trying to deal with what happened.

- If you find yourself dwelling too much on your resentment and what might have been, write it all down. What happened, why you think it was unjust, what should have been done, and most important of all, how you feel. Putting it all on paper is the first step to getting past it and on with your life.

- When you are gone, you're gone. Believe it or not, after all the sweat you put into your job, and as important as you were to the company, after you are gone, *no one will call you to ask your advice on anything.*

- Up till now, your time has been filled by work. Most of your life you worked to achieve things. In school it was to get your home-work done and do well on tests. At work it was to complete proj-ects on time, meet sales goals, come in under budget. Now there's a big hole in your schedule because all that is gone.

- You will feel the need to be "productive" every minute and feel guilty when you aren't. But, in fact, it may be a good idea to settle back and enjoy yourself a little while you have the time.

  That's the hardest thing to learn. You can't work at finding a new job every minute, and even if you could, it wouldn't be pro-ductive. There are times when there's nothing you can do. Take a break—you've earned it—and have some fun.

- Even though you don't have to accomplish something every minute, you do have to keep your synapses crackling by keeping yourself mentally active and challenged, even without the stimu-lation of the job. Do this to keep your brain from turning to cement and to keep a positive outlook.

  Keep current on the world of work. Things change fast, even in six months. Even as you were reading this sentence some consul-tant thought up a new fad that will take business by storm, and you'd better know about it. Read *Fortune, Forbes, Business Week,* or the *Wall Street Journal.* Not all of them; one is fine.

  Plan to spend a portion of each day doing something that you have wanted to do but haven't had time to. Reading the classics, painting or sketching, woodworking, embroidering, redecorating, playing music (actively playing, not listening to CDs), or writing short stories. Watching the soaps is not on the list.

- Keep to the actives, away from the passives.

Active	Passive
Reading	Watching TV
Reading something that makes you think	Reading *People* magazine or *Reader's Digest* only
Up at normal time	Sleeping in
Nautilus, swimming, biking, walking	Watching TV
Working at a hobby	Eating, drinking, or sleeping to keep from being bored
Learning something new	Not challenging yourself
Doing something different every day	Sticking to the same old routine
Meeting new people	Staying within your current circle of friends

- Keeping fit can be fun, and it makes everything else better. It should occupy some of your time every other day.
- Be patient. Some things take time to develop. Let's say you have always wanted to write a book. Now you have the time, and, full of hope, you get started—and find that writing is impossible. "I've been at the word processor all morning, and all I have to show is a few pages of garbage." Well, sit at your word processor every morning for a couple of months and you may have a page or two worth reading. Your dreams for free time may not be any easier to accomplish than any other lofty goal in life. Keeping at it and improving as you go is most of the fun anyhow.
- Join a local support group. You'll feel better and get some helpful ideas.
- Do some volunteer work. Or increase the time you already spend volunteering. You'll feel good about yourself from helping others and meet some good people.

Nontraditional Careers

"Between two evils, I always choose the one I never tried before."
                                    —Mae West

If you feel it is time to do something entirely new with your life—or if you have no other choice—you have lots of options. They fall into two broad categories: working for others and working for yourself.

Working for Others

Go with a smaller company. This is where the action is today, and just because you have been working for a behemoth doesn't mean you can't be happy with a little firm somewhere. Lots of people are; in fact, many large companies are having problems attracting good people because more and more new college graduates and experienced executives alike are heading for smaller firms, where they have broader responsibilities and more say in the company's future.

In the class of 1989, 70 percent of Stanford MBAs went with large companies. In the class of 1994, only half did. And many of them did that only so they could get experience and go with a small company or go out on their own later. "If my career is going to be at risk, at least I want some control over it," says one manager, who was downsized from a giant company and now works for a small importer.

Here's what to consider:

1. Look at companies you have worked with—there might be opportunities with suppliers, consulting firms, or customers. Ask your friends about possibilities with their companies and with their suppliers and customers.
2. Determine where your expertise could fit in and what responsibilities you could handle. Usually, those responsibilities will be broader in a small company than those you had before.
3. Check out any company before accepting an offer. How sound is the company? What are its sales and profit trends? What does the future look like in terms of customers and competition? You don't want to join a firm in trouble and find yourself out on the street again after three months.
4. If you can, start part-time. That way you get a foot in the door

and can see how well the company is doing and how other employees feel about working there.

5. Don't be surprised if you have to settle for a smaller salary, but try to get performance bonuses or equity in the business.

6. Be ready for culture shock if you go with a smaller firm. One executive I know went from a giant to a medium-sized company, and he broke up a meeting by asking, "Who does our speechwriting?" Of course, the answer was (as it was for much of the other work) "You do your own." Another executive I know, after years with a big chain, went with a retailer that runs small stores. "I used to go through the store in the morning and make a list of what needed to be done and then call in my people and parcel out the work. Now I make the list, then turn around and do it all myself."

7. Probably you will work harder but have more fun than you did in a big company.

8. There is no more or less security. You can be rightsized out of a little company as well as a big one.

Move into the service industry. Look at service companies, even if you have not been in one before. Ninety percent of the 2.7 million jobs the U.S. economy created in 1994 were in the service sector, and many of them did not require you to ask, "Fries with that, sir?" Nearly half of the jobs created were managerial, professional, or technical. And that trend will continue. The U.S. economy will add 25 million jobs by the year 2005, almost all of them in service industries. Areas of greatest growth will be retailing, restaurants and bars, teaching and schools, health care, and computers.

Try temporary work. More and more managers and professionals are turning to temporary work. Despite its lack of security and the need to look constantly for new positions, many are enjoying it. Some say they weren't all that secure when they were employed on a regular basis, and by doing this they at least get to work with many types of companies. There are agencies that place management-level people in temporary assignments—some for a few weeks, some for a year or more.

Go into the family business. One option may be to finally give up and go to work for Dad. But first you probably should:

1. Examine the reasons you didn't go into the family business in the first place. Are those reasons still valid?
2. Look at the business: Is it something you are interested in? Can it grow? Is there enough there for two or more families (your parents' and yours—or, in some situations, brothers and sisters, cousins, uncles and aunts, and grandparents)?
3. How will you get along? Who will do what? What decisions will you make, and which will your parents make? Can you work for the family? When and how will the business become yours?

Working in the family business can give you some security and a start in an established business. Families working together can be tricky, however.

Working for Yourself

This is not for everybody. But it may be a lifelong dream of yours, and even if it is not, it may be something you will have to do someday. So you should be actively thinking—even if you have only an hour a week to spend on it—about what kind of business you could start.

You should be clear about the answers to these questions:

What are your major strengths and skills, and what are your main interests? What type of business do they point you toward?
What product or service will you provide? And who will you sell this to? What uniqueness can you bring to the marketplace?

Here are some working-for-yourself options to pursue:

Buy a business. Tips for buying a business:

1. Make sure it's in a field you know. You can probably learn a new area, but most failures occur among people who go into businesses they aren't experienced with and who find themselves in Chapter 11 before they figure it all out. What expertise do you have that will make this business work?
2. Hire an accountant you trust to examine three to five years of financial statements to determine the soundness of the business and uncover problems such as unpaid taxes, overdue receivables, employment agreements, and so forth. How long has the

company been in business? What has the pattern of sales and
profit growth been?

3. Try to determine how well the business meets the needs of customers and how well it will fare five years from now. What are the
principal products and services? Are they likely to be salable five
years from now, or are they on the way out? What competitors
are moving in? How powerful are they likely to be?

4. Get to know the employees. How well trained are they? What is
their overall attitude toward their employer and their jobs? How
about suppliers? Are they in place and fairly stable?

5. Take a look at locations. Where are branches, stores, distribution
centers, and other facilities located? Are they in the right demo-
graphic areas for the business? What will the situation look like
five to ten years out? Where are competitors?

6. What patents or ideas-in-development does the business have?

7. Is the asking price reasonable? How will you raise the money?
What return can you realistically expect on your investment?
How easily can you get financing and on what terms?

8. Is this a business that interests you, that will keep you excited
over the years?

Buy a franchise. This is like buying a business, only you get more
support in terms of marketing, training, and product. You also incur
certain obligations to the franchiser—which may be so extensive, in
fact, you'll end up feeling like an indentured servant.

1. Decide on the type of franchise you want; something you are familiar with and interested in.

2. Look at what's out there. How do others of the same type do?
What are their sales and profits? Be careful. Most franchises to-
day are fringe start-ups and not established successful ones like
Coke bottlers, McDonald's restaurants, and car dealerships.
Many solid organizations such as Kentucky Fried Chicken, Pizza
Hut, and Taco Bell aren't taking on new franchisees in the
United States. Magic Organic Mushroom franchises might be
available but may not have a very exciting future.

3. Do a reality check: What's the failure rate? How good is the parent? What services/products does it supply? Do you have to buy
them? At what price? How much of your sales or profits do you
have to shovel off to the parent? What is the litigation rate?

Don't laugh. One sign of trouble in franchise land is that franchisee complaints against parent companies are growing at the rate of 50 percent per year.

4. What is the reputation of the franchise? How satisfied are customers and franchisees? Go talk with them.

5. What training and support does the franchise provide? Is it realistic and adequate? How much does it cost?

6. How restrictive are franchise rules? Can you live with them or will they stifle your creativity?

7. Don't get rushed into anything. Read the fine print. What are your obligations, and what are the obligations of the parent? (In many contracts you will have ten times as many obligations as the parent company does.) Get everything in writing, even descriptions of the company's operations and locations. Before you sign up, consult the Better Business Bureau, your accountant, and your lawyer. The Federal Trade Commission requires that you get a detailed disclosure statement at least ten days before you sign up or fork over money. Get it and let your accountant and lawyer look it over.

8. What is this going to cost you? You may have to shell out as much as $50,000 to join up, then have to buy equipment, invest in training, take over a lease, and purchase inventory. This can add up to some big bucks. Do you want to risk your entire savings on it?

9. Does the agreement state whether the parent can open additional franchises in your area? Competition is tough enough without competing with your own company. Many franchise fields are overcrowded today, or are rapidly becoming so, because franchisers are in business to build sales, even if that means oversaturating a market.

10. If it doesn't feel right, don't sign. You might be better off just starting your own company.

11. For more information, order the *Franchise Opportunities Handbook* ($10) from Superintendent of Documents, U.S. Government Printing Office, Washington, D.C. 20402; or *Evaluating Franchise Opportunities* from the Federal Trade Commission, SBA Box 15434, Fort Worth, TX 76119.

A franchise will give you some protection and security. Franchises have lower failure rates than other start-ups, at least that's what most of them claim, but they aren't foolproof. In fact, it seems as though the great days of franchising are nearly over. You will have support if you are with a good firm. You may have to borrow to buy in, but some will help you with low-interest loans.

Start your own. If you have a skill or experience in a certain area, a hobby that could be marketable, and a network of possible customers, this may be for you. More and more new graduates are starting their own companies—some because they can't find a job with an established company, others because they don't want to become a corporate suit. And many experienced people, downsized or fed up with the corporate life, are going out on their own. Here are some suggestions for you if you are a budding entrepreneur.

1. Be sure you choose a field you know about. Write a business plan. Figure out what your business will be, who your customers will be, and why they should buy from you rather than from the ten thousand competitors out there. What will make you unique in the marketplace? If you can't think of anything very convincing, back away from this one and pick another option.
2. How will you finance it? Will you be able to raise the money? Will you be able to meet debt service, payroll, rent, and other expenses?
3. Build a business you can sell. Keep as much equity as possible. Run the business with the idea in mind that it is going to be your retirement.
4. Starting your own business is lots of work and can be lots of fun. There is a high failure rate, but failures often happen to people who start businesses in areas they know nothing about, or who have rosy dreams of having lots of free time to travel and play golf, or who are convinced that because they are so good at what they do customers will come and competitors will wither away.

Become a consultant. Consulting is the easiest business in the world to start. Anyone can do it, any day of the week. There is little initial investment (maybe stationery, business cards, an answering machine, and a "for deposit only" stamp in case a check comes in). You don't need a license or special training.

Starting up is easy. Getting clients is another story.

- Decide what you have to sell.
- Determine who your target customers are: your old company, companies in the same industry, other industries. Do you want to specialize by industry or by professional area?
- Figure out how you will market your service. Remember, market to prospective clients' needs, not your own. Clients will buy your service if you can improve their businesses. They won't buy because you are desperate and starving to death.
- Getting work as a consultant is based as much on the ability to fit in and work well with the client as on technical skill. And fitting in and getting the client comfortable with you may take time. (I visited one of my clients ten times over six months and talked with just about every senior officer before the company gave me the first piece of business. But they have grown into a very good client.) Expect that just getting work can take as much as 40 percent of your time.
- A real plus in consulting is that overhead is low—especially if you work on your own and work out of your home. When you bill a client, you get to keep most of it.
- It can be very compelling work and a lot of fun.
- Many people try it; only a few make it. Consulting takes persistence, discipline, and a tolerance for rejection. It also takes courage, because sometimes the things you recommend are not popular and will meet resistance. And you need patience. After four calls on a prospective client you may think you have a job lined up and then find that nothing happens for six months. Then, when you have given up, your phone will ring.

Let's see if you have the makeup to be a consultant—the questionnaire that follows will help you measure your CQ (consulting quotient).

CQ PERSONAL AUDIT

Do you agree or disagree with each of these statements?

1. I can support myself for six
   months without an income while
   getting my business established.　　　Agree_____　Disagree_____

2. I don't mind being by myself.　　　Agree_____　Disagree_____

3. I can handle rejection and
   don't take it personally.　　　Agree_____　Disagree_____

4. Objectively speaking, I have
   skill and knowledge someone will
   pay me to share with them.　　　Agree_____　Disagree_____

5. All my life I have had a burning
   desire to run my own company.　　　Agree_____　Disagree_____

6. I would not mind an annual income
   that fluctuates wildly from $300,000 to zero.　　　Agree_____　Disagree_____

7. I can sell sell sell.　　　Agree_____　Disagree_____

8. I have a network of possible customers.　　　Agree_____　Disagree_____

9. I have done this kind of work before
   and can, in all modesty, say I'm good at it.　　　Agree_____　Disagree_____

10. I can get out of bed each morning and
    go to work even when no one
    is checking up on me.　　　Agree_____　Disagree_____

Give yourself one point for every time you marked "Agree." If you scored 7 to 10, you have a good chance at succeeding. If you scored 4 to 6, you are a long shot—and 0 to 3, forget it.

A word about being an entrepreneur. It's a dream and a nightmare, a course not to be taken lightly: 40 percent of the 80 million jobs in the Small Business Administration database disappear six years out (from 1980 to 1986). You get no guarantees. BRG, a consulting firm in New York City, contends that only one fifth of the managers and professionals they work with have the personality and strength to make it on their own without the support of an organization.

In trying to get yourself established, you may waste time you could have devoted to getting reemployed, and you may use up your savings. If you succeed, you may find yourself working longer hours than you ever did before and making less. On the other hand, 74 percent of millionaires in this country own their own businesses, and even if you don't become one, you can enjoy the same freedom and satisfaction.

A survey by economist Theresa Devine of Penn State shows that the earnings for self-employed men may be losing ground to inflation faster than those of men employed by others. Self-employed women are actually gaining ground, but make far less than the men. Ninety percent of self-employed people, though, like their jobs better than the ones they had in corporate and hope to stay on their own.

Some successful entrepreneurs will tell you they made it through hard work, talent, and sound management skills. To be realistic, there is usually some pure luck involved. You'll need all of those to make a go of this.

If you are determined to go ahead, read this:

TEN MISTAKES YOU SHOULDN'T MAKE AS A NEW ENTREPRENEUR

DON'T

1. Assume you are so good that customers will flock to you, and you won't have to worry much about competition or marketing.

2. Forecast high. It is easy to add 20 percent to your sales estimate each year; actually getting more sales is another question.

3. Assume the sale. Don't count your money until the customer actually forks it over. "Sure" sales have a way of evaporating.

4. Go into a business you have no experience in, depending on your excellent management ability to make it a success.

5. Expect you will change. If you find it hard to motivate yourself to work hard now, you probably won't suddenly become a tiger just because you start your own business.

6. Overestimate your ability. Can you handle marketing, sales, finance, human resources, distribution, operations, and everything else by yourself? Probably, you can't. Get outside help.

7. Start with an unclear mission or no mission. If you aren't clear on what your business is, and how it is unique in the marketplace, your customers will be confused or discouraged and won't buy from you.

8. Focus on your needs rather than the customers'. Customers aren't going to change their schedules, procedures, or specifications to accommodate you. You must understand their needs and be flexible enough to meet them.

9. Bet the farm. Don't put your life savings into a new business venture. As good as you are, your business has a good possibility of failing. Get financing another way, or hold back some to live on if you need it.

10. Look for the life of leisure. If you start a full-time business, it will consume all the time you have and then some for the first five or ten years.

Other thoughts on working for yourself:

- When you kiss corporate good-bye, the paychecks stop. Although you know this, it still is going to come as a shock because you are used to having those dollars roll in every month, no matter what.

- Ditto benefits. Do you know what it costs to buy medical insurance on your own? Eight million dollars—or at least it will seem that much.

- You can't take other company supports with you either. No PC, no fax. Your old firm is just not going to be happy if you send stuff over for your old secretary to run through the word processor. And, believe it or not, many of us who are self-employed don't have executive jets. In fact, your years in a big company may make going on your own more difficult for you because you've gotten used to all the support systems.

- You may find you are as stupid as you thought your old boss was, and can't run a toaster. Not everyone has what it takes to be an entrepreneur. Many who try it find they cannot cope without the support of a company organization. You may fail—then what? You need a contingency plan.

- Everything takes longer than you think it will. Loan from the bank? Commitment from your first customer? Learning to use that new computer? Writing a brochure? Finding the right employees? Make your best estimate, then double it.

- Having your own business gives you certain tax advantages—things you can legally write off, but it also brings new tax burdens: Social Security, state corporation taxes, disability, unemployment. You also have to pay an accountant and probably a lawyer, so self-employment brings nice new fees you never had to worry about before.

- You must live with uncertainty. You lived with it even when you were employed, but in your own business it is ongoing. Valued customers go elsewhere, likely prospects reject you, vendors are difficult to negotiate with, and key employees quit. You must learn to live with this and handle the stress involved.

- The joy of receiving a payment from a customer and putting it in your company's account, the fun of paying yourself each month, is much greater than getting a check from an employer.

- With everything involved, if you can make it, it's a great way to spend your life.

SBI: Be prepared for any eventuality, even if things are going well now. Explore alternative career options and begin laying the groundwork for new directions in your life.

Part III

COMMUNICATION SKILLS

8

OBFUSCATION AND OTHER SKILLS
How to Speak and Write

"The market quickly reached new high ground, breaking its neutral trading pattern. A market or stock that is breaking out has begun to make an important upside. These tend to materialize in the early phases of major uptrends and portend meaningful upside potential. This sequence of price movement is not a blow-off but a momentum squeeze that now appears to be under way."
—Market update from a major brokerage firm

You Must Communicate Better Than Ever

Every year I run dozens of seminars around the country for managers and professional people. Usually, to get things warmed up, I ask participants to introduce themselves and talk about their strengths and areas they would like to improve. Areas for improvement are many: time management, delegation, motivation of people, product knowledge, and on and on. But in seminar after seminar, week after week, number one is communication.

I ask them what they mean specifically. "I would like to be able to speak in front of groups." "I would like to be more confident talking in meetings." "I wish I could write better." "I want people to pay more attention to what I have to say."

My experience is not unique. CEOs and senior executives agree that good communication is the single most important factor keeping organizations competitive today. Companies are so dependent on good communications, and so worried that their people are lousy at it, that they devote more dollars and more time to improving communications than to any other management skill. A recent survey of human resource executives in major companies showed that communication is number one on the list of subjects taught in management development courses.

Even with that, things are getting worse rather than better. In another study, done in 1994, 80 percent of companies surveyed said their employees need to improve writing skills, up from 65 percent the year before; and 75 percent said employees have a major problem with speaking, listening, and talking with customers and other employees, up from 62 percent the prior year.

Your ability to communicate may be the single most powerful tool you have to increase your value to your employer and to make yourself marketable inside and outside your organization.

It is truly a survival skill in today's workplace. Your skill at expressing yourself, persuading, influencing, and capturing the imagination of your listeners or readers can improve your chances for getting on the short list for the next promotion (if one ever comes along), and even more important, it can boost your chances of staying off the short list for the next downsizing.

Your writing and speaking put the color and texture on the picture others have of you and determine how well they respect you and how committed they become to your course of action. People make all kinds of judgments about you by the way you communicate, and they get lots of opportunity.

Think of how much of your time, every day, you spend communicating: writing letters, reports, memos; talking with your people, with your boss, with others in the organization, with customers and vendors—talking with people on the phone, through voice mail, fax, or on the computer; in person—one-on-one—or in meetings. How much of your time? Fifty percent? Probably more than that. Maybe it is easier to list those things you do each day that *don't* involve communicating.

Communicating for Your Future

You probably think you're a pretty good communicator. And you probably are—that's just the point. Pretty good. So are lots of others. With a little effort you can be better than the others, stand out and be recognized as someone who has a valuable talent a company badly needs.

The ability to communicate has certainly served me well. It helped me get a lot higher in my corporate career than I would have otherwise, and it got me involved in major corporate change, company meetings, executive retreats, strategic planning sessions, corporate videos, speeches, and many other activities of importance—much of it work beyond the scope of my job description, but high-powered and highly visible.

More recently, communication skills enabled me to go out on my own and do what lots of people dream of—form my own company. Most of the work I do depends on my writing and speaking skills.

Something I was born with? I don't think so. I still have a college theme with the professor's comments: "Concept very good, writing fair." And I have an old videotape of one of my first front-of-the-room presentations. Totally embarrassing. From that faltering start, I worked hard to develop communication skills. Midway through my career I was put in charge of a large human resource development function, where I managed dozens of people who were great communicators. I had to improve because I wanted to be able to lead by example. I read, went to classes, learned from my people, and most of all, practiced. Over time, I started to get better.

Not that it's any easier. Even after eight books, dozens of articles, and thousands of corporate communications, I still struggle with words. I agonize over what I have written, wondering how it will sound to others and whether it will do what I want it to. And, even after thousands of hours in front of the room, I still sweat when I have to make a presentation or lead a seminar. But I've learned a lot over the years and worked hard to apply it. And I can save you some time in your learning process by passing some of that on to you.

Why Is Communicating So Difficult?

How many memos and reports do you get that are so full of jargon and convoluted sentences that your eyes glaze over before the second paragraph? How many times do you listen to a speech by the CEO or someone else high up enough to have a private bathroom and think, "This person is really boring, and besides, he isn't saying anything relevant to me"? How many times have you come out of a meeting thinking, "What a waste of time"? And how often do discussions with your boss or your subordinates end up with mixed signals and misunderstanding?

Why do people have trouble communicating? After all, we've been at it a long time. We learn to talk at two, read and write at five or six. With all the practice we've had, why can't we do it well? There are several reasons.

- Words get in the way. Many of them have imprecise meanings, or are vague, or are even the wrong words for the thought. And it's hard to string the right words together to make compelling messages.
- Nobody listens. We are lousy listeners, partly because we are never taught to listen. We take courses in reading, writing, and speaking, but nobody teaches us how to listen.
- People evaluate everything against their own needs and prejudices. And they may decide to forget what someone says even before they've had a chance to say it.
- People believe some forms of communication are beyond them: "I just can't write, I don't have that talent." "I would rather have a root canal than get up in front of a group." "I spend my whole life in meetings, and nothing ever comes of them."
- Nobody has time. There are fewer middle managers after all the delayering we've gone through, and those who are left supervise more people and can't spend as much time with each one individually.
- Many "survivors" are doing the work of two or three people today and are so pressed for time they can communicate only in sound bites.
- Every communication has to compete with an avalanche of information people receive today—in person, in meetings, via memos, E-mail, voice mail, videoconferences, faxes, computer printouts—messages coming from every direction.
- Nobody believes anyone anymore. Many people are suspicious of what companies, bosses, and even peers and subordinates tell them. Old notions of trust have disappeared. "No more layoffs." (Wanna bet?) "You're a valued member of the team." (Does that mean I'm next to go?)
- Many of your communications—think about it—are done with your own goals in mind, as you try to find that magic combination of words that will make people do what you want them to instead of communicating to your receivers' needs.

Okay, those are the problems. What are the answers? Here's where to get help in using the full voltage of communications to increase your value to your employer and to yourself.

Type of Communication	Where Covered
Speaking to groups	This chapter
Writing	This chapter
Speaking one-to-one	Chapter 11: Yes Sir, Yes Sir, Yes Sir: Dialogues with Your Boss
Meetings	Chapter 16: Staying Awake: How to Get Things Done in Meetings
Listening	Chapter 9: I Don't Mean to Interrupt, But — How to Shut Up and Listen

Let's get started. What is communication anyway?

The *Random House Dictionary* gives us this definition of *communicate*: "To give or interchange thoughts, information or the like." Seems simple enough, but it becomes very complex when you throw in the word *interchange*. That means exchanging ideas and thoughts, and involving all parties in the communication process, not just the sender. Keep that in mind as you read the Ten Commandments of Communication.

Ten Commandments of Communication

1. Keep it short. No one has time to read something that is twice as long as it should be or sit through an hour-long presentation that could have been given in one sentence. You don't, why expect others to? You should communicate with people as concisely as you can, and without boring them to death.

2. Keep it focused. Decide on your objective—what you want to get across to your receivers. Try to stick with one theme per communication. Prepare your message, then go back and take out everything that doesn't support your objective.

3. Keep it simple. Use little words that everyone understands. The more precise the better. Don't assume everyone understands. They don't, so explain everything, especially jargon, acronyms, or code words, and especially mysterious terms that only people in your line of work understand.

4. Use an "opening grabber." Start off with a story, a fact, or an anecdote that will get your listeners' or readers' attention and make them want to find out what you have to say. Tell your receivers up front why paying attention will benefit them.

> "One day last month I called the office trying to get in touch with Charlie—I was with a customer who was out of product, so I needed Charlie right away. It took me three calls and over ten minutes. Someone on the central switchboard didn't know who Charlie was and connected me with the wrong department. They transferred me and lost it. So I had to dial again. Then I got put on hold and waited forever, hung up, and dialed again.
> You all know our phone system is a disaster. But our team has been meeting with phone company engineers, and what I'm going to tell you in the next couple of minutes is the answer to your prayers."

Be sure to stress benefits, not features. "Your new voice mail system can store up to fifty calls." That is a feature. "You won't miss any more customer calls." That is a benefit.

5. Never apologize. "A lot of people are better qualified on this subject than I am" shows you are modest, but it also is the weakest way to present any communication. It tells your receivers that they shouldn't bother to listen to or read what you say, because it's not going to be any good anyway. Also, don't use too many qualifiers: "I think," "It might," "We could," "If all goes well." They all tend to weaken your communication.

6. Stay with the active, avoid the passive—which is boring.

> "It has been established that sedentary office workers are more prone to various diseases than those who are physically active."
> Yawn.
> "Move your butt or you'll get sick."
> Oh, okay.

7. **Edit everything.** First drafts are usually horrible; they're supposed to be. Try again. Good communications need to be worked on.

8. **Be honest.** People have been lied to too much—not only in business but by advertising agencies, politicians, lawyers, and just about everyone. Don't try to fool people. They will know it when they see or hear it. If you don't know, say so. If you can't divulge information, say so.

9. **Be a good receiver.** Receiving information is a communication skill, too. When you get a memo or report from someone, read for comprehension. When someone speaks, listen. Try to get something from every communication.

10. **Ask questions for clarification.** If you don't understand something, ask for an explanation even if you think everyone else in the world understands perfectly.

Speaking to Groups

Believe it or not: In early 1995, Martin Keeler, VP of Finance at Roanoke Radicchio Corporation, gave a speech that was so boring, he fell asleep in the middle of it and dropped in a heap on the stage. Fortunately for him, all sixty people in the audience were also sleeping and never noticed.

Imagine yourself sitting in an auditorium. It is after lunch, and a speaker is up at the podium droning on while pointing out details on a complicated slide. The lights are down, and your eyes fog over, then close. Your head tilts to one side and you begin to slump before you catch yourself and sit upright (did I snore?). A gallon of Nyquil couldn't have done a better job. Probably you are drowsing off just thinking about it.

Now, switch the scenario. You are the one up at the podium. You are looking out at an audience of about a hundred sitting around the dimly lit room. You have worked three weeks on this presentation, and you know management is watching. Your boss is staring at you.

You are sweating, and you can feel your heart thudding in your chest. You feel as though you might squirt right out of your skin and shoot through the ceiling like a little Saturn rocket.

While you are freaking out onstage, someone out there is snoring.

Why the difference? The difference is that human beings were never intended to get up and talk to groups, and so weren't given good speaking genes.

But one thing we have is the ability to adapt, and we have learned over the years how to do lots of things we weren't designed to do. Speaking is one of them. Speaking is a learned skill. Some people may start off with more of a knack for it than others, but basically it is learned.

For you, it is worth some pain in learning, because the ability to get up in front of a group and give a good talk will enhance your reputation (and your perceived value to the organization) way beyond what the act of speaking is worth.

Here's what not to do.

LOSER'S GUIDE TO GIVING AN AWFUL PRESENTATION

1. Start with a joke, a lame one if possible, and watch the audience squirm.
2. Follow your joke with something really boring, like your background.
3. Wing it. You know your subject, don't prepare much, just get up and talk about it.
4. Talk to your shoes. Don't look at anyone in the audience.
5. Use lots of big words and formal language. While you're at it, talk in a monotone.
6. Use visuals, but stand in front of them so no one can see them. Put pages of text up on the screen and read them to the audience.
7. Show your modesty by telling the audience you don't know as much as others do about your topic. That way they will be sure not to listen to you.
8. Have about thirty things you want to talk about and unload them all on the audience.
9. Say "In conclusion" and then go on for another half hour.
10. End by saying, "If there aren't any questions, I'll close." Walk quickly away from the podium but forget to unhook your lavaliere mike so you pull it out by the roots.

Winner's Guide to Memorable Presentations

Now that we have the awful stuff out of the way, we can get to giving memorable presentations, using the 3-G process:

Get it together
Give it hell
Get better

Let's look at each.

Get It Together

Every presentation you give, whether it is a five-minute report in a staff meeting or an hour presentation in front of a thousand executives, is your moment in the spotlight. If you wow the audience, people who don't know anything about your performance on the job will assume you are outstanding, and they will ask your opinion on subjects unrelated to your speech because they will assume you know what you are talking about.

There are no "minor" presentations. Every one you give deserves your best effort.

The best way to get your nerves under control when you are about to speak is to prepare so well that you are 90 percent confident with your material and can concentrate on how you say it. The most important part of a presentation is not getting up and giving it, it is practice. Keep that in mind as we go along.

Giving a presentation in the next few weeks? Use the following process, beginning with the Presentation Design Worksheet, to make it a winner.

PRESENTATION DESIGN WORKSHEET

1. **Decide on an objective.** What do you want to accomplish? Do you want to give information, get support, or get action? Whatever it is, knowing that will help you build a better communication. Try to stay with just one objective, one main point for your presentation.

Your objective for this presentation—what you hope will happen as a result of it:

_____

_____

_____

_____

_____

_____

2. Consider your listeners. Think of your audience. What benefits can you offer them? Why should they pay attention, and why should they spring into action as a result of your talk? List all the benefits you can:

__Benefits:__ _____

_____

_____

_____

_____

_____

3. Create your content. Keep your objective and your audience in mind. Then think through what you are going to say and develop specific points you will make. Content consists of

Opening grabber
Body of the presentation
Closing call to action

Opening grabber. Start with a story or statistic that will get everyone's attention and pique their interest in what you are going to tell them.

Ideas for your opening grabber

_____

_____

_____

_____

_____

_____

Having trouble? Do this. Write the rest of your presentation, read it through, and find the most powerful, most attention-getting statement, anecdote, or fact, pull that out, and make it your opening grabber. If that doesn't work, think of something really outrageous you would never say to the audience and then tone it down so you can use it.

Outrageous:	"Good morning, losers."
Toned down:	"Want to increase your sales by twenty percent? I'm going to tell you how one rep did that."

You might want to use a prop. A shopping bag full of items to support your objective, a company product, a book to quote from, a garden tool—anything that will get attention and make your opening more dynamic.

Body of the presentation. Start by listing the main points you want to make. Be sure, as you develop your points, that each of them supports your objective. Take out any that don't. Then brainstorm examples, statistics, anecdotes, and quotes you can use to back up each of your points. These make everything come alive and help the audience remember.

Key points

_____

_____

_____

_____

_____

_____

_____

Examples, anecdotes, facts, etc., to back up key points

_____

_____

_____

_____

_____

_____

More thoughts on key points:

Show the need and present a solution. People are used to seeing problems solved in a short period of time on TV, and expect it everywhere. Got one of those bad headaches? Nuke-U-Pain pills will cure it in a fifteen-second commercial.

Restate your main theme or most important point. Lay it out at the beginning, build on it in the content, and restate it at the end. That way, even those who are sitting out there thinking about the weekend will catch something.

Visualize: Ask your audience to think "What it would be like if only we could . . ."

Closing call to action. You have to tell your listeners what it is you want them to do, or they won't do anything. If you want members of the audience to take on a project, change something, think differently, or buy your product, ask for it, so they know exactly what you want and will be motivated to act.

Don't let your presentation fall flat because you don't ask for the sale.

What to cover in your closing

_____

_____

_____

_____

_____

_____

4. Practice. Remember, it's your reputation—you can't afford to do any presentation, no matter how insignificant it may seem, without practicing.

Out loud.

Sometimes words that look good on paper don't sound so hot when you say them. Paragraphs that flowed easily into one another on paper seem disconnected. Familiar words become hard to say and make you stumble. And clever stories and anecdotes seem strained.

Use your first run-through to revise and strengthen the content. Use the second to work on your delivery and to make further adjustments to the content. Use the third to make your delivery as good as you can get it.

As you practice, replace vague words with ones that are more specific, eliminate words you have trouble saying, and get rid of weak qualifiers such as "I think," "maybe," and "could" or "might."

This is your chance to take something that sounds like an address to a morticians' convention and make it friendly. In fact, you should try to say things as though you were talking to a good friend. I don't know why people feel they have to sound stiff and formal when they are in the front of the room, but many do.

Cross out "major corporate initiative" and put in "big job." Ash-can "My talk is a compendium of disparate subjects, but I will attempt to delineate between topics," and make it "I've got a lot to cover, and I'll let you know where I am at every step along the way." You will be more relaxed, your audience will be happier, and the overall effect will be a better connection between you and your listeners. Formal language creates distance between you and the audience. Conversational talk creates intimacy.

As you practice, rely less and less on your script and concentrate on eye contact with the audience. If you want the security of a full script, highlight a key word at the beginning of each paragraph so you can glance down, see that cue word, and say the rest of the paragraph, looking up at the audience, in your own words.

If you want to get away from being tied to a script, take those key words and make an outline. While you are splitting from the script, split from the podium, too. Put your key words on three-by-five-inch index cards and hold them in your hand while you are at center stage.

Don't try to memorize your talk. That seldom works and may get you in real trouble. Work from an outline, at least. Or use your visuals as your guide.

If you can practice with an audience, do it. Ask a few people you respect to sit through your speech. You will owe them big-time for agreeing to do this, but their comments and suggestions can help a lot. Get out your camcorder and videotape your practice; then review the replay with a critical eye (and ear).

Here's what you and your "audience" should look for. Ask them to fill out a copy of the critique and return it to you.

PRESENTATION CRITIQUE

Please complete and return to the speaker after the rehearsal.

1. How good was the opening? What got my attention? What could the speaker have done to make it more dynamic?

_____

_____

_____

_____

2. How good was the speaker's manner? Was the speaker warm and inviting or did the speaker look like he or she was having an appendicitis attack? How could the speaker have been warmer and more welcoming?

_____

_____

_____

_____

3. Did the content make sense? How well did it flow from point to point? How understandable was it? What could the speaker have done to make the content clearer? More interesting?

_____

_____

_____

_____

4. How captivating was the delivery? Did the speaker vary pace and emphasis, or talk in a monotone? Was there good eye contact, or did the speaker avoid looking at the audience? What could the speaker have done to make the delivery more professional?

_____

_____

_____

_____

5. Was the delivery confident, or did the speaker seem nervous and unsure? What distracting mannerisms should the speaker avoid?

_____

_____

_____

_____

6. How well did the speaker use visuals? Did they help the flow of the presentation, or were they unclear, awkward, in the way? What could the speaker do to improve the visuals?

_____

_____

_____

_____

7. How good was the ending? Did the speaker "ask for the sale" or just dwindle off without letting you know what was expected of you? How could the speaker have better inspired you to action?

_____

_____

_____

_____

Give It Hell

Okay, time to get up and do it. You've gotten ready, practiced, and brought your presentation to the point that you are very confident with it, and now it's time to Give It Hell.

Just before you go on, warm up. Say your opening grabber out loud, just the way you will do it. You can do this in an empty conference room or in your car on the way to the presentation. Find a place. The ten minutes you spend doing this will raise the level of your whole talk.

When you know your opening cold you can concentrate on smiling and making friendly eye contact with the audience. Believe it or not, you can look like you're having fun up there. At the outset, your manner (the way you present) is at least as important as your matter (what you present). It's the way to win the audience and get them on your side for the whole presentation.

Research shows that people who are persuaded were influenced 8 percent by content (what was said), 42 percent by appearance (how the presenter looked), and 50 percent on style (how it was said).

First of all, look around at everyone and smile. That will show you are cool as a Caribbean daiquiri (even though you may want to run screaming out the fire door) and will relax the audience. Then, start off with high energy and keep yourself there. That doesn't mean you should talk like a human Uzi—say words at a normal conversational speed but with emphasis on key words and thoughts. Every sentence you speak has a word you want to emphasize. Mentally highlight that word and punch it when you say it.

Pause after important points for emphasis and to let the audience think. Two seconds of silence in front of the room feels like a week, but practice your pauses so you are comfortable with them and can use them.

Things to watch out for:

Frowny faces. As you look out at your audience, at least at first, you are going to see a bunch of grouches glaring at you. This doesn't mean they don't like your presentation (usually, anyhow), but it does mean they are concentrating, trying to get into what you are saying. I recently gave a talk, and a guy in the second row sat through it looking as if he were waiting for a lethal injection. Afterward he was the first up to tell me I had given a great presentation and had really made him think. You just can't tell by looking—don't let those grim faces throw you.

After you get going, you'll see some nods and maybe a smile or two from people scattered around the audience. I love those people and deliberately (desperately) look around for them. They help to bring the tension down and build confidence. Locate these people and check in with them once in a while to keep your self-esteem high.

Visual-lock, or talking to your visuals. When you are using visuals, your natural tendency is to look at them. Don't. Glance if you must, but face the audience and talk to them. Also, don't stand in front of your visual. Use a light pen as a pointer.

Another type of visual-lock is talking to your script or to the floor or ceiling. Look at your audience. Find one of those friendly faces on one side of the room and make eye contact with that person. As you talk, switch to a person on the other side. That way you will seem to be looking at everyone in the audience.

Afraid of losing your place? As you glance down to pick up a key word from your script, put your finger near the key word in the next paragraph, so when you look down again, you'll see exactly what comes next.

Tics and tremors. Nervous habits can so annoy the audience that they lose track of what you are trying to tell them. Watch for these on your practice video and try to eliminate the worst of them. They include verbal distractions such as "er," "um," "like," "you know," and the ever popular "okay?" A few are all right; a whole string of them can be irritating. They also include physical quirks like constant pacing, rocking, scratching your nose (or anything else), or rattling change.

Mechanical man. If your gestures make you look like a robot assembling a Toyota, ease up a little. Speech coaches have harped on gestures so long that people are forcing themselves into all sorts of unnatural hand and arm movements. Do what feels natural and comfortable for you. If you want to put your hand in your pocket, go ahead. The world won't come to an end. Watch what you do on videotape, then try out more natural gestures in front of a mirror.

Brownout: Low energy, monotone, lack of emphasis. Any of these give the audience the impression you are not much interested in what you are saying—if you aren't, why should they be? One cause of brownout is reading from a script. Don't do that. Say what you want to say *in your own words*. Let your personal warmth and enthusiasm come through.

Some of the warning signs that you are losing them are that they are:

looking at their watches
rummaging through papers
yawning
walking out

If you see those signs, quicken your pace, punch out those key words, smile, look at them, show you are interested, and if that doesn't work, wind up and get off fast.

To understand brownout, try this. Say in a monotone, "The sky is blue." Pretty boring, eh? Now experiment with other ways to say the same line. Try saying it as though you are full of wonderment at "blue." "The sky is *blue*?" The audience will think (1) you are going to give them some new insights about the sky, or (2) you are weird. Go for it and hope they come down on number 1.

WHY DO YOU SUPPOSE POLITICIANS TALK IN CAPITAL LETTERS? Because they want you to think they are energetic, in command, and willing to fight for what they believe. You may get sick of hearing them holler all the time, but a little of that can help you impress your audience and avoid brownouts.

Most of the above problems are caused by the stress of speaking. Legend has it that JFK used to calm himself down by imagining his audience sitting out there in their underwear. Go ahead if it works for you and you can keep from laughing.

How to Use Visual Aids

Probably you will want to use some snazzy visual aids with your presentation. Visuals make things more interesting for the audience, help them keep track of where you are, help them remember, and can act as an outline for you.

GUIDELINES FOR VARIOUS TYPES OF VISUALS

Type of Visual	Use for	Guidelines
Handouts or notebooks	Complex material Put it here, not on slides	Number the pages. Cover them in order so the audience doesn't have to hunt around.
	Backup material	Don't mix in articles and backup materials—put them at the end.
		Give handouts all at once, not a piece at a time.
Slides	Large audiences	Never use right after lunch with the lights out. ZZZzzzzzz. Put key words only on slides, not text.
Computer visuals (See next page.)	Same as slides	Use only if you are well trained in running them.
	Adding motion and interest	Resist making them too complex or busy. They should support your message, not distract from it.
Overheads	Visuals you can write on Low-budget visuals— you can make them on your laser printer	Introduce some color accents, but don't use colored foils (except yellow); they are too hard to read.

Flip charts	Small groups	Write in big letters so everyone can see.
	Recording ideas	Don't write sentences. Use key words and headlines only.
Videos	When you want to rest	Cue up beforehand so you don't have to sit through five minutes of leader.
	Providing an entertainment break	Never let a video stand alone. Have the audience discuss it, or they will forget.
	Getting across a point	

Thoughts about computer-generated visuals

With your laptop, some software, an LCD projection panel, and a little training, you can create dynamite visuals. Computer visuals:

Save preparation time and expense. You can do them yourself instead of using graphics experts to make slides.
Allow you to work anywhere and make last-minute changes.
Make it easy to customize presentations for an audience.
Allow you to use motion and animation.
Give you the option of writing on visuals with an electronic pen.
Enable you to add sound to your visuals.

Remember to:

Keep your visuals to one topic each.

Use key words only. Think headlines. Never put a page of text or a financial statement on a visual, flash it up there, and say, "You can't read this, but . . ." Visuals are for headlines, to help the audience follow you. Handouts and notebooks are for detailed text.

Keep visuals to no more than five short lines.

Build your visuals to follow your talk exactly—in other words, points 1, 2, and 3 on your visual should be in the same order they are in your script.

Handouts or notebooks should have the same content in the same order.

Use artwork, charts, and color to make your visuals interesting. For visuals with text, don't use ten colors. That's confusing and too hard to read. Use two colors for words, one for background. For instance, on slides, your main titles could be gold, subheadings white, background royal blue.

Rehearse use of visuals. Always run through slides right before your presentation. They have a way of jumping around in the tray and getting mixed up.

Mark your script or outline to signal visual changes, or have someone change them for you. Otherwise you'll be talking about a point on slide 5 and you'll still have slide 2 on the screen. Plan how you will indicate points on your visuals without standing in front of them. Highlight points on the visual itself, or use a light pen.

Involve the audience. Even couch potatoes are not used to sitting passively for long periods of time without doing something. (CPs, after all, have remotes to play with.)

If your presentation is going to go on for a while—say, more than twenty minutes—build in an exercise or problem so the audience has a chance to work in pairs or small groups. Instead of telling them everything, give them a chance to figure it out. This will help them remember and will keep the energy level up. Ask for volunteers to report back and tell the whole group what they decided. This can work in large groups—I've seen it done in groups of several hundred—as well as in small ones.

Handling questions. One way to involve the audience is to ask for questions. Do this at the end or at the end of major sections. Keep in mind, if you open up for questions in the middle of your talk, you may have a problem getting back on track again.

Repeat questions before answering them. Some people in the audience might not have heard.

Acknowledge all questions and keep a positive or at least neutral tone. Don't ever make anyone feel he or she has asked a dumb or unimportant question—even when that's the case.

Some questions are really statements or challenges: "Don't you think, in light of what happened in our Chicago plant last year, we should dump this program?" When you get one of these, you can defuse it with questions of your own: "Joe, could you tell us why you feel that way?" "What specifically would you like to have happen?"

Remember, you can always use the group to help out. "Joe doesn't feel we should continue with this program—how do the rest of you feel?" They might cut Joe to ribbons, but they won't unless you ask.

Watch out for hypothetical questions: "What would you do if there were a class-action suit against your company for price-fixing?" Just smile and say, "Since we don't have a class-action suit against us, and we don't engage in price-fixing, I'd rather not try to answer that."

Also, don't get trapped into answering forced-choice questions: "Does our reengineering program mean we are more likely to downsize or to close this facility altogether?" Obviously, neither one may be the case, but you probably will be tempted to try to make a choice. You don't have to follow the questioner's lead. Give your own answer.

Video Presentations

Maybe your fifteen minutes of fame will come from a video you make to communicate with employees or customers. If you are about to do one, here are things to keep in mind.

Keep it short. Twenty minutes of a talking head—especially an amateur head—is deadly. Viewers will feel uncomfortable and embarrassed for you. Keep it under ten minutes.

As with any presentation, stay with one main point. Don't try to cram everything into your presentation; you'll lose your audience.

Use visuals. Anything that supports your main points and adds variety to your video.

Look at the camera as though you were talking with a friend. Don't stare; you'll look too owllike. Glance at your script, or at others if you are on a panel. Use facial expressions. Smile for happy news, frown for sad news.

If you're going to be on video, practice on video. Watch yourself and use the Presentation Critique sheet. Be particularly sensitive to nervous mannerisms. Bad enough in person, they are awful on video. Keep your hands away from the front of your face—in fact, keep them at chest level or below. Watch sideways glances; they look sneaky. Listen to the pace and tone of your voice—do you sound convincing? Be aware of interest level. What you think is dynamite stuff may seem flat as roadkill on video. Is the presentation lively, or is it dull and draggy?

You'll look fat on video, and your hair will look like a squirrel's nest. Get used to it.

Watch the pros. Tune in to your favorite newscasters or talk show hosts. Watch their facial expressions and gestures—they look natural and not forced. Listen to the way they punch out certain words and change the pace, and how they match facial expressions to what they are saying.

Get Better

Every presentation you give should build on your last and improve it. To become a great presenter, learn from each experience. Review your videotape. Ask someone you trust in the audience to critique your performance using the Presentation Critique. Feel great about what you did well, and agonize over what you screwed up—and figure out how to do it better next time.

Make notes on things you want to improve. Pick one or two to work on next time. Don't try to improve one hundred things at once.

Before your next presentation, go back and look at your notes. Build those improvements into your next presentation.

Writing

> "It has been determined that henceforth all access to security-sensitive areas in our principal building, such as MIS, the executive office, and R&D, will be controlled through the usage of a Security-Ident Card. Security-Ident Cards may be obtained, upon authorization, through the Corporate Security Department by all personnel who have established a certifiable work requirement to have access to these areas."
> —John Martin, VP Security, International Escargot

Why is it that a normal person, who might say to someone in the hall, "Hey, Fred, you need a security card to get into MIS," feels it is necessary to use a stilted, incomprehensible style when writing? After years of studying this problem, I can tell you I don't know.

But that's what seems to happen when people fire up their word processors, immediately switching from conversational to formal, dense language. As though no one will understand or pay attention if they write like humans instead of IRS agents.

Terrible writing is easy to spot. Usually it is based on:

Foggy ideas no one can understand
Big words even though little ones will do
Long, twisted sentences covering many subjects
Tangled verbal underbrush such as obscure jargon, acronyms, form numbers, and abbreviations known only to the writer
Vague words and statements that sound impressive but mean nothing
Arrogant style
Boring content
Complete disregard for the customer (the reader)

Maybe it's not so surprising that people have trouble writing. It is hard to do, even for professional writers. It's not like talking, where words disappear in the air and repeats, partial sentences, even grammatical lapses are the rule. When you write you can't catch puzzled expressions, scowls, or smiles, and you can't answer questions. What you write has to stand on its own, and knowing that, you strain to get it perfect. It is that effort that gums up the message.

I'll try to help you do better.

Guidelines for Good Writing

1. Understand that writing is not a God-given talent. It is demanding work—you aren't the only one who is Microsoft-challenged.
2. Always write with the reader in mind. Be considerate, be friendly, be interesting, and be clear. That's what the reader wants. Ask yourself: Will the reader understand? Am I making this clear? How does it sound? *Would I want to read this?*
3. Focus your work. Decide ahead of time what your topic is and what you want to happen. If you can't describe what your message is in one sentence, maybe you shouldn't bother writing. When you do figure out what the purpose is, make sure everything in your letter, report, memo, or other message supports it. Delete everything else, and save those thoughts for other communications.
4. Write everything in the simplest, most direct way you can. "It is

imperative, from the date of this writing and henceforth, that our print media campaigns be consolidated into editions with maximum circulation." Huh? "From now on, let's advertise in the Sunday papers." Oh. Use simple words and short sentences. Don't try to impress people by making your writing more complex than it needs to be.

Cormac McCarthy has been widely praised for the power and beauty of the writing in his novels.

> Before they reached the turn at the top of the hill there were three more shots from the road behind them. They turned onto the main track south and went pounding through the town. Already there were lamps lit in a few small windows. They passed through at a hard gallop and rode up into the low hills. First light was shaping out the country to the east.
>
> —*All the Pretty Horses*

Hard to find a word longer than two syllables, isn't it? And look at the sentences. Short, strong sentences. You probably won't be writing novels, but the point is clear. Your message will be much more powerful if you keep it as simple and short as possible.

5. Use headings and subheads in long reports to help the reader know where he or she is.
6. Use bullets to indicate points.
7. Be consistent. If you start a list with action verbs, continue that all the way through.

> "Here are the steps in the process:
>
> 1. Develop the new staffing guides.
> 2. Get approval of management.
> 3. Print 100 sets.
> 4. Communication."

"Communication" is jarring when you read that, isn't it? That's because it is not consistent with the rest of the list.

8. Take out every *that* and *which* you can. Also take out unneeded fillers and qualifiers.

> "I think that we should go ahead with the Carson matter. As you know, it is a matter that most people feel is highly important."

The two *that's* add nothing and take up space. Delete them.

"I think we should go ahead with the Carson matter. As you know, it is a matter most people feel is highly important."

"As you know" is a filler. If they already know, you don't have to tell them.

"I think we should go ahead with the Carson matter. It is a matter most people feel is highly important."

As a matter of fact, if they already know, why write the sentence at all?

"I think we should go ahead with the Carson matter."

"I think" implies you are not sure and weakens the sentence. Can it.

"We should go ahead with the Carson matter."

9. Avoid boring, overused words and phrases such as "time-frame," "in depth," "in regard to," "ballpark," "interface," "viable," "parameter," "input," "maximize," or "bottom line." Why not use something new and more interesting?

10. If you are having trouble writing simply, explain what you are trying to say to a coworker or to your spouse. Then write down what you said. That's your message. There's no rule against writing in a conversational style.

    If you get tangled up in the middle of a sentence, break it in two. If a paragraph goes on for more than a quarter of a page, split it in half. Visually, short paragraphs are easier to wade through.

11. Just as in presentations, begin with an opening grabber. If you are having trouble finding one, throw out the first paragraph or two of something you have written and begin with what's left. Often that will be the point of what you want to say anyway.

12. Get your message in that first paragraph. Most readers, swamped with paper and bombarded with electronic words, have no hope of keeping up, and scan most things hoping to grab the meaning as they whiz by. Besides, you are not running a treasure hunt—why hide what you want to say somewhere in the fifth paragraph?

13. If you are word processing, print out your draft on paper and edit it there before going back to your computer. You are used to seeing words on paper, and somehow words fit together differently on paper than they do on the screen.

14. Don't waste all afternoon thinking up the perfect opening or the perfect way to say something. For your first draft, just write what

comes into your head. You are going to edit it anyhow, so you don't have to live with it for long. Keep on plowing through without taking time out to evaluate what you have done. The point is to get started—the act of writing generates ideas, and many times, while you are writing the third or fourth paragraph, a good opening paragraph will pop into your head. I don't know why. Don't analyze it too much, just go with it.

15. Make your message fun to read. Support your main points with anecdotes, statistics, quotes. "I was there and saw this . . ." is a good interest-getter. Expert opinion is good. "Eighty-four percent of those we surveyed said . . ." is an eye-catcher. Use charts and other visuals when you can.

16. Stay away from the passive voice. "It has come to the attention of management . . ." is a guaranteed yawn. It is bureaucratic and causes people's eyes to snap shut. How did it come to the attention of management? Who ratted on us? Does anyone care anyhow?

It's okay to say "I." And clearer. "We" is faceless and less friendly. Let's say you get an E-mail that goes like this:

"We got your message of the 25th. We will look forward to meeting with you on May 1st. Joseph Benson."

You show up and look around. Only Joseph himself is there. Where the heck is everybody?

17. If you are writing a long report, organize it by sections so the reader can get what he or she wants to out of it.

18. Number the pages. It is very awkward to discuss something when you have to say, "It's on the page after the one with the graph on it, the one that begins 'Point number two.' It's about a third of the way into the report." How about "Turn to page eight" instead?

Finally, if you want to learn how to write well, write. Write as much as you can. Read what others have written critically, in light of the guidelines above. It's worth any effort you put into it.

Title

Your title should accurately describe what's in the report. Finish the sentence: "The main purpose of my report is_____." Somewhere in there is your title.

Findings and Recommendations

This is a short summary of what you found and what you want people to do with that. A page or two is enough, and it should be able to stand on its own, because it is all many people will read. This is also called the Executive Summary. Write it last.

Introduction

Include why the report was done, when it was done, who was involved. This is a one-pager.

The Report

This is a more detailed look at the findings and recommendations for those who want more information. If your research involved going out and talking with people, include (anonymous) quotes in this section. If you hear "Our systems are not up-to-date enough to keep up with customer needs" from several people, include it as a typical comment you heard in your interviews.

Appendices

Include statistical information, charts, lists, reference material, bibliographies, and other supplemental information that would clutter up the main report.

How Technology Is Changing the Way You Communicate

Technology is having a major impact on all types of communication. You have access to more information more easily than ever before. Technology is breaking down old barriers between departments and between levels in the organization as information flows everywhere.

It allows you to work anyplace. Computers, E-mail, and faxes have created virtual offices from which you can communicate just as though you were in the work space next door. This has created more than a few side effects. How do you supervise people who are spread out all over? How do you discipline yourself to produce when you work outside the office? What do you substitute for the social aspects of the office?

Technology is changing the way you deal with customers. Now you can tap into information from all over the organization to find the answers to customer problems and requests quickly and accurately, or you can allow customers to tap in directly.

The Internet will revolutionize the way you communicate, if it hasn't already. On the Internet you can call up vast stores of information from databases all over the world. You can instantly access knowledge and advice from libraries, newspapers, professional societies, and colleges and universities.

Many companies are experimenting with the Internet: IBM, AT&T, Ford, Federal Express, Merrill Lynch, J. P. Morgan, Bank of America, and Dun & Bradstreet are going on with company, investor, and product information. Some have electronic catalogs on the Internet.

The World Wide Web, powerful new software, is making it easy to navigate the Net, and software enables your laptop to reach into the Web for information, conversation, tickets, merchandise, new programs, and much more we don't even know about yet.

The Web will enable you to place, receive, and pay for orders without talking with anyone or filling out any forms. It will allow you to work with colleagues in remote locations on design projects just as though you were in the same room. The Internet will take over your PC, telephone, fax, TV, and your life.

Technology subjects you to a whole new set of illnesses:

Carpal tunnel syndrome—pain caused by repetitive actions, such as typing all day at a computer. Newly designed keyboards are helping with this.

Voice mail rage: "You have twenty-seven messages."
  "!!@!#&&*@#%@!"

Technophobia: Instructions that come with computers and software are impossible to decipher. That's why there are all those books on the market to explain them to you. Learning can be a frustrating experience—in a recent survey, 41 percent of periodic computer users said they felt like throwing something at the screen. People over forty-five seem to have mega-problems with computers—many don't type, and they didn't grow up with high tech: "If I touch the wrong key, I'll blow it up."

If you doubt the impact of technology, consider this: Computer engineers and scientists, and systems analysts, are the fastest-growing occupations for college graduates.

Work on your communication skills. Good speaking and writing will serve you well. They will help you stand out from the crowd and increase your value to your employer.

SBI: Communicate with the needs of your audience in mind. Emphasize the benefits to them and make it clear what you want them to do.

9

I DON'T MEAN TO INTERRUPT, BUT—

How to Shut Up and Listen

"A good listener is not only popular everywhere, but after a while he gets to know something." —Wilson Mizner

Listening is the forgotten part of the communication process. In school we are taught how to read and write. We learn social graces and how to be with other people. Some of us take courses in public speaking. No one teaches us how to listen, and until very recently, listening was not even regarded as a skill to be learned.

Of the four basic communication skills (listening, speaking, reading, and writing), listening is used the most and is taught the least. Writing is used the least and is taught the most.

That may change. As people work more in teams, as time becomes more precious and they struggle to make every minute count, and as they partner with suppliers and even competitors, they realize they have to listen to make sense out of the complex issues they deal with. And they learn there is more to listening than just sitting there with the eyes at half-mast while someone else talks.

As you develop your listening skills, you will improve your ability to:

- Understand others' thinking.
- Build on others' ideas.
- Reach agreement.
- Keep on the subject—and run shorter meetings.
- Avoid going back over the same subjects time after time.
- Gather accurate information from others, including customers.
- Get along better—*people like to work with others who listen to them.*

Why You Don't Listen

Listening is hard work. I don't know about you, but it tires me out. When I run a workshop, at the end of the day I'm shot—not so much from presenting material or guiding the group, but from listening. I have to listen to what people say; I can't let my mind wander off—and that is pretty exhausting. Listening for extended periods of time is not natural for me—or for you either. Here's why:

1. **Your mind does not like to pay attention.** Try as you might, after a few minutes your mind strolls off to the beach or the golf course. Then it changes course to rehash a tough conversation with the boss the other day and make it come out more in your favor. It may allow you to listen a little before it meanders off again to think about fixing the car, going shopping, cooking dinner, and all those things you have to do after work.

After "listening" to a ten-minute presentation, you will probably remember half of it. Two days later, you'll be able to dredge up 25 percent. That's partly faulty memory, but it also has to do with not listening.

People rarely see themselves as outstanding listeners. In a recent survey, respondents rated themselves an average of 55 on a scale of 100. Only 5 percent rated themselves 70 or higher!

2. **You think faster than people talk.** Most of your cohorts talk at about 125 to 140 words per minute; you think four times faster than that. You think in concepts, not individual words, and can leap far ahead of the speaker who is slogging along word by word: "Second-quarter earnings were down two percent. Here's what is behind that. . . ."

By the time the CFO has said that, you have already thought of a dozen reasons why earnings were off. So why listen to a twenty-minute explanation?

3. **People are boring.** They dwell on irrelevant details, insist on using arcane jargon so no one knows quite what they're talking about, and stumble around verbally trying to express half-formed ideas. Your noggin says, "Time to take a hike."

4. **You rehearse your responses while people talk.** The boss says, "I saw your note on the delay in the Crumrine project . . ." and you immediately start thinking up reasons for the delay. You might miss the part where he says, "It will work out all right; we can't implement it till next February anyhow."

5. You have too much on your mind. It's hard to listen to anyone when you've just learned the Reengineering from Hell Consulting Group is coming in next week and you've just bought a house.

6. Listening puts you in a "second-class" role. Or at least it seems to. Speaking is active and controlling; you're in charge. As a listener, you are not doing anything visible, and that may make you feel less important than the speaker. The bottom line? You'd rather hear yourself talk than someone else.

7. You think the speaker is a loser. You don't like the speaker, or you don't trust him or her. Maybe the last few things the speaker told you turned out to be not true. So you take a little mental holiday. Why listen to someone who has nothing of value to say?

8. You don't believe much anyone tells you anyway.

9. You can't hear. There's too much noise in the room, the speaker is whispering down at the other end of the table, or your eardrums are getting flabby.

With all that working against you, it's no wonder you don't listen to everything. But there are a few simple things you can do to listen better, understand better, and get twice as much out of each conversation you have.

Nine Steps to Better Listening

1. Make sure you can hear. If you are missing words, move closer or ask the speaker to talk louder. If you have continual problems hearing people, it may be that listening to all that rock music has blasted something loose and you need some medical help.

2. Shut up. You can't hear what's being said if you are talking, too, or if you are talking to yourself mentally—rehearsing your responses or tearing apart what the speaker is saying.

3. Look for something you can use. No matter what is being said, however irrelevant or boring, try to find some meaning in it. Listening for your own benefit will help keep your attention where it should be in case something important comes along.

4. Work at understanding. Go for the real meaning of what the speaker is saying. If you aren't clear, ask questions. Use open questions like "Can you tell me more about that?" or "What other alternatives did you consider?" Often, you will need to ask a second or third (digging) question to get the clarity you want. Use neutral questions; stay away from questions that seem challenging or argumentative ("Why" questions can seem confrontational).

Keep active. Takes notes, write down key words. It helps you stay with it. Mentally summarize what was said once in a while.

Don't beat yourself up if your attention wanders and you drop out for a bit. You probably haven't missed much, and sometimes you get good ideas when you wander off. Write your ideas down and drop back in.

5. Judge the content, not the speaker. If you don't like the speaker, try to get past that. Focus on the meaning of what the speaker is saying and find some truth in it, even though you don't have much respect for the person who is talking. Anyone, even people you wish would disappear, can bring something of value to the table.

6. Paraphrase. When you absolutely positively have to focus on what's being said, tell yourself you will repeat the speaker's thoughts back to him or her. Actually do it if the situation permits. This is the technique I use in leading workshops, because often I *do* have to repeat thoughts back to the group. You can also let the speaker know you are listening by nodding affirmatively, saying, "Yes, I agree," or "I understand what you are saying." Watch out for weaker phrases like "That's interesting" or "Is that right?" They are tip-offs that your mind is on the Concorde heading for Paris.

7. Evaluate. When you are satisfied you understand what the speaker said, you can evaluate it. Wait till the end; then think of the positives first. What do you like about the idea? Decide that before you nuke it.

Evaluate based on:

Content. What the speaker said, not on how he or she said it or whether or not you like the speaker.

Credibility. Do you believe what was said? Was it well thought out and rational, or based on flimsy evidence?

Usefulness. Will it do you any good—make your work easier, make you more effective?

Usability. Is it practical? Can it really be done, or is it a dream?

8. Give feedback. If the speaker has asked you to do something as a result of what was said, let the speaker know what you plan to do (or not do).

9. **Act.** Surprisingly, this is part of listening. If one of your people outlines an idea and asks for your support, you can go through all of the eight steps above, but if you don't do something, your subordinate will always feel that you were nice and polite, but you didn't listen.

How to Get Others to Listen

You can bet that others are as listening challenged as you are. What do you do when you are raining down words of wisdom and no one is listening? Here are some strategies for getting the attention of others.

1. **Make sure they can hear.** Try to keep away from phones, machines, jet planes, and Bon Jovi concerts. The quieter and calmer the place, the more chance that your listeners can hear you.

2. **Start with an attention-getter.** A story, anecdote, or fact will amuse or surprise the listeners.

3. **Tell them what's in it for them.** If you can convince them that they will benefit somehow from listening, they will.

4. **Speak with energy** and at a fairly rapid pace. Listeners pay more attention to someone who plunges ahead than to someone who dawdles along and leaves long pauses between words and thoughts.

5. **Get them involved.** People listen least to lectures and speeches. They pay much closer attention and retain more if they actively participate in give-and-take, problem solving, or brainstorming.

6. **Tighten up your thoughts.** Whether you are talking to a group of several hundred or just one-on-one with a peer, focus what you are saying, say it as briefly as possible, and include only relevant information. Don't wear the listener(s) down with long discussions of minor details or bring in semirelevant personal war stories.

7. **Use the "I" technique** to keep the listener from tuning out when you are offering criticism. The "I" technique puts the emphasis on what the listener's behavior does to you rather than on the listener's shortcomings. Instead of saying, "You haven't made your sales goals in the last two quarters," which prompts the listener to rush off mentally, thinking of excuses, say, "When you miss your sales goals, I worry because I know that gives people the wrong impression of your ability."

8. **Take a break.** If you have a long session, or sense that the listeners are losing energy and getting bored, take time off. Let them get some coffee, or just stand up and stretch.

9. **Ask for feedback.** "Do you understand what I am saying?" "What would you say is the main point in all this?" "How do you feel about it?" "Do you have any questions?"

10. **Ask for the sale.** If you want your listeners to do something as a result of what you are saying, ask them. To keep their attention, you might tell them up front you are going to be asking them to do something.

Reading Listeners' Clues

Your listeners can tell you a lot without saying anything, or by the way they speak. Observing their nonverbals and their speech patterns can let you know how well they are buying what you are saying and whether you need to change your tone, pace, or content.

Similarly, when you are the listener you will want to watch what clues you are giving the speaker.

On the next page are nonverbals and speech patterns along with what they usually mean. I say "usually" because there are always people who do the opposite of what is expected and screw up your perceptions.

CLUES TO WATCH FOR

What to look for	What It Usually Means	
	Listener agrees, likes	Listener disagrees, is bored
Nonverbals		
Posture	Sitting forward, leaning in	Leaning away
	Arms relaxed	Arms crossed over chest
Hands	Relaxed, natural gestures	Clasped. Holding on. Chopping or clenched fist gestures. Fingers drumming.
Location	Moving closer	Hiding behind desk, moving away
Eyes	Good contact	Looking away, studying papers
Face	Smiling, looking interested	Frowning, looking uncertain
Speech Patterns		
Speech	Normal, calm	Loud and fast (could indicate tension)
	Using supportive words, sounds	Silence, muttering
	Sympathetic tone	Sarcastic tone, annoyance
	Speaks directly to the issues	Dances around, says "To tell the truth," "Frankly," "To be honest with you"
	Uses "we"	Uses "I"

SBI: When you want to be sure to listen, tell yourself that you will have to repeat what the speaker has said.

PART

IV

FOLLOWER SKILLS

10

YOUR BOSS AS A HUMAN BEING
Leading Your Manager

"The longer I study effective leaders, the more I am persuaded of the underappreciated importance of effective followers." —Warren Bennis, management expert

"We need to train nonsupervisory people so that they can handle responsibility, just as we have been training managers."
—Anthony Carnevale, former Vice President of
National Affairs, American Society for
Training and Development

Take a minute and think about your boss. Okay, what does that picture look like?

Maybe what you're seeing isn't too pleasant—after all, bosses have a way of being exasperating. On the other hand, you may love your boss and think he or she is just wonderful.

No matter how you feel, one thing is sure—you have a strong opinion about your boss. Very few people say, "The boss? Gosh, I don't know. . . ."

Here are some boss comments I've heard recently:

"The boss is so busy it's tough to get to see him. He's got so many
    people reporting to him."
"The boss never talks to me. A lot of the time I'm not real sure what
    the priorities are."
"I'd like to know how I'm doing. No one ever tells me. Appraisal? It's
    a joke. The last one I got was in a taxi on the way to the airport.
    About ten minutes of meaningful discussion about my performance. Just the three of us: the boss, me, and the cabdriver."
"The boss is a good person, but she's swamped—we all are. . . ."

"The boss is an idiot."

"The boss could throw more challenges my way. I'm using about half
my talent in this job."

"The boss tries hard, I'll say that for her, but . . . well, let me tell you
what she did last week. . . ."

Sound familiar? The implication always seems to be: "However I feel
about the boss, good or bad, I could do better if I had that job."

When you think about it, having a boss is probably pretty low on
your list of favorite things. Right down there with dental work, canceled
flights, and paying a lot for a muffler. You never liked it when your parents put a damper on all those things you wanted to do, why should
having a boss now be any better? It is just not natural for people to be
comfortable with any kind of authority.

The old captain of industry—the fearless tyrant, standing on the
forecastle (or wherever captains used to stand), waving a cutlass and
shouting orders—is now supposed to get out with the deckhands and
facilitate. Facilitate! Become a coach, not an order giver, someone who
relies on involvement, communication, and recognition rather than
kicking ass. In the jargon of the day, a leader.

The wisdom in that is that most of the problems we face today—
quality, productivity, and service, for example—are people problems
and can be remedied if people are better trained and motivated.

Changing from captain to coach isn't easy, but many bosses are trying to shed old habits and learn new ways. They are struggling with a
new world, where not everything is understandable and where old
methods don't work. For a lot of bosses it's a tough transition.

Today, bosses supervise more people because organizations are flat-
ter, and they have a tougher time communicating with everyone. They
work with people who have little or no loyalty to the company, people
who are demoralized with worry that they will be reengineered into
oblivion. Bosses are faced with meeting unrealistic goals and trying to
attain higher and higher quality while their staffs and budgets are being
cut. And they are whipped around day after day with change and conflicting signals.

Bosses are totally exposed. The boss may make a thousand decisions
a week—big ones, little ones. Each decision is examined microscopi-
cally by everybody. And if one of those thousand decisions is a bad
one—*hold on*—the whole department (and neighboring departments,
who will hear about it soon enough) will be gleefully yakking about how

dumb the boss is. Subordinates who have been semicomatose, playing computer games for weeks, will suddenly become interested in what's going on at work. People love to see the boss screw up.

Bosses disappoint us, frustrate us, make our eyes roll in disbelief, and infuriate us. Of course they do; they are human beings just like everyone else.

Everyone should have the boss's job for a while. I mean it—if everyone had firsthand experience with how tough it is, people would shut up about how bad the boss is and just be glad they aren't in that job.

New Expectations

We need to rethink our expectations for bosses. As followers, we need to be more accepting of the fact that underneath it all, bosses are just subordinates who got pulled out of the pack and were given a chance to manage, often with no guidance. (Yesterday you were a salesperson out on the road; today you are a sales manager. Congratulations. Go to it!) Bosses are trying to figure out what to do, just like you are, except that their "what-to-do's" are harder than most.

Also, we need to accept more of the responsibility for what's happening with the boss.

If you are wishing your boss would become a real leader, don't sit around and wait. It won't happen all by itself. You should be taking an active role in setting goals and priorities, opening up communications, getting feedback, and in general leading your boss. The boss needs your help. Nobody can do it alone today. When you do help, you will increase your value in the boss's eyes, and you may get more freedom, more important work, and more recognition. At the very least you may go further down the list of people to be squashed.

The New Boss-Subordinate Relationship

> "The difference between a good boss and a bad one is that a good one lets you do your job."
> —Roger Smith, CEO, GM

It is too bad we still have to talk about bosses and subordinates today, because the terms are outdated and have bad implications. *Subordinate* comes from the Latin *sub*, which means "under," and *ordinary*, which means "common." A subordinate, then, is someone who is lower than common. *Boss* comes from the old Anglo-Saxon word meaning "sea lion."

Up until ten years ago, the rules for the boss-subordinate relationship were pretty clear. The boss was there to make you do things by the book, pass down messages from higher management, and give you one-minute reprimands when things went wrong. You were supposed to do what the boss said, work hard, dress for success, and get ready for the next promotion.

That was before we were overwhelmed by global competition, downsizing, TQM, technology, boomers, busters, and Xers.

All those have changed the boss-subordinate relationship dramatically over the last few years. To understand the nature of that change, my company recently did a survey of CEOs, senior executives, top consultants, and educators on the new boss-subordinate relationship. Here are a few of the findings:

HOW THE BOSS'S ROLE HAS CHANGED

Old Role	New Role
Formal, structured	Collegial, cooperative
Give commands, orders	Help, develop, coach
Micromanage	Delegate, empower
Go it alone	Work in teams

HOW THE SUBORDINATE'S ROLE HAS CHANGED

Old Role	New Role
Seen and not heard	Participate in decisions
Rely on company, boss	Take charge of own work, career
Accept and go along	Confront, challenge, question
Wait for others	Initiate

Notice that much of the boss's responsibility has shifted to subordinates, blurring the sharp distinction between the roles of managers and subordinates. The balance of power has moved. While bosses used to have almost all the power and subordinates none, power is shared today.

That gives you an opportunity to help your boss form new habits that will make life better for you. You can step up, take charge of the relationship, and build it the way you want it. Actually, the boss may welcome your help.

Here's a true story: On a Wednesday afternoon, Alex Edwards was hard at work in a corporate office in New York City, when he got a call from the senior vice president of operations. "Plan to be in San Diego on Friday morning," the SVP said. "We are going to have an all-day meeting at the branch office out there."

Surprised but curious, Alex said, "I'll be there, but let me ask you— coast-to-coast in one day is pretty hard travel—what's going on?"

"Something has just popped. We've found a manager out there who *talks to his people.*"

Alex and about forty other managers from around the country arrived in San Diego to hear the branch manager tell them about 20 percent sales increases he attributed to an involvement program in which he spent an hour or so a week meeting with groups of people at all levels. In those meetings, employees brought suggestions for improvements in customer service, delivery, and packaging, and ideas for building sales, cutting costs, and getting the job done better and faster.

Many organizations have employee involvement programs, quality circles, and the like. But the astounding thing about this particular venture was that it was thought up, not by the boss or a team of consultants, but by a *plain old employee* who wanted more say in what was going on but didn't have a forum for doing that.

The branch was getting windfall sales increases, the boss learned something about involvement, and the employee who had the initiative and the courage to suggest it gained a whole new measure of respect . . . not to mention fame, because the system was adopted throughout the company and quickly became known as "Mary's Meetings" after its founder.

Maybe you can think of other instances like this, where subordinates have stepped in and given the boss firm direction. Where someone has taken charge to improve his or her own work situation.

Can you do what Mary did—give the boss firm direction and improve your work situation? How good can you be at leading your boss, training him or her to build a working relationship that suits you better? Follower skills will help.

Follower Skills

For years, organizations have been training people to be leaders. Conference centers around the country are filled with people taking courses on leadership, and there are mountains of leadership books and videos on the market. But there is very little on how to be a follower. That is curious, because all of us are followers. Even if we are bosses, we're also followers, and it takes skill to be a successful follower.

Getting Started

Consider these things when working on your follower skills:

1. Realize your boss is human, and is probably trying to do a good job. Be tolerant of mistakes the boss makes—at least what you, in your wisdom, see as mistakes.
2. Change your thinking from "what the boss is doing to me" to "what I am doing to manage this relationship." You have every bit as much responsibility for making the relationship work as your boss does—in fact, more. Your boss isn't going to change to accommodate you, so you will have to take charge of at least 51 percent of everything that happens.
3. Be careful not to make it seem that you are trying to take over the boss's job. Make it clear you recognize who is boss, and that you are working to be supportive of the boss's direction.
4. Keep in mind your boss may be much more open to suggestion than you think. You'll never know till you try.
5. When discussing any major issue with the boss, take ownership of the problem. "It's my problem to fix, but I want to talk with you about it, because I need your support."
6. If your boss is one step below Attila the Hun, don't despair. You can learn a lot from rotten bosses. Keep a log of what not to do, and when it's your turn to lead people, don't do those things. When you are really frustrated, remember, you probably won't work for this boss forever.

7. Be patient and persistent. Changing the relationship with your boss takes time. Keep at it and you will see results. But not right away.

8. Keep looking at yourself. In today's blameless society, it's easy to push your own shortcomings off on your boss: "The boss gave me a bad rating. He has it in for me." Maybe, maybe not. There is a chance—hard as it is to admit—that your performance is lousy.

Building Follower Skills

Now that you have more power in the relationship, you should know how to use it. When we asked survey participants, "What are the major sources of power subordinates have to build more productive relationships with their bosses?" their responses were (in order of importance):

Being professional
Having the "right" attitude
Communicating well
Meeting the boss's needs
Being visible
Taking charge

Let's look at each of these more closely.

1. **Being professional means:**

- You have the technical competence and knowledge to do your job effectively. You know more than your boss, so the boss has to rely on you and look to you for your expertise.
- You know the business. You keep up-to-date on how the company is doing, where competition is going, strategic issues, new products and services, and what is happening in the industry. You should be able to talk business with the best of them. Also, you should see beyond your own area and think in terms of how the work you do affects the entire organization, the customer, and the bottom line. All this will help you be viewed as a corporate person, not just someone tied to one department.
- You know where you are going. If you don't have clear goals, don't wait for the boss to tell you. It may never happen. Take a look at

corporate goals, at department goals, and then form your own goals to support them.

- You take the initiative to manage yourself and your area. The boss is too busy trying to lead an army of other people to spoon-feed you every step of the way. You know your job better than the boss does anyhow, and you should go do it. Think of yourself as running your own business within a business.
- You are prepared. You always do your homework and are ready for every meeting with the boss or anyone else—you know your stuff.
- You are dependable. You do what you say you will do, and you establish a track record of meeting goals and deadlines, following through.

2. Having the right attitude means:

- You are optimistic—about your work and about the future. This can be tough (1) if you have a very difficult boss, and (2) if your company is collapsing around you. But negative people are not very pleasant to work with. You know that from those you have to deal with. Try not to be one of them.
- You are a good team player and can function well in a team environment. Good teamwork can heighten your reputation all over the company.
- You support diversity.
- You are willing to learn. You are flexible and open.
- You think in terms of the customer. You form long-term customer relationships with "customers" inside and outside the company. You tie your work as closely as possible to satisfying the customer. You have the respect of your customers, and that earns you the respect of everyone in the organization.

3. Communicating well means:

- You keep your boss informed as to what is going on in your area. You alert your boss to problems and changes, and their implications. You share information with the boss and keep surprises to a minimum.
- You involve the boss in plans and decisions you know he or she is concerned with, and see that the boss is brought into ongoing projects and team actions at appropriate times.

- You initiate discussions on goals, problems, progress. You don't wait for the boss to get around to it. You disagree constructively when you think the boss is on the wrong track. You stand up for what you think.
- You use technology. You use it to keep in touch wherever you are and to gain instant access to information. You use technology to empower yourself to make informed decisions.

4. Meeting the boss's needs means:

- You show respect for the boss. You may not like working for this particular boss, but you should show deference to the fact that he or she is in that job and you aren't.
- You support your boss's goals and make the boss look good. You do something every day that will move your boss's agenda ahead. You use your special talents to make the boss look competent (even if you wish the boss would be aboard the next space probe). For instance, if you can write well, and the boss has trouble, offer help in writing speeches and reports. If you are good with numbers, and the boss isn't, offer to help with budgets or sales projections. If you are at ease with computers, and your boss is still using a slide rule and mechanical pencil, offer to teach the boss or to input the stuff yourself.
- You create solutions, not problems. You never go to the boss with a problem without also suggesting a solution. You use your creative skills to come up with new ideas and approaches.
- You are "easy to do business with." You try to work with your boss the way the boss prefers, and you modify your own behavior to make the boss more comfortable in your relationship. The Boss Profile on the next page will help. Circle those words or phrases that best describe your boss's preferences.

BOSS PROFILE

Communication

How does the boss like to communicate?	Face-to-face E-mail Phone Fax Written reports
How much detail does the boss like?	Mountains of data Some detail Outlines and overviews only
What is the boss's discussion style?	Makes small talk Likes to get right to the point
What does he or she prefer talking about?	People and relationships Tasks, the work Opinions, ideas Facts, data

Time Use

How does the boss use time?	Always in a hurry, everything is urgent Laid back, things will get done
How quickly does the boss act?	Fast Slow, deliberate

Decisions

How does the boss approach planning?	Plans thoroughly before acting Jumps in and goes ahead
On what does the boss base decisions?	On facts, uses information On emotion and gut feeling
How does the boss approach risk?	Plays it safe A risk taker
How quickly does the boss decide?	Makes fast decisions Needs time
How much does the boss involve others?	Decides alone Gets input from others Often delegates decisions

Based on what you have circled, determine how you can accommodate your boss's preferences and be seen as someone who is "easy to do business with."

Area	Boss's Preferences	What I Can Do to Accommodate
Communication		
Time Use		
Decisions		

5. **Being visible means:**

- You work on high-visibility teams or projects. You volunteer for a team or a task force that is working on big company issues, work that is close to the business, even if you are there only in a support role.
- You improve communication skills so that you will stand out as someone who is good in front of the room, writing, or facilitating meetings.
- You are active in community or charitable activities, especially those supported by your company.

6. **Taking charge means:**

- You empower yourself. You get your boss to give you more responsibility and set you free to make decisions about your work. You don't necessarily take on *more* work, but you get more control over what you do, with less time referring decisions up the line and waiting for approvals to come down.

  Be careful, because you will be taking away some of your boss's authority. Think about what decisions you can and should make that are now being made higher up. Make a list of them, and then list the *benefits* to your boss and to the organization. Always talk about empowering yourself in terms of benefits to others.

  Some benefits to the boss might be:

  Free up time to work on more strategic stuff
  Get rid of routine work
  Avoid interruptions
  Have more satisfied customers because their needs get met faster
  Build business

  Some benefits to the company might be:

  Streamlined decision making
  Faster response to customer—the company will be easier to do business with
  Reduce costs
  Do more business with satisfied customers
  Develop employees
  Give employees more satisfaction in their work

- You sell ideas. You use influencing skills to get the support you need.

  You make sure you get your fair share of the boss's time. When you do get time, you use it well. You build the relationship and bargain for scarce resources you badly need: staff, budget dollars, information, office space, and equipment. As always, you stress the benefits of your ideas.

Those, then, are your follower skills. Put them to work for you and you will build your esteem in your boss's eyes and increase your value to the organization.

> **SBI:** You must take 51 percent of the responsibility for the relationship between you and your boss.

11

YES SIR, YES SIR, YES SIR

Dialogues with Your Boss

Boss: "Here's what I think we should do. . . ."
Subordinates around the table: "Good idea!" "I agree with that!" "Let's do it!"
Boss: "Let me tell you what it is first."

Talk with the boss? Maybe you'd rather dine on nuclear waste. That is, if your boss is abrasive, crabby, uninterested, closemouthed, or maybe too busy to listen to the nickel-and-dime stuff you have to say. And what the heck, you can just go ahead and do your job without talking with the boss anyhow.

The truth is, you have to talk with your boss. Like it or not, your boss has a big say in what happens to you next month and next year, and building an open, productive relationship with the boss can only help you.

As in other parts of the relationship, you will have to take some initiative in seeing that discussions happen, especially if the boss is a reluctant communicator.

Think CPR. It can be a lifesaver. Make your communications

Candid

Positive

Regular

"Candid" is scary. It is much less stressful to tell your boss good things and just agree with what he or she says. But bosses need honest information, and they need to hear the downside as well as the positive.

As we'll see, there are ways to give your boss bad news, even to disagree with your boss, that will preserve his or her self-esteem and won't jeopardize your reputation—and may even enhance your value in the boss's eyes.

There are few people bosses can depend on to give honest answers, and in most cases, bosses come to rely on those people more than others. You have to decide if you want to be one of them. There is some risk involved, but you can lower it by being positive.

"Positive" means looking for the upside of every situation and framing your communication around that. If you are disagreeing, do it in a constructive way, trying to make things better in the future. If you are reporting a disaster, do it in a problem-solving mode, with potential solutions in mind.

"Regular" is tough, too. Your boss probably has a small army reporting in, and has more pressure on time than ever before. Everyone wants to see the boss, and you will have to struggle to get time. As appealing as it may be to wait until the boss asks you in, you need the boss for too many things to let communication slide.

Let's talk about some specific kinds of dialogues you may have with your boss. Keep in mind that *dialogue* means here "a conversation between two people to exchange ideas and reach an amicable agreement."

Finding Out What the Boss Expects

Never assume you know what the boss wants. More than one person has been put in thumbscrews after working all year on the wrong thing. If you don't have goals spelled out, or even if you have goals but haven't talked much with the boss about them, get on the boss's calendar for a discussion.

Tread lightly here. The boss probably thinks everything is crystal clear (it may be in the boss's mind), and by wanting to talk about goals you'll imply it isn't. But, remember, you are being candid.

You also want to make the dialogue as positive as possible, so do your homework.

As was suggested in Chapter 5, sit down with the boss. Take your Time Allocation–Brainpower Chart with you. Tell the boss you have done some serious thinking about your job and want to make sure you are concentrating your time and energy so you support the company the best you can. Take the boss through your chart and get the boss's agreement.

Review your goals with the boss on a regular basis, and especially when you have reached major points along the way. Don't wait for the boss to ask, and don't wait for appraisal time to come around.

Finding Out How You Are Doing

Everybody hates appraisals. Bosses don't have time to fill out the forms and talk with their people, but human resources hounds them till they do. Many managers feel uncomfortable sitting in judgment of other people and finally reducing them to appraisal numbers. "You've worked your tail off all year, handled fifteen major projects, opened a new office in Bakersfield, brought in ten new customers, and single-handedly turned the company around. Congratulations, you are a three." And then dealing with the anger that follows.

Subordinates hate to hear all those criticisms and to be confronted with all their mistakes, some of which they didn't even know were mistakes until appraisal time.

At its worst, appraisal is a giant evil machine that grinds through the organization, leaving everyone bruised and bloody as it goes.

Appraisals can do more harm than good and make everyone feel lousy. That's why almost every company I know is busily designing new forms or redoing rating scales. But, unfortunately, appraisal may be the only time you have any kind of performance discussion with the boss, and you see it as something you have to endure—then you can go back to work and recover.

If you're nodding in agreement with the above assessment, it may be the fault of the appraisal process, it may be the fault of your boss, but more likely, some of the fault has to lie with you—because you are not participating the way you should in your own appraisal. It is managers *and subordinates* who make appraisals work.

Let's see what you can do to make appraisal more of a helpful experience for you.

How to Get More Out of Your Own Appraisal

Appraisal time is coming up. Your manager is getting ready, and you should be, too. Here's how:

1. Prepare

> *"Get your facts first, and then you can distort them as much as you please."* —Mark Twain

- Remember, appraisal is a dialogue, not a one-way communication. You should be ready to participate in the discussion at least as much as your boss does.
- Make sure you have the facts. Your boss keeps a file all year on your hits and misses. You should, too. Make notes if you have discussions (praising your performance or criticizing it) with the boss. Keep a log of major successes and mega-screwups so you remember what happened. Things get hazy six months out, and you want to be as candid and accurate as possible.
- Get a copy of the appraisal form and fill it out on yourself, even if the boss doesn't ask you to. Try to be objective.
- Write objectives for the coming year.

   Write five to ten goals for yourself, not goals focused on more of doing the same things better, but goals that will allow you to take on more responsibility, explore new horizons, and make you more valuable to the organization. You want to end up next year knowing more than you do now and having broader experience. Even if you don't get complete agreement in the appraisal discussion, this is a good time, maybe the only time, to plant the seeds.

2. Practice

- Anticipate where and why you and your boss may have different opinions on your performance, and practice your responses to what the boss will say. If you feel there will be disagreement as to what happened, or as to the value of your work, practice giving your view of it.
- Practice out loud, so you can hear yourself say the words, and keep working on them until they sound right. Remember, you are trying to be positive as well as candid. If you sound defensive or

whiny, or if you tend to make excuses and blame others when you are practicing, try another approach. Focus on solutions, not problems; the future, not the past.

3. Participate

- Once the discussion begins, don't just sit there and fume. You are at least an equal partner in the discussion. After all, it's your appraisal.

  Make yourself a partner, so you have as much airtime as the boss does. When you are criticized, use a problem-solving approach and talk in terms of how you can improve, meet goals, and do even better—with the boss's help, support, and encouragement. If you want the boss to be more involved in something you do, this is a good time to ask: "You've worked with these big accounts a lot in the past, do you think you could travel my territory with me a couple of days a month?"

- Use your listening skills. Listening is participating, too. Use digging questions to get more details and a better understanding of what the boss is trying to tell you. If the boss's first reply doesn't spell it all out, ask another question to clarify.

- Be willing to disagree if the boss hasn't got it right. After all, you have your file of what happened, too.

  When disagreeing, stick to the facts, what happened, and don't attack the boss's judgment.

- Focus on results. Your interest should be on the customer, building business, controlling costs, improving the bottom line.

- Focus on the future. One of your responsibilities in the process is to guide the appraisal discussion away from the past to how you will learn and grow and contribute more in the future. This moves your appraisal discussion from a (possibly negative) review of what happened to a positive look at what can happen in the year(s) to come.

  The boss is under pressure to make the appraisal a record of the past. It has legal implications if he or she should ever want to dump you. It also is tied to salary, and on the off chance there is an increase in the future, the size of it will depend on your rating.

  That's all well and good, but once the boss gets through yesterday's news and heaves a sigh of relief, the appraisal may be pretty much over. It will be up to you to pull the discussion through to

the future so that a good half of the appraisal discussion will be on what's coming next.
- When it's over, thank the boss.

4. Follow up

Take the appraisal discussion seriously, especially the goals you have set with your boss. Get to work and start implementing them. If the boss has agreed to send you to a seminar, sign up right away, don't wait three months—the whole world will have changed. If you have been given more responsibility for making decisions, start doing it right away, before the boss forgets.

Discussing Performance Between Appraisals

Some bosses give feedback in regular coaching sessions or in one-on-one progress report meetings; many do not. If yours doesn't, schedule them. Get on your boss's calendar, telling your boss, "I need to talk with you once in a while, because I need your help and advice." What boss, no matter how swamped, would refuse that? Do it on a regular basis, so you both expect it.

- Don't crowd the boss. Schedule one-on-ones with restraint. Don't show up every other day.
- Keep the sessions short. Get right to the point; tell the boss what's going on and what you plan to do. Ask if you are on the right track. Ask for blessings, advice, and support as needed, then get out.
- Keep to one topic per session. One project, one problem. Keep subjects as close to sales, costs, or customers as you can—important subjects, at the heart of the business.
- Avoid surprises. If you see a problem rumbling over the horizon, use these sessions to talk with the boss about it. Better to take some heat now than to have the boss hear about it later from the CEO.

Receiving Criticism

As exemplary as your work is, in the course of doing eight million things each month, you may screw one up, and—amazing as it may seem—it may be your fault!

Bosses react to failures in various ways. There are bosses who feel their job is to watch you carefully and whack you as soon as you make a mistake. Others are more philosophical and will talk with you about it supportively, and in due time.

At any rate, you are with the boss, you know you have blown it big-time, and he or she is about to let you have it. You can suffer through it with your head bowed, thinking what a miserable garden slug you turned out to be, or you can use this as an opportunity to raise the boss's respect for you.

It all depends on how you handle the situation.

First, remind yourself you are human, and as such tend to make mistakes sometimes.

Second, listen openly. Ask questions to clarify, not to challenge. But listen; don't immediately jump to mounting your defense.

In fact, don't be defensive. You don't have to agree with what the boss is telling you, but your attitude should be "I understand what you are saying." Keep it on a positive note.

Be careful of excuses. Other departments or other people might have let you down, or there might have been outside factors that killed your effort, but if it was your job to manage it, you have to take the rap. Be candid and point out reasons for the failure in a matter-of-fact way, but end up by saying, "But overall, it was my responsibility and I should have handled it better. I wish I could do it over. I would do it differently."

The truth is, the boss does not want to hear you whine about how others' poor performance has done you in. It's much better to own up and take what's coming. In fact, accepting blame in today's no-responsibility world can be so disarming that your boss will view you with new respect.

Third, look on it as a way to improve. Maybe you actually were less than perfect, and maybe there are ways you could have done better. Your boss may have more experience with this sort of thing than you do, and might even have a good idea or two.

Fourth, think about what the boss has told you; it might work.

You may not want to run in to the boss on a regular basis, asking, "Beat me, whip me, criticize me," but if you are initiating discussions with your boss, expect that some criticism is going to come along at some point and be ready to handle it in a way that will help, not harm, you.

Giving the Boss Bad News

There will be times you will have to give the boss bad news, disagree with the boss, or even be critical. You will have to weigh the pain and benefits of doing any of these, but in the spirit of open communication you should probably come down on the side of being candid. Most bosses will accept it, some of them gracefully, and will appreciate your directness if you do it right.

You can give bad news in a positive, constructive way. Just because the message is negative, it doesn't have to create an adversarial situation. In fact, your willingness to stand up and give negative information when it's necessary will give you more credibility with the boss. Here's how to do it.

1. Practice what you are going to say, especially if it deals with a sensitive topic. Anticipate your boss's reaction and how you will respond.
2. Always start with a positive. Something your boss agrees with, something good that happened, something you liked.
3. Be direct and honest.
4. If you are giving criticism, maintain the boss's self-esteem. Remember, the boss has feelings, too.
5. Always have a solution. Never go into any kind of discussion of this kind without thinking through a way to improve or resolve the situation.

   Be direct. Be positive. Give the boss hope that better days are ahead.

Getting Your Boss to Buy Your Ideas

> *Subordinates:* "We want to get an eighteen-wheeler and
> fix it up so the side opens into a stage. Then we can go
> around to the dealers and put on a musical to introduce
> our new product line!"
> *Boss:* "I told you people, no more brainstorming
> sessions."

Organizations are constantly talking about the need for innovation
and creativity, but few can tolerate it. Ideas are very dangerous in the
workplace. They represent new and untried ways of doing things, and
they might fail. The penalties for failure, even small failures, are often
so severe they outweigh any benefit that might accrue from a new idea.

So, when you tell the boss your idea about the eighteen-wheeler, the
boss will see it as threatening and will immediately run through a Massive Mental Defense checklist:

MMD CHECKLIST

How will this look to *my* boss? How about when the CEO gets wind of it?

What are the chances this won't work? Can my record stand one more goof-up?

What's this going to cost? How much is an eighteen-wheeler anyhow? A lot, probably. What will it do to my budget? Is it a careful way to spend the company's money?

Has anyone loused up with something like this before?

How will it look to the public? Will stockholders think we're throwing away their
money when they see this rig rumbling down the highway?

What about accidents? Suppose the driver rams into someone's Miata?

The checklist run-through can convince the boss this is a bad idea in
seconds, and he or she will tell you all the negatives. With some bosses,
that will be the end of it (unless you know more about selling ideas), and
with others it's just a holding action until they get used to the idea.

Here are some things to think about before you spring your mar-
velous idea on the boss.

- Try to link the idea to something the boss thought of or did in the
  past. That way it becomes partly his or her idea. "Boss, remember
  when you rented that Model-T Ford for the trade show? That

worked so well, we were kicking that concept around and we came up with something like it. . . ."

Better yet, try to get the boss involved in the brainstorming session so the idea really is partly his or hers.

- Do a cost-benefit analysis ahead of time so when the boss says, "That would be pretty expensive," you can say, "It will cost us—for rental of the eighteen-wheeler for the season, painting the trailer, gas, oil, driver, a singer, and insurance—$160,000. We figure that investment can bring us about two million in additional sales. Here's our plan. . . ."
- Think of some alternatives, in case the boss is dug in against the idea. "Suppose we get a big van instead and give it a great paint job with the company logo all over the sides." "Maybe we could just use tapes instead of hiring a singer."
- Don't pass any monkeys. If you have an idea that is going to take some time and energy to implement, offer to do it yourself so the boss doesn't see it as another big boulder being loaded on his or her shoulders.
- Dispel feelings that it will never work by finding examples of other departments or other companies that have used similar ideas successfully.
- Get some allies. If someone the boss especially respects likes the idea, be sure to tell the boss that, or have the person come along when you approach the boss.
- Offer small bites. The safest course in any new plan is to test it on a small basis. "Why don't we rent a truck for a couple weeks to try it out in the local area? Instead of painting the trailer we can hang a banner on it. Let's see how it works."

If, despite your best efforts, the boss kills off ideas time after time (and you are pretty sure it is not because you are coming up with really stupid ideas), you might want to talk with the boss about it. It's okay to talk about what is happening in the relationship. "Boss, I've got a problem I need your help with. I don't seem to be getting very far in getting you interested in ideas and suggestions lately. Am I doing this wrong, or should I just stop bothering you with this stuff?" Sometimes the boss may not even realize he or she has been doing this, and will try to be more open next time.

Getting More Support

Support comes in many ways, some of which your boss can control and some not. Resources are scarce, and everyone is competing for a bigger piece of the pie. Every person in the organization is under pressure, as you are, to increase quality, speed up production, lower costs, and improve service—and do it with fewer resources. The boss, no matter how high up or powerful, has a finite amount of budget money to spend, and a limitation on head count.

Support can be in the form of (starting with the most difficult to get):

Additional staff
Budget dollars
Selling to higher management
Getting support of other departments
Helping to resolve problems
Training
Recognition

You have to be able to compete like a demon for resources. Show the benefits to your boss of the resources you need, and spell out the return on the investment.

Always start by showing how you can help the organization meet its goals. Spell out how giving you support will benefit the boss and the company, and what they will get back on the investment. Don't begin with a list of things you need, no matter how badly you want them, but talk about building better relations with customers, improving quality, lowering costs, speeding up delivery, increasing sales, and the like. Going in with "Gimme, gimme, gimme" in this age of scarce resources will not work very well.

Sell the concept first, and you'll have a better chance that the resources will follow. If you focus on the customer, on sales, and on the bottom line, you will get your boss's attention—and, quite possibly, support.

Keep the boss involved in your work as it progresses, if only to give short updates on how you are doing. The more involved you can keep the boss, the more ownership the boss will have and the better your chance to pry lose some additional support.

Moral Support

You need it. Without pay increases and promotions, what else is there but a little recognition once in a while?

If the boss is quick to criticize but never gives praise, you will have to try to change that. Let's say you have just completed a project and everyone feels you have done a great job on it. Or you have just landed a customer the company has been after for some time. Kudos all around. From the boss, nothing.

Go in and remind the boss what you did.

Boss (grudgingly): "Well, I thought it was not too bad a job."

You: "Thanks, boss. I need to hear that from you. I don't know if you know this, but it seems I don't hear much from you when I do something good. Some people may not need to, but I work best when I get feedback, when you let me know what you think of my performance, good as well as bad."

A little encouragement can influence the boss to give some praise next time. And maybe more criticism—but, hey—you tried.

Resolving a Difficult Working Relationship

Suppose you and your boss are just not hitting it off. You are uncomfortable talking with the boss, and the boss seems to be annoyed by you and not receptive to what you are doing. It may be that the boss treats everyone that way and the behavior does not reflect on you or your work. It may also be that there really is a problem—but whatever, it's causing you great stress.

You could try Alex Carlswell's solution. After fighting with his boss, he invented something called the Stressball, which uses a computer chip and speaker to make the sound of shattering glass when it's thrown against the wall.

Or try the Japanese method. The Japanese, it is said, have special rooms with punching dummies so workers can go in and slug away their anger at their bosses.

But, being a rational person, you may want to tackle the problem directly. The boss may have no idea he or she is seen that way. I have had managers tell me, "One thing I have is a warm, open relationship with my people," and then hear those same people say the boss is as friendly as an IRS agent. "Confide in the boss? I'd rather kiss a shark."

At any rate, when you have had it with the stress the relationship is giving you, go in and talk candidly with the boss. Tell the boss you want to discuss a problem, that it is your problem, and that you want some help in fixing it. Tell the boss you have the feeling he or she is not comfortable in the relationship and that you want to know what you can do to make working together smoother.

The boss may have no idea what you are talking about, or may pretend not to. Have some specific examples that have to do with on-the-job situations, not the boss's personality.

Here is a planning sheet you can use to work out dialogues for dealing with a difficult boss. For each one you use, plan how you will make the dialogue candid, positive, and regular.

DEALING WITH A DIFFICULT BOSS

Describe the dialogue you want to have with your boss:

_____

_____

_____

_____

_____

_____

_____

Plan how to manage that dialogue:

How to make it candid:

_____

_____

_____

_____

_____

_____

How to make it positive:
_____
_____
_____
_____
_____

How to make it regular:
_____
_____
_____
_____
_____

The Bottom Line on All This?

1. It's okay to talk with your boss about making the relationship between the two of you more productive.
2. Plan and practice your approach.
3. Own the problem; take the burden of fixing it.
4. Make your discussions candid, positive, and regular.
5. When all else fails, there is always the Stressball.

> **SBI:** Take the initiative to talk with your boss. Make your discussions
>
> Candid • Positive • Regular

LEADERSHIP
SKILLS

12

GOOD-BYE, MANAGEMENT

The Lore of Leadership

"Most of what we call management consists of making it difficult for people to get their work done."
—Peter Drucker, management guru

"Managers can't know it all; they must depend on their people."
—Donald Pierce, former CEO,
First Fidelity Bank North

"I worked twelve years to become a manager, and now, by God, I'm going to manage something."
—Anne Marvin, supervisor,
Toledo Transmogrification Corporation

I've been lucky. I've worked for fourteen bosses in the course of my corporate career, and most of them were bright, decent people who gave me a lot of support and guidance. A couple were not so great.

I have, in turn, managed hundreds of people in my career. Being a manager was exciting for me, and I could not do the consulting work I'm doing today without that experience. I loved working with my people and helping them grow in their jobs, and I was proud when I was able to promote one of them out.

But the best part of that experience is that I grew from a manager to a leader. In the beginning I didn't even know I was doing that. At first, insecure and ignorant of what a supervisor was supposed to do, I kept a pretty tight rein because I didn't want people screwing up or goofing off. As I grew more confident, went through some difficult situations and came out whole, and got some good guidance from others, I started to move toward leadership.

And I think in later years I was a pretty good leader. Some of my former employees, who have nothing to gain or lose now, have made a point of telling me that.

As a manager, I did a fairly good job of maintaining the status quo—keeping the organization going. As a leader, I began to change it, improve it.

If you supervise people or act as a team leader—or work in any capacity where you interact with others and influence them—you have to be *both* a manager and a leader, keeping the organization going *and* growing.

Simply tending shop isn't enough anymore. Your company is changing to respond to the marketplace, customers are changing, employee expectations are changing. Becoming a leader and moving your organization ahead has to be high on your list today.

Why All the Fuss About Leadership?

Many companies, especially the big old blue chips, grew to be over-managed and underled. I was doing some work for one of them a few years ago and wondered about a couple of things I saw. Once, an executive was kidding me about my colorful flip charts. "In this company, we use only two colors: black for headlines, green for subheadings." While I was contemplating that and wondering how people lived under that level of conformity, I went to plug in a slide projector and noticed that the outlet had a number on it. I looked around the room—every switch and every plug was numbered. I walked down the hall—there were numbers on everything. "In case a switch goes bad, maintenance can tell exactly where it is," I was told.

That's a company that paid attention to details. In those days it had plenty of extra people around to do that. And while they were becoming more and more professional at how they managed the company, they were burdening themselves with procedures and safeguards that made it impossible to respond to customer needs. Meanwhile, competitors were taking share of market away from them.

A good dose of leadership would have enabled them to develop their people and turn them loose so that they could have responded to customer needs quickly and creatively.

Management serves its purpose, don't get me wrong. In the age of mass production, people did what they were told and weren't expected to think much. Managers passed information up and down the line, told employees what to do, followed up to see they did it, and everything worked well. If workers moved along at three-quarters speed, if there was a lot of waste and inefficiency, if products came out with quality problems, not to worry. There wasn't much competition, customers had to buy what was available, and there was plenty of money coming in to cover up mistakes.

But global competition, technology, changing employee attitudes, and stockholder demands for better return on investment have changed all that. And the role of the boss will never be the same.

Old Manager	New Manager–Leader
Is the boss	Is a sponsor, facilitator, team leader
Follows chain of command	Works with anyone; begs, borrows, and steals to get the job done
Makes the decisions	Fosters participation
Hoards information, parcels it out	Shares information
Is expert in one discipline—e.g., marketing	Tries to be knowledgeable in many disciplines—a "renaissance manager"
Demands long hours	Demands results

(Adapted from "The New Non-Manager Managers" by Brian Dumaine in *Fortune*)

With the move away from traditional management has come a whole dictionary full of euphemisms for the function. "Servant-leader" is one; and if you don't like that, try "facilitator," "post-heroic leader," "virtual leader," "un-manager," "sponsor" . . . anything but "manager," which conjures up an order-barking autocrat.

What Is Leadership Anyway?

"Virtuality at the mental level is something I think you'd find in most leadership over historical periods."
—Newt Gingrich,
Speaker of the U.S. House of Representatives,
as quoted in *Business Week*, January 23, 1995

I have been teaching leadership for years, and I am pretty much up-to-date on it. But to make sure I could explain to you exactly what leadership is, I went back and reviewed about twenty books and thirty articles on the subject. And notes from several seminars I've attended, and a few I've run. Now that I have done that, I can tell you with confidence that I am not sure what leadership is, or if it can really be attained.

Every CEO who has ever turned a profit, and a few who haven't, has written a book or made a video on leadership. Baseball, football, and basketball coaches are vying to tell you how they do it. Generals, politicians, and consultants all want to share their wisdom. College professors who have a lot of experience at . . . well . . . being college professors are anxious to teach you how to lead. There are books on leadership lessons learned from Attila the Hun, the Mafia, Jesus, and Soko (a chimpanzee). Collectively, the experts have come up with lists of leadership attributes that include every virtue known to man (or chimp), so overwhelming in scope they can send would-be leaders racing back to blue-collar jobs.

It is worth noting that very little is said, in most of the stuff on leadership, about getting anything done. That, of course, is supposed to be a by-product of leadership, but the emphasis is on input (what leaders do) as opposed to output (what happens as a result of leadership). Consider that as you develop your role as a leader.

If there is such a thing as leadership, we certainly aren't practicing it. Most of us are disappointed in leadership. We want our leaders in government to be honest and to pass laws that will make our lives better. They aren't always, and don't always. We want our business leaders to be fair and to provide us with decent opportunities. They aren't always, and don't always.

Let's see if I can distill some usable wisdom from all the expert advice. Here's a simple interpretation of the manager and leader parts of your job:

You'll naturally concentrate here	You'll have to discipline yourself to move in this direction
▼	▼

Managers	Leaders
Maintain, tend shop	Build, make things better
Focus on today	Have a vision for the future
Administer	Innovate
Follow policy	Find new ways to improve
Control	Turn qualified people free
Focus on numbers (budgets, reports, etc.)	Focus on people—motivate, train, listen, build teams
Push quantity, productivity	Push quality, continued improvement
Follow orders	Take charge; solve problems; decide, don't go to the boss for every little decision
Look inward—running own organization	Look outward—company goals, customer needs
Give orders	Help people do their jobs—coach, train, remove roadblocks
Operate on past experience	Continually learn and grow

Management versus leadership is not just an academic distinction. You must be both a manager and a leader to survive and succeed in today's workplace, and knowing the difference between the two will help you understand where to concentrate.

Here's a simple definition of leadership.

> Leadership is attracting people to a cause and inspiring them to work to their potential in support of that cause.

Note that you don't have to be one step from sainthood to be a leader, and you don't even need to supervise people. You don't have to be a CEO or a four-star general to be a leader. You may not be *the* leader, but you can be *a* leader.

Attracting people to a cause. First you have to have a cause, one that people will want to hook up with, and be able to tell them about it in a convincing way. Your cause doesn't have to be some grand scheme for saving the world. It can be a vision to make your department better— for instance: "We show the highest possible concern for our customer in everything we do, every day." Leaders must add value, so your cause has to:

Be related directly to the support of the company's financial or other major goals; for example, something that will build business or cut expenses, and/or

Build relationships and help keep customers, and/or

Improve teamwork, quality, technology, or communications in the company

Inspiring them to work to their potential in support of that cause. Well, this is a tall order, because most people won't work to their potential in support of their own causes, much less yours. But it is a good goal to have because it sets a high standard.

Inspiring people is a big leadership challenge today, especially when your people have gone through years in which the company has done everything to *uninspire* them. Inspiring people doesn't mean *making* them work to their potential—managers have been trying to do that for years and have not been able to. It is creating an environment in which people can figure out what has to be done and then want to do it as well as they can.

Leadership is a lonely cause. Sometimes trying to be a leader as well as a manager can be hard on you. There aren't many rewards in leadership—at least not immediately—and there can be some pain.

The management side of your job is more visible, at least in the short term, and probably you get pulled toward it and away from leadership. Your boss knows if you are getting your reports in on time, if you are staying within budget, if you are following policy. On the other hand, leadership activities such as developing your people, coaching, and motivating them are less visible and harder for your manager to recognize.

Ed Williams, a guy I know pretty well, was promoted to run a large department at his very traditional employer. Within a few weeks he had pretty much convinced upper management they had made the wrong choice—what they saw was a department in chaos. People were out of their offices and work spaces, congregated in the halls. Meetings were noisy, and there were sounds of laughter coming from the conference rooms. One of Ed's people made a mistake in handling a customer situation, and Ed apparently had not set up a system to head off errors like that. Ed did not always know where everyone was, and sometimes couldn't tell his boss the exact status of his people's work. "You've got to get control of this," Ed's boss told him.

But things didn't change. And management was thinking about taking Ed out of that job, but before they did, they decided they could overlook Ed's unconventional methods because quality work was coming out. Productivity was high, and completed projects had creative new twists to them that made them appealing and easier to sell. After a year, no one had left—unusual for a department that large. And although it used to be a struggle to get people to transfer into that area, people were lined up to go there.

Ed would be the first to tell you he is no organizational genius. He practices a few basic principles of leadership, like turning qualified people loose and having respect for people and their ideas.

But the first months were tough ones for Ed, because he was moving away from old orderly company management values toward leadership, which can be messy.

What leadership will do for you:

Help your company serve customers faster and better, because empowered employees can make decisions without going up through the hierarchy.

Produce better products and services, because people who participate in decisions take more ownership and try harder. And people who have freedom will use more creativity.

Produce better people, because you have to coach and train people before you can turn them loose.

Create new forms of loyalty. Not to the company or to the department or even to you, but to the work and the atmosphere in which it is done.

But leadership won't:

Give you more control. You'll have less, and that will take getting used to.

Eliminate mistakes. There will always be mistakes, but you will have greater tolerance for them. What you'll lose will be more than off-set by what your people will learn.

End internal competition and rivalry. You can help your people with teamwork, but there will always be a "me first" attitude in today's unstable workplace, with its insecurity and fear. In fact, competition is healthy as long as it is aboveboard.

Reduce training expense. If you are looking for budget dollars, you won't find them here. Employees at all levels will have to be exposed to more training and education—with managers and subordinates receiving similar training to enhance personal performance.

Bring back loyalty to the company to where it was fifteen years ago. Too much has happened in most companies. But leadership can increase loyalty to the job and can bring more job satisfaction.

In my seminars, I ask participants to take what they have learned about leadership and develop a leadership oath for themselves that will guide them and help them concentrate more on the leadership part of their jobs. You may want to do the same thing. Review the material above and write your leadership oath. Put it somewhere where you can see it every day.

LEADERSHIP OATH

I promise, as a leader, I will

_____

_____

_____

_____

_____

_____

_____

_____

_____

_____

_____

What It Takes to Be a Leader

Assertiveness?

There is a myth that the most assertive people—those who continually speak out, take charge, confront others, have a high sense of urgency, and do a lot of telling—have what it takes to be the best leaders. They get further faster and are the ones who move into the executive suite. Less assertive people—those who are quieter, take more of a support role, are slower, and ask rather than tell—may as well resign themselves to lives in middle management at best. That is the myth. It is not true.

Extensive studies in which assertiveness is measured show that the business population is evenly spread along the assertiveness continuum, that there are just as many low- as high-assertive people, and that goes for people in mahogany row as well as those at lower levels. My own experience, which has involved doing assertiveness work with thousands of managers, professionals, and salespeople, bears this out. No matter how you measure success—level in the organization, income, sales figures—there are as many low assertives at the top as there are high. Hard to believe, isn't it?

But think a minute.

Leadership argues for a less assertive style. The whole concept of supporting others and facilitating rather than commanding calls for lower assertiveness. Where a high-assertive person, driven to get a project done, might run roughshod over people and have trouble delegating, a less assertive person will concentrate more on building relationships and take more time to develop people. With less need to control, low-assertive people have an easier time delegating and letting others take charge of and take credit for work they do.

A high-assertive person, with a high sense of urgency, will make decisions quickly, while a lower assertive will take the time to involve others.

The truth is, you can be just as effective and just as successful if you are low assertive as if you are high assertive. Having said that, I want to throw out one caution. Since the myth does exist that high-assertive people are the best leaders, always behaving in a very low-assertive way can hurt your image. On the other hand, continually staying in a high-assertive style can turn people off and make it hard for them to follow you.

It is best to pull away from either extreme and move toward medium-assertive behavior, especially when you are working with someone whose assertiveness level is different from yours. What that means is, if you are high assertive, back off a little. If you are less assertive, pick it up a little.

QUICK ASSERTIVENESS CHECK

Low-Assertive Behaviors	High-Assertive Behaviors
Quiet, reserved	Talkative and outgoing
Takes time to decide	Decides quickly
Cautious	Risk taker
Asks questions	Makes statements, tells
Team player	Takes charge
Supports others	Challenges
Cooperative	Competitive
Slow	Fast
Type B	Type A
Total	Total

Circle the one choice that is most like you in each pair. Pick the one that is really you, not what you would like to be. Add up the circles. The column with the most circles is your assertiveness level, and the more circles in one column, the more toward that behavior you tend to be.

Now that you have determined whether you are high or low assertive, you can check on degree. Subtract the number of circles from the column with the lower number from the total circles in the column with the higher number. Put a mark on the chart on the next page to show where you are on this assertiveness scale.

Example: If you circled five in the "Low-Assertive Behaviors" column and four in the "High-Assertive Behaviors" column (5–4= 1), put a mark in the 1–4 quadrant on the low-assertiveness (left) side of the scale. You are a little on the low-assertive side. If you circled eight on the high assertive and one on the low assertive (8–1=7), mark the 6–9 quadrant on the right side of the scale. You are a high-assertive person.

Assertiveness Scale

	6–9	1–4	1–4	6–9	
Low					High

It does not matter where you are on the scale. In fact, wherever you are, one fourth of the business population is there with you. What matters is your ability to adapt your behavior, especially if you are in one of the 6–9 quadrants, to make others more comfortable in your relationship with them.

If you are 6–9 on the low-assertive side, push yourself to:

Speak up. Express your opinion and promise yourself you will say at least one thing in every meeting.

Decide more quickly—maybe you'll be only 90 percent right.

Take more little risks. Do something new every day.

Make more statements. Be direct and do a little telling.

Push yourself to be a little more dominant.

Challenge more. Gently if you like, but if you disagree, say so.

Try to win once in a while.

Speed up a little.

If you are 6–9 on the high-assertive side, hold back a little so you can:

Shut up. You don't have to express your opinion on everything. Listen for a while to what others have to say, or if they don't volunteer, ask them.

Slow down a little on deciding. Be more deliberate, get more facts.

Be more cautious. Pull away from high-risk stuff.

Ask more questions. Listen to others. If you dominate everything, you'll never get any input.

Give up a little; you don't have to run everything.

Challenge less. Some people don't like to be told they are wrong.

Accept coming in second once in a while.

Slow up a little.

(Adapted in part from the workshop *Producing Results with Others*, TRACOM Corporation, Denver, Colorado)

SBI: Push yourself to develop and use your leadership skills. If you don't, you will find yourself spending all your time on management work and never move ahead.

13

YOU CAN DO IT! (I HOPE)

How to Motivate People in a Scary World

> "Everyone has an invisible sign hanging from his or her neck saying MAKE ME FEEL IMPORTANT! Never forget this message when working with people."
> —Mary Kay, CEO, Mary Kay Cosmetics

> CEO at a managers' meeting: "We are in a tough situation in the marketplace—I don't have to tell you that. Our competitors aren't resting; they are moving ahead at full steam. We have got to rededicate ourselves, to strive even harder to make this company the great company we all know it can be."
> Mary, in the back row (to herself): "I'm working seventy hours a week now. What does he want?"

Every day managers struggle to find just the right combination of words that will get everyone juiced up and ready to sacrifice themselves for the good of the company. When that doesn't work, they fool with pay, sprinkling incentives here and there, convinced that everyone will kill themselves if there's an extra $1.75 to be made. The funny thing is, if you get those managers to tell you what really motivates them to high performance, words and money aren't near the top of the list.

Motivating People When the End of the World Is Near

Motivation is inspiring people to high performance. It is the noblest of the leadership functions—and about the hardest to do. I am not talking here about getting people to do their jobs well. That is important, of course, but motivation is about *high* performance. Getting people so turned on they will produce way beyond the ordinary.

What inspires people to high performance today? In many organizations, unfortunately, fear is the motivation. Fear of losing their jobs. With reengineering, companies have inadvertently hit on a motivator that isn't listed in any textbooks. People do extraordinary things when they are afraid, but, of course, fear is not a good motivator because:

It doesn't work over long periods. People get burned out. And try to escape, one way or another.

Fear often motivates people to give the *appearance* of high performance while they are doing something less.

Fear paralyzes. People who are afraid become very cautious. They stifle any creativity they have and close down communications with others, especially the boss—no bad news goes upward. Fear also hurts teamwork: "Why should I make the other guy look good when the company may have to choose between us?"

If the climate in your company is riddled with fear, how do you go about motivating people? First, address the uncertainty and fear, then put real motivators in place.

Address the Uncertainty and Fear

Clear out the weeds and brambles so there will be a place for motivation to grow. If your people are afraid of the future, you may not be able to alleviate that fear directly, but you can enable them to deal with it.

If your people are uncertain about their careers, encourage them to develop strategies so that they can deal with anything that comes along.

If your people are discouraged because there are no promotions and hardly any salary increases, make their jobs more meaningful—give those who qualify more responsibility, involve them, give them new challenges, put them on teams and task forces—and generally provide them with compelling reasons for coming to work in the morning.

If your people have been misled by management in the past and don't trust anyone, be sure you are direct and honest with them. If they can't believe anyone else, at least they can look to you for a straight answer.

Put Motivators in Place

Several years ago, when I was head of Human Resource Development for JCPenney, I was asked to do a workshop for the annual executives' meeting. Sounds routine, but that meeting was a major event in the company and only a select few high-level executives and line people got to attend. The chairman had decided that communications needed to be improved throughout the company, and assigned a group of district managers to put together a workshop for the meeting.

District managers were great at getting business, but pulled up short on how to design a workshop. At the eleventh hour, the job of doing that fell to me. For several days (and nights) I worked at peak capacity. I not only had to design the workshop, produce visuals and notebooks, and make arrangements with the conference center, but I had to run a pilot and train executives to lead it. The story has a happy ending—the workshop scored the highest rating of any event at the meeting.

But the point is, something was motivating me to work a lot harder than usual. What inspired that high effort?

My list is this:

Freedom to create: No one told me what was to be in the workshop—in fact, no one knew what *should* be in it. That's why they called on me in the first place. So I was free to do it my way.

Hope for recognition: Somewhere along the line the chairman might tell the executives, "That workshop was done by Bill Yeomans," or I might get a note from him saying, "Thanks." Both happened.

A chance to be involved: I got to attend the meeting.

Pride: Wanting to show that I could do it, that I was very competent in my job.

Fear: Yes, there was a certain element of concern. I am a pretty confident person, but there was always the nagging thought that this was a first, there was no precedent for it, and what if they hated it? I tried very hard to make sure they didn't.

Notice that nowhere on my list is "Chance to make more money." That never entered my mind.

Now it is your turn. Think of a situation where you pulled out all the stops and worked like never before, far beyond your usual level. Write down what happened:

_____

_____

_____

_____

_____

_____

Now try to figure out what motivated you to work that hard. List those motivators below:

_____

_____

_____

_____

_____

_____

Look at those motivators. Chances are, your people are motivated by the same things you are.

Each year, in the workshops I lead for managers, salespeople, and professionals, I ask people to talk about situations in which they were highly motivated and to rank their motivators—the same sort of thing we just did above. I have heard many wonderful stories of high motivation and have also found that motivators don't seem to vary much by company, by industry, or by level in the organization—time after time, the motivators come out like this (in order of importance):

1. Freedom: to do the job, to innovate, to make decisions
2. Appreciation, recognition
3. Involvement
4. Challenging work
5. Empathy, caring on the part of the boss

Good pay ranks about seventh.

Remember, I am talking here about motivators that inspire people to high performance. My list compares almost exactly with lists in classic studies on motivation. Freedom always ranks number 1 or 2, for instance, and pay always falls somewhere down the list, lower than you would expect it to.

Let's take a look at each of the above motivators and see what you can do to make sure they are all there for your people.

1. Freedom to innovate, make decisions. This is empowering your people, and is a high calling for you as a leader. But you can't just turn people loose and expect them to succeed.

First of all, agree with each of your people as to what is expected. A recent Harvard Business School study found an important motivator for salespeople was clarity of task. It's obvious, when you think about it. People can't be inspired if they don't quite know what it is they are supposed to be inspired about. There has to be a positive relation between effort and results.

Second, determine degree. Are you asking your subordinate to take the assignment, do it, and come back when it's done, or are you asking him or her to check with you every step of the way? There's a big difference, and you should get an understanding on this at the outset. Be clear on what decisions they can make on their own and what you have to approve.

Start-to-finish responsibility is a high motivator, but you can give that only to people who have shown they can do the job—or have the potential to learn it. What have they done in the past? Have they used judgment and common sense? Have they gotten the work done on time? Have they done quality work? Are their customers happy?

Turn them loose to do as much of the work themselves as they can. When they demonstrate competence, turn even more over to them.

Third, provide the support and resources they need to handle their freedom. Training is one kind of support; equipment, systems, budget dollars, time, and staff are others. You must be willing to share any information that will enable them to do their jobs and remove roadblocks that might be in the way.

Fourth, follow up to see how things are going. If they are not going to your expectations, provide additional training or pull back on the degree of freedom. If they are going well, give some recognition.

2. Appreciation and recognition. Provide appreciation and recognition, even for small successes. People work harder knowing there is something in it for them. Part of that is having the boss say, "You did a good job."

That is Supervision 101. But day after day in my workshops people tell me, "I catch hell when something goes wrong, but I never hear about the good things I do." Even bosses say, "We really should take the time to tell people when they've done a good job. We don't do enough of it."

Why is it so hard to show appreciation and give recognition for good work? Probably because:

Some bosses believe people are paid for doing good work and don't need to be recognized for doing what they are supposed to do. These bosses may assume that people know when they are doing good work anyhow and don't need to be told.

Some bosses, in the press of everyday work, just don't get around to it.

Others find good work in others threatening and don't want to call attention to it.

Some worry that if they give too much praise, people will expect salary increases.

A few are just insensitive worms.

Mostly, bosses don't give recognition because they are insecure in their boss-subordinate relationships. When the boss says, "Good job," the boss is giving something away. If the boss says, "Good job, a heck of a lot better than I could have done!" the boss is giving a lot away. It takes a secure, confident person to do that.

But it is exactly that kind of boss who has the best motivational climate. Think back on the last year or two and what kind of feedback you've been giving to your people. Has it been on the side of appreciation and recognition, or was most of it negative? Not that you shouldn't correct mistakes and help people learn from them; you should. But if that is all you do, and if you miss the chance to tell people when they have done something well, you are bypassing a big opportunity.

Recognition is easy to do. It doesn't cost anything, and it doesn't take much time.

Don't wait until the end of the project or the end of the year. If you see some progress, even little improvements, show your appreciation.

When you do have to give criticism, do it in a way that will motivate the employee, not make him or her want to hibernate for a year. Focus on performance, not personality. Stay with the facts. Be constructive and use a problem-solving approach: "What can you learn from this? How can you do it better next time?"

3. Involve your people:

1. *Boss to you:* "I was thinking about that Johnstone situation last night and made some decisions. Here's what you should do."
2. *Boss to you:* "Let's spend a few minutes on the Johnstone situation and see if we can't decide where we go from here."

Which approach do you like better? Which are you going to be more committed to? A no-brainer, isn't it? It is just great to work toward goals you have set yourself, your own goals, rather than those dropped on you from above.

A client of mine installed Employee Work Improvement Teams as part of its quality program. In its very first session, a warehouse person came up with an idea that saved $50,000 and got the products out the door faster.

Management was surprised at this suggestion, which was a very simple change in procedures. When they asked the employee why he hadn't told anyone about that before, he said simply, "Nobody ever asked me."

That employee felt he had no forum for expressing ideas, or if he did, no one would take them seriously. How many great ideas are lying around unused because you never asked?

Besides providing you with great ideas, involvement is motivating for those who are . . . well . . . involved.

Part of a quality team, one woman in that same company was caught in a downsizing. When the boss told her that she was being laid off, her first response was "Can I still come in for my team meetings?"

Many companies have formal involvement programs. GE's Work Out program is well known and involves all GE employees. It is run through "town meetings," off site, led by outside consultants—

managers are locked out. Solutions developed by the Work Out groups are later presented to managers, who have to decide on the spot, in front of everyone.

But you don't have to wait for a company program. Increasing involvement is easy enough to do in your own area. You don't need a lot of approvals or a very complicated program. Remember these involvement guidelines:

If you use involvement groups, keep them small, under ten. Let them decide on a time to meet, during working hours; for example, two hours every other Tuesday.

Set parameters. Groups should work on improving customer service, cutting waste (including time), reducing expenses, improving quality, and the like—ways to improve their operation or move the company ahead. Off-limits topics are pay, benefits, and your performance as a manager—these are not bitching sessions. You may want to select initial topics for groups to work on, just to get them going in the right direction.

Accept all group recommendations positively—if you shoot down ideas you won't get many more. Never kill off a recommendation in the same session you hear it. Thank the group for good work. Ask questions for clarification.

Tell the group what will happen. You want to think overnight about the recommendations and let them know tomorrow, or ask the group to go ahead and implement its recommendation. Time is important here—note that GE asks managers to decide on the spot. That way days don't slip by without an answer.

Give the group recognition for recommendations that are implemented.

You don't even need a group to get involvement. "Hey, Joe, what do you think we ought to do about this Johnstone situation?" is a great way to involve people one-on-one—if you do it consistently and if you take Joe's suggestions seriously.

4. Create challenging work. Connect the work to something that is meaningful to the employee. A learning experience, a challenge, a chance to improve or acquire a new skill, an opportunity to make new contacts or to become familiar with a new field. And, always, a chance to do important work for the company.

As organizations flatten and promotional routes disappear, people are in their jobs longer. And that can turn excitement into boredom.

OLD CAREER PATH

First year:	Learn the job, new and exciting
Second year:	Even better, know the job, improve on it
Third year:	Polish it up
Fourth year:	Get promoted to a new job

NEW CAREER PATH

First year:	Learn the job, new and exiting
Second year:	Even better, know the job, improve on it
Third year:	Polish it up
Fourth year:	Been there, done that
Fifth year on:	Yawn
Unless . . .	the job changes and takes on new dimensions

One of your responsibilities as a leader is to help your people find creative ways to make their jobs more challenging. This takes some original thinking, especially with people who are doing well and know their work backward and forward.

One way is to give them more freedom to innovate and make decisions, as discussed above. Encourage your good people to expand their jobs, to upgrade the work they do so that it affords them new challenges and makes life more interesting to them. The company is changing, customer expectations are changing, competition is changing. How can your people change in ways that will respond to all that?

Ask each of your people:

What work is not being done that should be? What are department, company, or customer needs that should be addressed? How could you be involved in doing it?

What parts of my job could you do?
What decisions that I make should you be making? In other words,
  what do you have to ask approval for that you could approve yourself?

Some people will react to those questions by telling you they have
plenty enough to do already and can't handle any more, thank you.
Others (including some who are also swamped) will welcome the
chance to take on more responsible work. And all of them will appreciate being asked.

Work that gets people to learn new skills, acquire new knowledge,
and explore new fields is motivational. The more you can put your
people in situations where they learn and grow, the more turned on
they will be.

Work that is important is a motivator. Remind your people how their
work helps the company achieve its goals, how it helps build customer
relationships, how it contributes to the betterment of the community.
If they can see the importance of their work, and you remind them of
that from time to time, they will be motivated.

5. Use empathy, caring. I once worked for a guy who was on a rocket
to the top of the organization. He was passing through our department
on his way up, just to accumulate some experience there. He was demanding to work for, had a high sense of urgency, and expected a lot
out of people. I look back on the time I was with him as a couple of
years in a Cuisinart.

But as tough as he was, he was a very caring person. When I had a
personal loss, and at other times when I needed support, he was always
there. He was someone who pushed for high performance but cared
about his people as human beings. How could I not be motivated to
produce for a person like that?

Either you care or you don't. It is not something you can fake very
easily. But you can look at your people's needs, either at work or in their
personal lives, and think of what you would want from the boss if you
were in their place.

And there is plenty of need today. Drug and alcohol abuse, divorce,
single parenting, AIDS and other illnesses, layoffs, demotions, good
work unrewarded with promotions or salary increases.

Just saying "I know how you feel. I've been there myself" or "I'm
sorry you are in this situation" can mean a whole lot. Offering help is
even better.

One friend of mine told me she felt motivated working for a very caring boss who was a couple of levels up in the organization. "What made the boss caring?" I asked. "Well, for one thing," she said, "he stops by my office once in a while, sits down, and asks what I'm working on and how things are going. The big boss in my old department never came around."

Something that probably seemed ordinary and natural to that boss had great meaning to her.

Part of caring is showing that you care about your employees' success. The way you show this is to make it clear you expect them to succeed. Your words and actions should say to each employee that you want nothing but the best and know he or she can deliver. Be sure you're *not* giving the employee the impression you have doubts. Your expectations can have a lot to do with that employee's confidence and motivation.

Another part of caring is giving people hope: "I can't guarantee what will happen to you in the future, but I can do this—while you are working for me, I will help you learn and grow so that wherever your next job may be, here or elsewhere, you will be better prepared for it."

The Bottom Line on Motivation

- Everyone is motivated to do something. When managers talk about an unmotivated person, they mean someone who won't do what *they* want.
- People know what motivates them—and it may not be what you think. Ask them. A retail client of mine was in the middle of a program to improve customer service. Each store manager was supposed to come up with awards for outstanding service. Managers began giving out pins, days off, and gift certificates. But one manager wanted to be sure he was awarding something that would really motivate people, and he put together employee involvement groups to brainstorm. And they came up with the perfect award.

    Parking spaces.

    Winners were allowed to park near the store instead of a half mile across the parking lot, where employees normally parked.

Customer service ratings went way up in that store as employees worked for their prize. And the manager never would have thought of it without input from the employees.

- Change is always a threat, and there is plenty around today. The way to make change a motivator is to—as much as possible—give your people a say in managing the change.
- People are motivated when they see "something in it for me." Let people know how their work will benefit them.
- You can set a climate for motivation for all your people. Start by working with one person at a time, using the Motivation Planner below.

MOTIVATION PLANNER

Complete this checklist, then use it as the basis for discussion with an employee you want to motivate.

Employee:_____

1. Freedom to innovate, make decisions

How qualified is this employee to do this job?

What training does he or she need?

What decisions that I now make could this employee make?

2. Appreciation, recognition

How often do I show appreciation, give recognition?

What else can I do to recognize good performance?

3. Involvement

How often do I ask this employee's opinion? What are some recent examples?

How well do I accept this employee's ideas? What are some recent examples?

How could this employee be more involved in decisions affecting his or her job?

How could this employee be more involved in decisions affecting the department? The company?

4. Challenging work

How can I help this employee make the work more challenging?

How can I make the work more important?

How can I help the employee learn new skills?

5. Empathy, caring on the part of the boss

How good am I at showing I care? What are recent examples?

How does this employee perceive me?

My attitude toward him or her?

My tone of voice?

My enthusiasm?

My expression—smiling, warm?

My confidence in his or her success?

SBI: To motivate people in uncertain times, clear out the uncertainty and fear, and activate motivators: freedom, recognition, involvement, challenge, and empathy.

14

HERE'S HOW YOU SCREWED UP

Talking with Your People

> "We have been through a lot over the last two years. It
> has been painful for everyone, but it is behind us.
> "Read my lips: no new layoffs.
> "Incidentally, we have hired the Smaller Is Better con-
> sulting firm to help us put together our new organiza-
> tion, and their people will be around to talk with each
> of you. Please give them your cooperation. Remember,
> people are our most important asset."
> —CEO, Baltimore Body Parts Corporation,
> after a fifth downsizing

Communication is the link you have with the people who report to
you. The way you talk with your people determines how they see you as
a leader and helps them decide whether or not they want to follow you.

Let's look at some common situations you may face with your people
today, and see how to handle them in ways that will build your reputation as a leader. They include:

Reestablishing trust
Talking about careers
Giving bad news
Giving feedback

Reestablishing Trust

Rumors have been flying that your division is going to be sold off and
that there will be a staff reduction to make you more attractive to buyers. In a meeting with your people, someone asks about the rumor. You

say that you don't know if it is true or not. (You don't.) Does anyone believe you? Some do; a bunch don't.

Probably that's because they have been lied to before. Maybe not intentionally. Maybe the CEO said, "That's the end of the layoffs," only to find six months later that stock analysts and investors were clamoring for more. But if anyone has misdirected employees, they are going to assume that everyone will, including you. Even if they haven't experienced it themselves, they've heard about it from people in other departments or friends in other companies.

Let's say—for the sake of not making *you* a liar—that events elsewhere in the company have caused people to lose trust, and now they are skeptical about everyone, including you. How do you get trust back?

1. Communicate constantly. About everything. Let your people know what your plans are and what is coming up that will affect their work.

Get off business once in a while and talk on a personal level. Share some of your own feelings with your people, and your concerns. It's okay to be a human being, and it may even make you a better leader. Ask how they are doing, how they are feeling about their work. You won't get straight answers right off, but if you do this a few times, you'll start to learn things about individuals and about what's going on in your department.

Hold conversations with individuals and groups every day. Don't save everything up for the Thursday meeting. Continual, open communications will let people get to know you better and help establish trust.

2. Head off rumors. In every organization there is a Vice President of Malicious Rumors. No one ever sees this person or knows quite who it is, but it's that very person who hears the CFO say, "Profits were up substantially in the second quarter," then hurries out into the hall and whispers, "I just heard two hundred people are getting the ax."

Rumors usually are:

Negative. The really bad ones get the most attention and are the most repeated.

Exaggerated. They tend to get worse and worse as they zing along the grapevine.

Denied by management. At least at first.

Time-consuming. Juicy rumors take precedence over work.

True. At least partially.

Get to local rumors before they start. Been to an off-site department heads' meeting? Boy, the place has been buzzing while you've been gone:

"They're planning a pay freeze for the next two years."
"I heard they're bringing in that guy from the Backbiting Division to run this place."
"Ten people are going to be transferred to the Omaha office Monday."
"It's awful and we'll all die."

When you come back, get your people together and tell them what went on in the meeting. Do it right away. Don't wait until you've gotten through all your E-mail, voice mail, and mail mail. Rumors will be out of control by then, and you'll never convince anyone of the truth.

3. Be as honest and open as you can. When the boss tells you "This is not to go beyond this room," you have some limitations on what you can pass on to your people. But in most situations you can and should be open and direct. When you are talking with individuals about their performance or their future, be straight out. Your people may say, "I don't like what the boss told me, but at least the boss is honest."

4. Be dependable. Do what you say you will do. If it turns out you can't, explain why.

5. Make your people strong. Make it clear that you want each of your people to be prepared for any eventuality and you want them to take charge of their own lives. Also tell them that you will help and support them in doing this, but they have to take the initiative, because in this world there are no guarantees.

6. Respect everyone. No one will trust you if the perception is that you don't respect them. The issue of respect comes up often in groups I work with—it seems to be in short supply today. People tell me in a hundred different ways, "I know my job isn't the most important in the world, and it may be routine and easy to do, but I do it well, I do my best, and I wish someone would show respect for that."

You can show respect by being courteous, by asking people's opinions, by showing appreciation and giving them public recognition, and by reminding them of the importance of their work to the company.

Talking About Careers

Your people are concerned that they will be fired, or if not, that they will be in their current jobs forever. Many of them won't even bring up the subject, but as a leader, you should take the initiative to talk about careers.

How do you talk about careers when the whole notion of a career (climbing up through the organization) is as outdated as the wagon train? How do you get people excited about moving slowly sideways? What do you say to people stuck in their jobs whose fathers were senior vice presidents and CEOs? How do you work up enthusiasm for the subject when your *own* chance for advancement carries the same odds as a sweepstakes letter from Ed McMahon?

If your people have no hope for careers in the traditional sense, give them hope of a different kind. Work with your people to:

1. **Expand their present jobs.** As they become qualified, help them broaden their present jobs to take on more responsibility, more interesting work (including some of yours).

2. **Help them learn new skills.** Give them new experiences, help them learn on the job by giving them special assignments, and, as budget allows, send them to outside seminars and workshops.

3. **Get them on teams.** Help them get team assignments that will broaden their knowledge of business, help them build networks by getting to know others outside your department, and make their workday more interesting.

4. **Get ready for changing jobs.** Encourage them to prepare themselves to change jobs if they run out of steam doing the same old work. Inside the company or outside if necessary.

And still—you should remind them that a few people *do* get promoted and you will coach and guide them so they have a better chance of at least getting on the list.

Giving Bad News

"Hi, Ed. You're fired."

Giving people bad news is part of your job, and today you have plenty of it to give. Probably you've done your share already, and it may be wearing you down. How many people can you downsize before you start feeling terrible? Probably one. Some managers have laid off hundreds.

Firing someone is actually a form of feedback. Terminal feedback. It says to the employee, no matter what the real reason for the layoff, "You weren't good enough." And it takes its toll not only on the fired employee and his or her family, but on you and on everyone else left in the company.

There is no easy way to do this, but there are methods that can help spare some pain (on both sides).

1. Convince yourself business is business. The termination decision may have nothing to do with what you want to happen or feel should happen. Often it has nothing to do with the abilities of the employee involved. Coldhearted as it may be, you have no choice, and thousands of other leaders are going through the same thing. And it may happen to you, too.

2. Maintain their self-esteem. When terminating someone, show respect and affirm that person's self-esteem and dignity. If termination has nothing to do with the person's performance, stress that fact. It is okay to show sorrow and to offer help in finding a new job. Be clear about dates of termination, severance, continuation of benefits, and other support the company will provide. Be clear that the decision has been made and that the employee has been terminated. (There have been managers who tried so hard to be nice during the termination interview the employees didn't know they were being fired.)

3. Feel remorse. Don't expect to recover right away from any termination, especially messy, massive ones. You will feel rotten, and you will face a workload that must now be done by a smaller and dispirited staff. You cannot take on everyone's burdens, however, just because they worked for you. You have to get on with your life, as they do. As a leader, you see yourself as a developer. But when you terminate, you are a destroyer, tearing down the organization you have built over the years. Expect to feel unhappy about that.

4. When it's over, it's not over. Despite your best efforts, some of the people terminated will hate you for it and make it clear they blame you for everything thereafter that goes wrong in their lives. And they will find ways to remind you of that from time to time.

5. Commemorate the loss. If there has been a large layoff, mark it in some way to show those laid off that they were valued and will be missed. Have drinks after work, or at least have coffee and cake in the office so that everyone can say good-bye.

6. Tend to the survivors. Sometimes they hurt more than the departed: There is such a thing as survivor sickness. Be honest with them. If you think there will be more layoffs, tell them that. If you think not (no guarantees), tell them that, too. If they are going to have to work like animals to get everything done, tell them that. Tell them how you feel about the situation (not bashing the company, but about your own personal sorrow in having had to disrupt so many lives).

Giving Feedback

You have too many people reporting to you, they're located all over the place in their virtual offices and hard to get to talk with in person, and they're all working hard, and probably won't be very receptive to criticism by you, even the helpful kind. But you have to find ways to give feedback because it is what helps people learn and develop.

Feedback is giving praise and recognition for work well done and constructive criticism in areas where performance could be improved. In most performance discussions there will be some of both.

Feedback Tips

1. Prepare. Have facts and examples. Not that you are going to grill your employee like an ax murderer, but it lessens the value of praise if it is vague and nonspecific, and it is hard to give criticism if you don't have the facts.

> *"Adam, I'd like you to work on your relations with customers."*
> *"What relations?"*
> *"Well, you know, how you present yourself when you are with customers."*
> *"What do you mean, 'present yourself'?"*
> *"Well, I've just heard things from customers."*
> *"What have you heard?"*
> *"Well, just that you sometimes don't present yourself well."*

Pretty weak, huh?

2. Practice. Out loud, ahead of time, especially if your feedback involves criticism. Be able to say what you want to say and state specific examples in support of it. If it doesn't sound convincing to you, work on it some more. Have a hoped-for outcome in mind, and practice that, too.

3. Direct feedback to performance, not personality.

4. Keep the human element. Remember, after all, this is just two people talking about work. Your employee has feelings, too, and has esteem to be protected.

5. Make it important. People are very sensitive about their own performance. Respect that by taking uninterrupted time in a quiet place to give your feedback, even if it's only a five-minute discussion. Don't do it casually, in the elevator, in the hall, in front of others. The one exception is, if you are giving someone recognition for a good job, do it in front of as many people as you can assemble.

6. Keep it simple—one topic per feedback session.

7. Keep it positive. Even criticism should be presented as a learning opportunity. "How can you do that better next time?"

8. Support your employee. Offer to provide whatever help you can, at the same time reminding the employee it is his or her job to correct the situation, not yours.

9. Get involvement, and agree on what is to be done, by when. Ask for the employee's ideas and input. Ask for the employee's reaction; find out if he or she understands, accepts, and is willing to act.

10. Don't wait. Whether you are giving praise or criticism, do it as close to the event as possible. If you wait to sandwich it in after everything else is done, it will lose its impact.

How well do you give feedback? Put a check mark on the scale after each of the questions below.

FEEDBACK SELF-ASSESSMENT

1. How often do you take the time to prepare before a performance discussion—get the facts, examples, think through what specific improvements in performance you want the subordinate to make?

Always	Sometimes	Never

2. How often do you practice before giving feedback?

Always	Sometimes	Never

3. How often do you focus your discussions on results rather than on personalities?

Always	Sometimes	Never

4. How often do you make a real attempt to keep the human element in your discussions and protect the employee's self-esteem?

Always	Sometimes	Never

5. How often do you assure the feedback will be given in private, uninterrupted?

Always	Sometimes	Never

6. How often do you keep feedback simple, focusing on one topic rather than a whole bunch?

Always	Sometimes	Never

7. How often do you keep feedback positive, treat it as a learning experience?

Always	Sometimes	Never

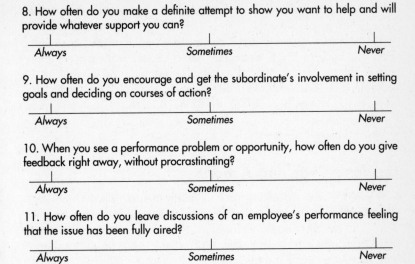

8. How often do you make a definite attempt to show you want to help and will provide whatever support you can?

Always	Sometimes	Never

9. How often do you encourage and get the subordinate's involvement in setting goals and deciding on courses of action?

Always	Sometimes	Never

10. When you see a performance problem or opportunity, how often do you give feedback right away, without procrastinating?

Always	Sometimes	Never

11. How often do you leave discussions of an employee's performance feeling that the issue has been fully aired?

Always	Sometimes	Never

Look at where your check marks are. What areas do you need to work on?

Coaching

Current wisdom is that managers aren't managers anymore, they are coaches. People manage themselves, and managers support them. Coaching has become today's prime leadership skill.

Coaching is an informal way of giving feedback on performance. It is less structured than performance appraisal, which is form- and time-bound, or corrective interviewing, which is a set step-by-step process. Coaching can be done at any time, doesn't need company paperwork, and can last minutes or hours.

Coaching is a conversation with an employee to improve performance. It is a great way to take a good all-around performer and help him or her get better.

Think of what a coach—say, a tennis coach—does. The coach knows the game inside and out. The coach knows how players are performing and helps them see things that hinder their game—actions they may not even know they are doing. The coach tells them about those actions and helps them improve. Maybe throwing the ball higher on the serve, going sooner to the net, moving with lots of little steps rather than great big ones.

At the same time the coach is giving criticism, he or she has to build the confidence of the players. The coach doesn't want players going into a match feeling they are failures and have no possibility of winning. If the coach is doing the job right, players will see the coach's suggestions as positive and motivating—something that will help them win.

Here is an outline for a strong coaching session.

Leader's Coaching Actions

When you see an opportunity for performance improvement, get ready to do some coaching. Let's say one of your sales reps, who does well in her job and brings in a lot of new business, is slow on follow-up. Several customers have remarked to you that she has promised things; then they have to call and call to get those promises fulfilled. "Not a big deal," they say, "but it would help if she would just do what she says she will."

Before you sit down with your sales rep, think through how you are going to approach this opportunity and how the conversation will unfold, so that it will take on a positive tone and not demoralize her.

Here are the steps in the coaching discussion:

1. Set the tone. When you begin your discussion, tell the employee you appreciate the good job he or she is doing and that you have a suggestion on how he or she could do even better in one area. State this as an opportunity you hope the employee will take advantage of. Keep this opening very positive in tone.

> *"Jennifer, congratulations on getting the Pittsburgh Pantaloon account. Nobody goes after new business like you do. You know by now I want to help you any way I can to be the top sales rep in the company, and I'd like to give you some feedback from customers that may help."*

2. Clarify the opportunity. State as clearly and simply as possible what the opportunity for improvement is and what could happen if the employee takes advantage of it (thus giving the employee a "what's in it for me?" handle). Note the term *opportunity*. If you think of this as an opportunity and not a problem, you will keep the discussion more positive.

When you have stated the opportunity, ask the employee what he or she thinks about what you said.

"Your customers really like you, and they are loyal to you. That's a real plus. Something that a few of them have asked for—I'll tell you which ones in a minute—is that you strengthen your follow-up. In other words, when you promise something, make sure the customer gets it right away and that the customer doesn't have to ask for it again. Is that a surprise, or do you see that as an opportunity?"

(Notice there is no "but" in these statements: "You're doing great, but . . ." If you use that approach, people will start listening for the "but" and won't hear the rest.)

Jennifer: "I know exactly what you're talking about, and I can tell you the names of the customers. Sometimes I get so excited about getting new accounts, I take too much time getting back to old ones. I'll take care of it. Thanks."

3. Reestablish the tone. The above scenario is easy. Suppose the employee reacts defensively?

Jennifer: "I may have made a few customers wait, but what do they want? I have three states to cover, and forty accounts. On top of that, I'm bringing in new ones all the time. Besides, when I give production a special order, I assume they will fill it right away. That doesn't always happen. What am I supposed to do?"

Here's where you have to step back in and get the tone of the discussion to the level you want it:

"I know all those things are true, and the fact is you are a great sales rep. All I am trying to do is to help you find ways to be the absolute best. Let me give you some specifics to think about. Here's what customers have said they would like from you . . ."

4. Establish mutual goals. Working with your employee, set SMART goals. Focus on outputs—what will come out of this, what will be accomplished. Let the employee figure out how.

SMART goals are goals that are:

Specific: "Customer service should be improved" is not a specific goal; it is too vague to ever be accomplished, and does not focus on the situation you want to fix. "Customer follow-up should be improved" is better, but not great.

Measurable: A good goal has an element of measurement in it: "Customer follow-up should be done within twenty-four hours."

Action-oriented: The goal as stated above is admirable but passive. Active is much more powerful: "Follow up on customer requests and promises within twenty-four hours."

Realistic and achievable: "Follow up on customer requests and promises within twenty-four hours. Fulfill the 10 percent of difficult requests within forty-eight hours."

Timely: Smart goals should state a time: "Beginning immediately, follow up on customer requests and promises within twenty-four hours. Fulfill the 10 percent of difficult requests within forty-eight hours."

5. Offer help. Find out what is getting in the way and help remove the roadblocks. Provide training or whatever else the employee needs. Show confidence that he or she can do it—remember, your expectations count.

"Jennifer, some of the other reps have been having problems with production on special orders, too. Why don't I set up a meeting with Ralph over at the plant, and we can sit down and see what can be done."

6. Follow up. Give recognition for even small improvements. If there are no improvements, start over.

Coaching Tips

- Don't let the session wander all over the place. Keep it focused on one topic.
- Don't let the employee get defensive.

"I know it isn't fun to hear criticism. The only reason I even mention it is that I want to help you do the very best job you can, and this is an area that can make a real difference to you."

- Don't dominate the discussion. Give the employee plenty of airtime to participate.
- After each coaching session, make notes on what you discussed and what you agreed on. This isn't to nail your employee, but is just a good habit to develop in case you need to recall what was said later on. Always make notes on any discussion of performance.

Performance Appraisal

Next to firing people, the thing you probably hate most is giving appraisals. You may be uncomfortable sitting in judgment of others, especially when it involves negatives, as appraisals usually do. Your people know, in today's precarious world, any negative on an appraisal can be a ticket for a front-row seat in an exit interview.

Appraisals have never been popular with anyone, and consultants, academics, and human resource people have been looking for better ways for years.

Getting 360'd

One of the new "breakthroughs" is 360-degree feedback. This concept is catching on among those who feel hearing about shortcomings from the boss is not enough and want to be whacked by the entire immediate world. In 360-degree feedback, superiors, peers, subordinates, even customers and vendors, fill out questionnaires on you and don't sign their names. Any of them may love you or hate you, may want to make you president or pull your coat over your head and rush you out the door. In today's cutthroat world of corporate survival, I suspect there is more than pure objectivity that goes into 360-degree feedback.

But it can have its value. According to the Center for Creative Leadership, two thirds of all people getting 360'd learn something about themselves. People who considered themselves open communicators, or supportive, or good delegators, find out they are not. One guy learned he stood too close to people and spit on them when he talked. Not very strategic information, but good to know if he wanted to build better working relationships.

This type of appraisal is not for the overly sensitive or people on the edge. It is for people who can tell themselves that learning how others see them, however painful that may be, is a growth experience. Especially if they are willing to do something about it.

Bringing Comfort to Appraisals

Appraisals don't always have to bring on anxiety attacks. You can do a lot to reduce the anxiety level and make your people more receptive to appraisals, mostly by making them part of the process. Here's how:

1. **Rule out surprises.** Use your coaching skills to talk about performance all through the year. Don't save up stuff for appraisal time and then unload it all at once—don't spring any surprises at appraisal time or bring up problems that you haven't discussed before. Don't set retroactive standards the employee hasn't heard of, and don't revise goals for the past year at appraisal time, now that it is over.

2. **Give your people plenty of advance notice** when an appraisal is coming up, and tell them:

You want it to be a positive discussion of performance and to focus on future growth.

You want their participation and their opinions on how well they met objectives, on successes during the year, and areas they want to improve. You may want to have your people fill out copies of their own appraisal forms.

3. **Do your homework.** I know filling out all those forms is a major abuse to your system, and you don't have time to do it, but the act of completing forms forces you to think through the appraisal. Knowing what you will cover and having the facts will build your own comfort level.

You may want to practice presenting information in a specific but not accusatory way, with an emphasis on problem solving. Anticipate what the employee's reaction might be to specific parts of the appraisal and practice handling any difficult situations you think might occur.

Conducting the Appraisal

Here are the steps for a smooth and productive appraisal discussion. If you follow them, they may not turn the appraisal into an all-time great motivational experience, or make it as much fun as Space Mountain, but at least it will not send either of you into therapy.

Step 1. Set a relaxed climate. This is tricky, since everyone is pretty sophisticated today. Employees know you have had appraisal training, and they might get impatient if you try to force a discussion about stupid stuff like the Super Bowl while they are waiting for the execution to begin.

Do what seems natural, and don't try to compel someone to relax any more than he or she can stand. Don't ask about the employee's family if you never do any other time. Don't talk about something in the news if you usually don't. Don't compliment someone on a new suit if you don't usually—it will sound contrived, and you may get sued for sexual harassment. If there is no relaxed way to begin with a non-work topic, start by asking about a current project or team assignment in which the employee is involved.

Have your discussion in a private place where you won't get interrupted. Conventional wisdom is to meet on some neutral ground that doesn't say "boss-subordinate." A conference room or empty office maybe, as long as people won't be walking in on you. Or, go out of the office entirely, although the idea of going to a restaurant or bar is not my favorite. It is hard to talk and eat at the same time, and why ruin a good drink by talking about performance? My suggestion is, if you have an office with a door, use it. It probably is the best and most natural place for the discussion to be held—and even if you go to another building and put on a clown suit, your employee still knows you are the boss.

Close this part of the discussion by outlining what will happen next: "We'll talk about your goals and accomplishments, discuss your overall rating, set goals for the coming year, and spend some time on your future development. Once again, I want this to be a positive discussion—its real purpose is to help you learn and grow in your job."

Step 2. Review goals and accomplishments. Go through goals you set with the employee and review how well he or she accomplished them. It is helpful if the employee completes this part of the appraisal, using as many facts and specifics as possible, before your discussion.

Remember that no one operates alone. Sometimes an individual won't be able to meet a goal, despite heroic efforts, because outside factors make it impossible. Suppose, for instance, an employee misses a sales goal in a year a competitor introduced a superior product at a lower price. On the other hand, sometimes goals are exceeded without any effort on the part of the employee. That same employee might go over a sales goal when a customer becomes dissatisfied with a competitor and calls in out of the blue with a large order. You have to take these factors into account when you are reviewing results.

This is a great time to give recognition for goals met or exceeded and to reinforce all those things the employee did well. It is also a good time to talk about what happened with goals that weren't met and what can be learned from the experience. Offer whatever support and assistance—coaching, training, or the chance to work with others who have more experience—the employee may need to avoid missing goals like this in the future.

Step 3. Give overall rating. Overall ratings cause a lot of trouble in appraisals. Let's say your appraisal program rates people from 1 to 5, with 5 being highest. First of all, anyone who gets less than 5 feels like a loser. Four out of 5 is good, but doesn't quite make it. To compound the problem, some bosses, for various incomprehensible reasons (like nobody is perfect), dictate that no one in their department can receive a 5, so everyone becomes a loser.

Over time, like grades in college, ratings tend to float upward, mostly because it is easier to tell people they are 4's or 5's than to tell them they are 3's. Also, as the workforce becomes more experienced, it gets better.

Top management people, who pride themselves on having the best team of employees in the world, somehow feel uncomfortable that their people are being rated highly. Companies spend millions hiring good people, coaching and training them, then wonder why they are rated so well. In many organizations, management periodically launches a campaign to push ratings down.

Human resources people write long scenarios to convince everyone that a 3 is not average but means the employee is doing everything the job demands. An all-around good job. People who have been rated 3 all along don't feel any better, because they know, whatever anyone says, a 3 is the middle of the pack. Then, to fit the model, many people who have been rated 4 in the past are now rated 3. All-around good job. Sure. So now, for no apparent reason, a whole bunch of people are alienated and demoralized, and hate appraisals worse than ever.

There is no good way to give someone a rating less than the top one. There is no good way to reduce someone's rating, but there are things you can do to make it easier. Let's say a person's performance has dropped, and that person has truly earned a lower rating. Here's one way to lower a rating: "Andrea, I know you are unhappy with this rating. I am, too. You should be unhappy, because you can do better. Your past performance has proven that. Let's see how you can do better in the future so you can get back to where you belong."

Sometimes a person earns a 5 rating based on extraordinary circumstances that required very high levels of performance. Celebrate the outstanding rating and discuss the events that made that rating possible, so the employee knows it may not be possible to attain that high a rating every year.

Step 4. Set goals for next year. This is often done outside the appraisal discussion, but this is a good time to get the process started and to review in general terms what next year will bring.

Step 5. Talk development. Here is a great creative challenge for you as a leader. Especially with any of your people who are doing a great job to begin with, and have been for some time. Where do you take them?

This is the most important part of the appraisal and is the one most often skipped over. What's past is past; there's nothing you can do about it. What you *can* influence is the future, and this part of the appraisal discussion sets the tone and direction for what is to come.

In preparing for the appraisal, try to think of ways to make the employee's job more challenging and build in experiences that will help the employee learn and grow. These might include expanded responsibilities, additional decision-making power, task force or team assignments, training programs, and leadership roles in company-sponsored charity and community service programs. Get the employee's input on where he or she would like to grow in the future, and try to direct development activities to support that.

This step serves another purpose. It ends the appraisal discussion on a high note, and even if there has been bad news in the appraisal, this gives the employee hope.

Don't be hemmed in by the appraisal form. The form is the starting place, but it may not reflect all the important parts of the employee's job. Discuss things like effectiveness as a team member, contribution to continuous improvement, and customer service whether or not they are on the form.

Training

Close your eyes and think of training. What do you see? I'll bet it's a U-shaped classroom with an instructor up in front writing on flip charts. Workshops and seminars are one kind of training, and can be very effective.

Unfortunately, many times they are not. That's because:

- Companies don't do enough of them. Training happens once in a great while, and people forget quickly.
- Workshops are not designed to meet the participants' needs. Sending people who don't supervise anyone to a supervisory skills seminar because it might do some good is a waste of time. They will learn skills they can't use, and will lose them in a month.
- Content is too theoretical. People want to learn stuff they can use back on the job. If what they get is concepts, that may be interesting, but of little use. When people go to a communications seminar, they want to be better communicators when they come out, and the workshop should help them do that.
- Workshops are amateurish. I once had the president of a small client firm tell me he wanted to borrow my seminar leader's guide so he could "read it" to a class. Here was a guy who had no idea of what training is about. People don't learn by having stuff read to them. But there are managers who just go ahead and put on seminars without knowing what they are doing. Holding attention, getting people into it, keeping control of the class, handling difficult personalities, keeping things on time, adjusting situations that aren't working well, and running the course so people learn from it take experience and skill.
- People are intimidated. Many have not been in school for a long time—and didn't like it when they were. They feel a workshop may be a test of their ability and may hurt their careers.

When you think of training, think beyond workshops. Here's how to begin:

1. Find out what people's needs are before you send them off to training. Your appraisal discussions with your subordinates should be a good source of development needs. Review them, and make a plan for each of your people.

   Always know what is in the training your people are getting. Attend seminars yourself, preferably beforehand, so you can evaluate their usefulness.
2. Use business problems as learning experiences. Make up teams to do research on actual problems, develop ideas, come to conclusions, and present them to you. You can build in some classroom training along the way on topics such as team building, problem identification, and creative problem solving.

3. Provide a challenge. Another way people learn is by being given a leap in responsibility. This doesn't have to be a new job; it can be a special assignment, a task force, or a new venture to manage. It has to be something the person has not done before that requires higher level skills and involves skills the person is apt to use in the future. Sink or swim is the analogy.

   Give away part of your job, for instance, and let one of your people handle it, mistakes and all. This is the best time to provide formal training, because people are most receptive to learning when they take on new work.

4. Get feedback. When you do send people to seminars, have them outline for you exactly what they learned and how they are going to use it on the job.

   Don't get too excited about what your people tell you when they first come back from a seminar. People have fun going to seminars (good seminars, anyhow) and are all charged up when they get back. Wait and see how well they use their new knowledge on the job and if there is any change for the better.

5. Help them use their new skills on the job right after they learn them, even if it means giving them special assignments. People learn best by doing. Keep that in mind as you develop your people.

6. If you put on company seminars, do it professionally. If that means investing in expert help, so be it. What you spend you will save many times over by not wasting money and time on a dopey seminar that does no one any good.

SBI: Constant, candid, constructive conversation with your people is the best way to motivate them and build commitment.

TEAM
SKILLS

15

THE GIPPER LIVES

Winning Through Teamwork

*"Sure, I'm happy I scored twelve touchdowns and signed
a forty-million-dollar contract with the sneaker company
at halftime. But the important thing is that the team
won the game."*

—Leonard Brewster, star running back,
Wilmington Wildebeests

The executive's ultimate fantasy? To have a workforce of people who
will pull together just like players on a winning team—who will get out
there in the mud and the slush and the driving rain and sacrifice their
bodies, their minds, and their lives for the company, giving each other
high fives and head butts after every success.

So strong is that fantasy that companies pay big bucks for motivational videos by coaches and sports stars, and millions more to hire
them in person to speak at company meetings, where they spout pro-
fundities such as "The team that puts the most points on the board
wins," "You can't score if you don't move the ball," and "Preparation is
the key to being ready." Despite all this help, building teams is a tough
struggle since people, by nature, put themselves first. As we know all
too well today, even sports figures, despite what they say after the
game, sometimes allow a little self-interest to sneak in.

But companies persist, thinking up new ways to put teams together,
new uses for teams, and in some instances organizing the whole company around teams. There are quality-improvement teams, employee-
involvement teams, high-performance teams, cross-functional teams,
problem-solving teams, self-directed teams, and teams to figure out
what the other teams should be doing.

Many of these are by-products of the quality effort, which, in turn, was an outgrowth of the Japanese management craze that sprang up in the 1970s when Americans discovered that other countries could make products, too.

The Power of Teamwork

Teams are a way of bringing parts of the organization together to solve quality, customer, marketing, or other problems. Or to plan and produce products and services. Teams, if they function right, can come up with creative new approaches, solve problems, streamline operations, and be great learning experiences for their members. Being part of a team can help offset lack of promotions and fears about being downsized. Good teams can help an organization meet its goals. They should be a very civilized way of doing business.

For instance, in self-managed teams, members are supposed to identify problems and come up with solutions, set work schedules and assign responsibilities, and at the same time hire and fire each other and do their own performance appraisals. The old manager becomes a team supporter, providing general guidance and support.

Self-managed teams get people involved, push decision making down, and give people freedom to innovate and run their own jobs.

Cross-functional teams (with members from several departments) can get things done faster, solve complex problems, focus the organization's resources on the customer, and help members understand other departments better.

But all is not totally rosy.

Problems in Teamland

- For all the commotion about teams, not many people are actually on teams. Sixty-eight percent of large companies have self-managed teams, for example, but only 10 percent of their workforce is involved in those teams.
- Teams are expensive. Ed Lawler, management professor at USC and an authority on self-managed teams, says, "They are high performance but high maintenance and expensive." In many cases,

management says it wants teams, but it doesn't want to spend the money to provide the training and budget resources teams need to function effectively.

- The benefits of working on a team can be unclear. Teams take time away from the main job, and managers often don't like their people going off to think up crazy ideas in some team meeting when they should be getting their work done. Performance appraisals often do not reflect performance as a team member.
- People don't naturally get along too well together, and just because they're on a team doesn't mean people will get all huggy.
- Team members usually have to run back to their functional bosses to get approval for a decision. This takes a lot of time and gets departments at each other's throats again. Some companies (Boeing, for instance) solve that problem with a no-messenger rule. Teams decide on the spot.
- Teams often don't communicate well or share information with other teams, so there has to be some process for integration—otherwise, teams will be just as stubborn as the departments they are meant to supersede.
- Some teams are formed to aid with reengineering, and in the past have come up with solutions that ultimately downsized some team members. People become wary of teamwork suicide.
- Several companies have formed teams just because it is the thing to do, and the teams have no clear idea what they are supposed to do.
- Some union officials believe teams are only another management ploy for getting more out of workers without paying them more. Or worse yet, they see them as union-busting devices.

What Makes a Great Team?

Despite the problems, teams are a way of life today in many organizations and can accomplish amazing things. Whether you are team leader or a team member, you should know what makes a great team.

Think of a team you were on (a committee, task force, or—okay—a sports team) that worked exceptionally well. What made that team great? List what the members did, or other factors that made that team effective.

1.

2.

3.

4.

5.

6.

Look over your list. Chances are it includes some of the following, which are generally considered to be the keys to great teamwork.

Members of *great* teams:

1. Know their mission.
2. Agree on goals.
3. Focus time and energy on meeting those goals.
4. Decide who does what.
5. Disagree openly but constructively.
6. Get everyone involved; get input from all members.
7. Protect new ideas and foster creative thinking.
8. Have access to information.
9. Have a spirit of cooperation.
10. Get things done.

Now take a look at the team you are on now. Use the assessment below to determine how well the team functions and to pinpoint areas for improvement. Use this questionnaire periodically with team members to check on the team's progress and plan for improvement.

HOW WELL DOES OUR TEAM WORK?

1. How clear is the mission of the team—why the team exists?

5	4	3	2	1
Very Clear		Fairly Clear		Murky

2. How well do members of the team agree on goals—what the team is supposed to do?

5	4	3	2	1
Very Well		Fairly Well		Didn't Bother to Discuss Goals

3. How well does your team focus its time and energy on meeting its goals?

5	4	3	2	1
Completely		Fairly Well		Unfocused, Wanders

4. How well does the team decide who does what?

5	4	3	2	1
Very Well		Fairly Well		Keystone Kops

5. How good are team members at disagreeing openly and constructively?

5	4	3	2	1
Very Good		Fairly Good		A Brawl

6. How well does the team get everyone involved?

5	4	3	2	1
Everyone Contributes		Some Talk More Than Others		A Few Dominate, Others Say Nothing

7. How well does the team protect new ideas?

5	4	3	2	1
Very Well		Pretty Well		Kills Them Off Promptly

8. To what extent do team members have the information they need?

5	4	3	2	1
Have It All		Have Most		In the Dark

9. How good is the spirit of cooperation?

5	4	3	2	1
Very Good		Pretty Good		Tug-of-War

10. How good is the team at getting things done?

5	4	3	2	1
Very Good		Pretty Good		Does Nothing

Scoring:

10–20   This may be a collection of people, but it is not a team.
21–30   Pretty weak. The group may get some things done, but with a great struggle.
31–40   You are approaching teamhood. With a little effort, the team could be great.
41–50   Gold Medal winner.

What is the team's greatest strength?

_____

_____

_____

_____

_____

What does the team need to work on? What is the biggest opportunity for making the team function better?

_____

_____

_____

_____

Let's talk about what it takes to lead a team and what it takes to be a good team member.

Being a Team Leader

You've been asked to lead a team to work on a company project such as "improving customer service." This is a nice juicy assignment—it is highly visible work, a prestige area to work in, and something that can make a difference. It can also be a way to screw up big-time.

Your Responsibilities as a Team Leader

1. **Define the charter.** Before you begin celebrating your new team assignment, determine what latitude your team has.

What is the exact nature of the assignment? That is, what will constitute successful completion of the project?
To whom does the team report?
What freedom do you and the team members have in carrying out the assignment? Can you visit company facilities and talk with

managers and employees? Can you talk with customers? What restrictions, if any, are there on your work?

Who will pick the team members? Do you have any say in that?

What resources will be available to the team? Will you have budget dollars? Can you use the company plane? (Oh, well, no harm in asking.)

Will the team have access to information it needs—for example, financial plans, profit goals, production figures, and strategic plans?

What about functional bosses of team members? Will the team operate on its own, or do team members have to run back to their bosses for approval?

Will team members be appraised on the results of their work? Will there be some recognition for them?

Wrong assumptions about any of these may derail your team. You may have to have a team meeting or two to write proposed answers to these questions if management doesn't have them for you. Get everyone's agreement, and you are off to a solid start—but do it at the outset, not after the team has been struggling for two months.

2. Build on strengths. Team members are selected for various reasons: a particular skill, interest in the project, experience in the area, general wisdom and creativity, and for political purposes. You may be given a team and have no say in who is on it, or you may be able to select your own team members. In any case, as the leader of the team, you must determine the strengths of each player, what he or she can contribute to the team, and how to best use that strength. Ask individual members for their views on how they can best serve the team.

3. Set ground rules. The team should decide at the start how it is going to operate, and you as the leader should get that process going. Here is a list of ground rules set by a team I was on recently.

TEAM GROUND RULES

We agree that we will:

Stay focused on our objective. Other agendas may be important, but we have only a limited amount of time. No war stories. We will stay on the subject, follow the agenda.

Get even input. Everyone has something to contribute, but some by nature talk less than others. We will encourage everyone to contribute and discourage anyone from dominating.

Respect ideas. We know new ideas may have things wrong with them, but we also know that flawed ideas are the basis for creativity and can lead to great new directions. We will not kill off ideas.

Operate informally and have fun. We will celebrate successes.

Encourage honest disagreement and conflict. But we will keep it confined to the issues and not extend it to a personal level.

Decide by consensus.

Be results-oriented and get things done.

4. **Develop a mission and goals.** Once you have agreed on how you will work together, get your team to define its mission, set goals, and work out action plans, so each member knows exactly what needs to be done, by whom, and when.

TEAM MISSION AND GOALS CHART

Mission:

_____

_____

_____

_____

Goal 1:

Action Steps	Responsibility	Completion Date

Goal 2:

Action Steps	Responsibility	Completion Date

Goal 3

Action Steps	Responsibility	Completion Date

5. **Herd the sheep.** Without a good Sheltie nipping at their heels, sheep have a tendency to wander off in all directions. Without a good leader, team members do, too. It's your job to nip—to keep them together. Since team members probably do not report to you organizationally, you will have to use skills such as facilitating and influencing to get things done.

6. **Break up fistfights.** There will be disagreements. That's fine, even desirable. But you must step in and mediate when conflict turns to anger. Stop the conversation, review the points of disagreement and the positions on either side of the argument, try to find areas of agreement, and when it becomes apparent neither side is going to move, state "This is an area we can't agree on right now. Let's put it aside and go on to other issues."

As the team leader, you should welcome conflict but emphasize collaboration.

7. **Build bridges.** Keep management (whoever formed the team in the first place) informed and involved in the project to keep commitment high. Sometimes people upstairs lose interest after a month or two, even in hot projects, and your team needs the resources and support that only higher management can give. In addition, you should stay in close contact with the direct managers of the team members, especially if they come from a variety of departments.

8. **Take prudent risks.** Assume that it is all right for the team to do almost anything that hasn't been specifically prohibited. Your team will

probably not come up with anything new and useful if you and the team members make all kinds of assumptions about what management will allow and what it won't. And so the team will decide on courses of action that are safe, conventional, old, and tired. That won't say much about you as a leader.

9. Make the work fun. Team participation should be the most fun anyone has at work. After all, being on a team is one of the few chances you get to set your own rules, operate outside the organization, and recognize accomplishments any way you want. Give yourselves lots of recognition, and throw a party when you accomplish something.

10. Create freedom: Encourage team members to feel free to be critical of the company and what is happening, free to express new ideas, free to come up with new solutions, and free to think outside established structure. You have a responsibility to see that all ideas, no matter how nuts they are, are protected and respected.

11. Assess performance. Periodically, you should ask the team to step back and rate its performance. Use the How Well Does Our Team Work? questionnaire. Have all members fill it out, summarize the results, then discuss ways to improve, especially in areas with lower ratings. You should also make sure that the work of the team is reflected in the performance appraisals of each member.

12. Get something done. You may have to push to get action. Team members have a lot of fun talking and arguing with each other and may want to keep on forever. Jump in and ask, "What have we decided to do? Where do we go from here? What do we do to get this off the ground?"

Functioning as a Team Member

The quality of work you do as a team member can enhance your reputation with people far beyond your own department.

Being part of a team can be a great opportunity, and much fun, but it has its responsibilities. To be effective, you'll have to make some trade-offs for the good of the team, and you may have to change some of your favorite ways of behaving. If you are used to dominating and controlling, if you have to win, if you can instantly analyze a new idea and find things wrong with it . . . well, all those things can wreck a team. Start by reviewing the team's ground rules and deciding what behavior changes you have to make to support them.

Some no-give things you must do to be an effective team member:

Show up on time for meetings.
Be prepared; complete your between-meeting assignments. If you agree to do something, do it.
Give your opinion, even if it is unpopular.
Back off—be willing to compromise.
Be playful and introduce unusual ideas when the team is brainstorming.
Give credit to others for their ideas and accomplishments.

What does all this mean to you?

Teams are here, for better or worse, and they can be great for you personally. They are fun, they can bring you and your teammates recognition, and they can help you expand your networks by getting to know people in other departments.

Try to get on a team or two. There's nothing that says you can't volunteer for a team if no one picks you, or form a team of your own.

Make sure the work you do for the team is top rate. You will quickly form a reputation on the team, and word will get around. Good teamwork can also offset the opinion of your manager if he or she is lukewarm about your work.

> **SBI:** Remember, you may have to change your own behavior to help the team succeed and to get the most out of the team experience.

16

Staying Awake

How to Get Things Done in Meetings

"I have discovered the secret to life: I don't go to meetings. If there were no meetings, everybody in the world could go home at one o'clock."   —Art Buchwald

Who am I to argue with Art Buchwald? I'm giving up going to meetings, too. I have gone to my last meeting. I will never ever go to another one. I will also make exceptions to that rule, of course. But that is just the point. I want to think of meetings as the exception rather than the normal way to waste a day. I want to exhaust all alternatives before I give in to going to a meeting. It has to be the last resort, not the first thing I think of doing.

And when I do go to meetings, I want to make them shorter and more interesting, and actually get something done.

What's Wrong with Meetings?

Meetings are a lousy way to get things done, because they involve people. Take out the participants, and meetings are fine. Just a table, some chairs, and maybe a flip chart or laptop, and everything is simple. When you add five or six people, the dynamics of communicating, agreeing, and deciding are as complex as the wiring diagram of a 747. And they don't work nearly so well.

If you are like most managers and professionals, meetings can kill half your workweek, and you may wonder if the payback is worth that kind of investment.

Problems with meetings include:

- No agenda or clear purpose for the meeting.
- Discussions that are not guided, so people spend too long debating the same issue, bring in new issues, tell war stories, and generally drift further and further from the original topic until nobody remembers what it was. The meeting runs twice as long as it should and becomes increasingly boring.
- People are hesitant or downright afraid to say what is on their minds, so little creative or critical thinking gets expressed.
- A few people dominate the discussion. It is the same ones every meeting. They may or may not have the most important things to say, but they say them anyway.
- Some meetings drag along like a two-hundred-minute hour. Time seems to hang forever, most of it wasted, with no end in sight.
- People are there who don't need to be. Topics are relevant to some, not others.
- No one "asks for the sale." Nothing is agreed on, and no one knows what they are supposed to do as a result of the meeting. And then the meeting ends and everyone leaves.
- There are just plain too many meetings.

But, with all their faults, some meetings are necessary. Especially today in the age of teams, because meetings are the main way teams get their work done.

Better Meetings

Here's how to cut meeting time and get more done.

1. **Think outcome.** Let's say you want to get the team together to talk about getting new business. In the past, it has taken about two hours to discuss topics like this, so you are tempted to schedule two hours. But if you spend time in advance designing the meeting, you might be able to knock off a half hour or more. Or you may decide you don't need a meeting after all and save two hours.

Here are some guidelines to help you:

- Start with the end. What would you like to have happen as a result of the meeting? When you think beyond the meeting itself to outcomes, you will begin to think in terms of what you want the meeting to accomplish rather than just what will go into the meeting. Write a hoped-for outcome and send it out with the agenda.
- If you have a hard time thinking of outcomes, you don't need a meeting. Scrap it, and use the time to do something worthwhile.
- Meetings aren't the only way to get group work done. Next time you have an overwhelming urge to call a meeting, take a cold shower. While you are cooling off, consider some alternatives:

Want to Accomplish	Possible Methods for Accomplishing
Inform people of something	Use E-mail, voice mail, memo, fax, one-on-one
Motivate them	Send around a Tom Peters tape
Entertain them	Send around a John Cleese tape
Get a decision	Use E-mail and ask for a vote
Get input	Use E-mail or a videoconference to get opinions from each member of the team
Get action	Use E-mail, voice mail, memo, fax, one-on-one, videoconference Ask each person getting the message to reply with exactly what he or she plans to do
Solve a problem, get new ideas	These are the best uses for meetings, because the team, working as a team, can be more creative than can individual members working alone

Felver's[1] Law: Anything that can be done outside a meeting should be.

---

[1] Felver was an executive who nodded off during an extremely long meeting and was downsized while he slept.

- Decide who should attend. Let's say you succumb and call a meeting after all. As you write your outcomes for the meeting, decide who can best contribute to attaining those outcomes. Is there anyone with technical expertise who will help? How about somebody who is wacky and can come up with new approaches? Or someone who typically helps a group connect to the big picture—like company goals or customer needs? How about a pragmatist who can bring the discussion down to something that will work? How about those who need to be involved—people who control budget money, or will have to implement what is decided, or could put up big roadblocks? How about inviting customers and/or suppliers? Don't forget diversity—not for politically correct purposes, but because meetings with mixed groups are livelier and more creative.

  While you are sorting through all that, remember this: keep attendance small. Five to eight is good; over ten and you won't get anything done. You don't have to have all the people on the team, or all those who were at the last meeting.

  As you design your list, think of who might introduce other agendas, who might be disruptive, who might try to take over, and who might be negative. Ideally you wouldn't invite any of them, but in the real world you might have to—see "Defuse difficult situations" on page 265—and plan how you will handle them.

- To save time, include background materials for people to read when you send out your agenda. If you are presenting a proposal and hope to get agreement on it, get supporters on board before you go into the meeting. Meetings are very political, so approach them with the politics in mind.

- Pick a good setting. Most corporate conference rooms are as inspiring as funeral parlors, and if you want creative thinking, you may want to go off-site to a hotel or conference center. If you have little money to spend, try a church or civic organization—many have space they will rent you for little expense. Or use your family room.

2. Set a strong agenda. Every meeting needs an agenda. An agenda is much more than a list of topics, it is a meeting map. Here's an example:

Date: 10/2/00

To: Joe
            Jennifer
            Anne
            Ned
            Adam
            Liz

From: Bill [you]

Subj.:   Sales Team Meeting

Time, Date, Location: 3:00–4:00 P.M., 10/12/00, Marriott
                             conference room A

Outcome: To find ways to get three new
                             medium-sized customers in
                             the next six months

Agenda

Time	Subject	Led by	Action
3:00–3:10	Review current customer list	Bill	Set priorities
3:10–3:30	Brainstorm new customer possibilities	Liz	Develop list
3:30–3:50	Develop strategies	Anne	Determine our approach
3:50–4:00	Agree on responsibilities, timetable	Bill	Get going

Note that:

- All attendees are listed so everyone knows who will be there.
- The outcome is spelled out very specifically. As opposed to something like "Build customer base," this purpose has a number, type of customer, and timetable. There is only one purpose, and the meeting is focused around it. The subtopics all support the main purpose.

- Liz and Anne run parts of the meeting. It is not necessary for you to lead all of your own meeting. In fact, if you want to participate in your meeting, you'll need help leading it. It is almost impossible to run the meeting and be a full participant at the same time. Make sure your co-leaders know how to run meetings and have the skills to guide the group.
- There's an action listed opposite each subject. This helps participants understand what is expected and what to work toward.
- The use of active verbs—*review, develop, agree*—implies that something will happen.

3. Get started:

- In the example above, team members shared running the meeting. As an alternative, to allow everyone to participate, you may want to ask someone outside the group to facilitate. The facilitator should keep the meeting on the agenda, on time, get even participation, run flip charts, and write up and distribute minutes. If you use a facilitator, explain to the group what the facilitator is there to do.
- If you run the meeting yourself, keep it on track, on subject, and on time. Be tough if you have to. Tell people the topic and the time you'll have to discuss it. Keep them on time and on the topic. They will thank you.
- Start on time. If the boss isn't there, start anyway.
- If this is a new group, you might want to get them to set ground rules before you start.

4. Guide the discussion:

- Restate the hoped-for outcome and review the agenda at the outset of the meeting, emphasizing the time allocated.
- As discussion progresses, summarize ideas and decisions made. Put them on flip charts or computer projections so everyone can see.
- Get input from the group: Ask for a comment or idea from each person in the meeting. Or, on sensitive issues, have members of the group write comments on cards, then collect and summarize them.
- Create an atmosphere of trust. Assure people that you will protect

their ideas and then do it. Make sure no one kills off ideas or embarrasses anyone else.

- Get even participation. Invite people who are quieter to contribute. Keep those who tend to dominate quiet at least part of the time.
- Use questions to control and guide the meeting and to get input, bring out ideas, and get even participation from all members of the team.

Questions are very powerful tools for leading a meeting. Here are various kinds of questions and how they can help you:

When You Want to . . .	Type of Question to Use	Examples
Get people to talk, get more information, stimulate discussion, generate ideas	Open (begins with "What," "How," "To what extent")	"What do you think we should do?"
		"If we do this, how will it affect our customers?"
		"What should our response to that be as a team?"
Get specific information	Closed (can be answered "Yes" or "No," or with a specific number or fact)	"What's the completion date?"
		"How much are we over budget?"
		"Are we on schedule?"
Get someone to talk, move discussion away from someone dominating	Direct	"Ned, fill us in on your work on that, will you?"
		"Anne, how do you see it from your perspective?"
		"Liz, how do you feel about what Jennifer just said?"

| Avoid answering a question yourself. Get others involved, find out what's behind the question | Return | "Jennifer, how would you answer Adam's question?" |
| | | "That's a good question, Ned. How would *you* answer it?" |

5. Defuse difficult situations. In every meeting, someone will (intentionally or not) get off the track. In really tough meetings it seems everyone does. Here are some ways you can handle tough situations and get your meeting back on course:

Situation	What You Should Do
Someone wants to add something to the agenda.	Say, "Anne, that is really important and we should talk about it. But we only have an hour for this meeting—maybe you should handle it at another time."
The big boss is there and people are inhibited.	Take the boss aside on break and explain what is happening. He or she will be flattered to be so powerful.
	Ask if the boss will excuse himself or herself from the meeting and let the group continue on its own. If that is not possible, ask the boss to plead for open discussion.
Someone is pulling rank.	Take the person aside at break and explain what is happening. Ask the person to hold back for the good of the meeting.
Old Fred is telling war stories.	Jump in, saying, "That's a great example, Fred. Now let's move on to . . ."
People are going for solutions before they understand the problem.	Interrupt and say, "I think we're getting ahead of ourselves a little. Let's make sure we understand what we're up against here before we get into what to do."
The group starts to wordsmith.	Interrupt and say, "It is hard to write something in a meeting. Let's get the general ideas out, and then we'll pick someone to draft it and send it around."

Someone is dominating the discussion.	Use a direct question to call on someone else. Or say, "Liz, we have heard from you quite a bit. Let's get input from some of the others."
You are getting major challenges from one participant.	Use an overhead question like "What do the rest of you think of that? Do you agree with what Adam is saying?" Many times they don't but won't say so till you ask.
A participant is negative and shoots down everybody's ideas.	Say, "I want to make sure we consider everyone's ideas, even if they aren't perfect. Let's get the ideas out. We can evaluate them later."
You can't reach agreement on an item.	Say, "It looks as though this is something we aren't going to agree on. Let's leave it for a while, then come back to it after we have gone through the rest of the agenda."
	Or, try to break down the topic; then find areas where there is agreement. Try to find acceptable compromise positions or alternatives for areas of disagreement.
	When compromise doesn't work, say, "I'd rather have everyone in agreement, but why don't we vote on this one, and that will decide how we'll proceed?"
There is open conflict between two participants.	Say, "Okay, you two. You're not going to agree on this, but the rest of the group seems to be together on it, so let's move on."
A participant is not talking.	Use a direct question. "Adam, what are your thoughts on this?" or "Anne, we haven't heard from you, how do you see it?"
No new ideas are coming.	Try this: "We seem to be stuck, and I think it is because we are trying so hard to find the solution. Why don't we take a ten-minute break and think of the wildest, most illegal, immoral, and unallowable approaches we can, and see if they don't lead us to new ideas?"

6. Keep a record:

- Use flip charts or computer presentations to record ideas and decisions.
- Write or type key thoughts only—headlines, not sentences.
- Use participants' exact words. If someone says, "We have to be done by the end of the month," write, "Done by end of month." Don't write, "Complete in next few weeks."
- If you use charts, write large so everyone can see. Printing is better but slower.
- If you are running the meeting, ask someone else to do the charts.

7. **Ask for the sale.** Every good salesperson knows that at some point in the sales call, it's important to ask for the sale. Otherwise, the call is over and nothing happens. The customer is not going to demand to be sold; he or she has to be asked.

The same holds true with meetings. You started off with a hoped-for outcome for your meeting, something you wanted to accomplish. Be sure, before you close the meeting, that you have agreement and understanding of what will happen next. Summarize what was decided and then get input on who will do what. By when. If you don't do this, you'll need to have another meeting. And there goes another two hours.

Then send out a summary. A simple one-pager like the one below can bring closure to your meeting and make the difference between a meeting that people leave and forget, and one that gets results.

Date: 10/15/00

To: Joe
            Jennifer
            Anne
            Ned
            Adam
            Liz

From: Bill [you]

Subj.: Sales Team Meeting Summary

Here's what we agreed to do in our meeting of 10/12/00.

Action	Responsibility	Complete by
Design brochure	Anne	12/1/00
Contact prospects # 1–4	Adam/Liz	1/30/01
Contact prospects # 5–9	Bill/Jennifer	1/30/01
Contact prospects # 10–13	Joe/Ned	1/30/01
Report progress	All	2/10/01
Make follow-up visits	All	3/15/01
Sign new contracts	All	4/1/01

How to Be a Meeting Participant

There it is on your calendar, a meeting tomorrow at 9:00 A.M. Good chance to relax and catch a few z's, huh? Well, not quite, because, as a meeting participant, you have responsibilities, too.

Your job is to contribute as much as you can to the success of the meeting and to help the meeting leader accomplish the desired outcome. Here's how.

1. Think outcome. What is the hoped-for outcome of this meeting? If one isn't stated, find out. Call the meeting leader and ask. Then think about what you can bring to the table, what you can contribute to increase the value of the time spent, and show your value to the team.

Remember, meetings are your showcase. Not only meetings you run, but any meeting in which you participate. Everyone there is exposed to your communication skills, your team skills, and your wisdom. Look on every meeting, no matter how annoying, as an opportunity to show what you can do—and be ready to do it.

2. Check out the agenda. If you don't get an agenda before the meeting, request one, or suggest one yourself. When you do get one, take a look at what topics are being covered and make sure you have input on each one that concerns you. Gather up any data you need to back up your opinions with facts. Do some research if you have to. But be ready to contribute.

3. Be involved in the discussion. Maybe you aren't comfortable speaking up in groups. That's okay, lots of people aren't. But the value of making yourself heard in meetings outweighs the effort in so many ways, you should push yourself to do it.

At any rate, make sure you are not one of the problem situations described above. Fix your own behavior first, then contribute to the meeting.

Try not to be too annoying. Here are a few well-chosen words that can make everyone uneasy and take the energy out of a meeting, words that turn a usually placid person like me into a rabid rottweiler.

Things you should never say in meetings . . .

"I know it's way past starting time, but let's wait a few more minutes for Jan to get here."

"Who called this meeting? Ha ha ha."

"That reminds me of something that happened in 1986, when I was out in the field . . . blah, blah, blah."

"Paradigm." (Never say "paradigm." What is it anyhow, and why is it spelled that way? If you say "paradigm," people will think you are a closet consultant, because consultants are always saying "paradigm"—and not only that, but shifting paradigms.

"I think we should meet every Tuesday and Thursday from now on."

"I know we are running into dinner hour, but we have only three or
four more items to cover and then we'll be done."
"We tried that last year and it didn't work."
GRRRRR.

4. Help with the sale. Be sure, before you leave the meeting, you
know what you are supposed to do. If it isn't clear, ask. How you handle
follow-up and do what you have agreed to do can make a lasting and fa-
vorable impression on everybody.

Things agreed to in meetings have a way of slipping away as people
get involved in the day-to-day back on the job. People agree to do
things and then don't. Be sure you aren't one of them. Do what you say
you will do.

High-tech Meetings

Many organizations are now using electronic meeting-support software (EMS) for more productive meetings. EMS enables laptop computers to be linked together on-site or in off-site locations. Meeting
leaders can poll participants, participants can vote anonymously, and
results can be tabulated instantaneously. Participants can also give
their opinions on issues, and those collective opinions can be displayed
on the computer screen (the electronic version of the flip chart).

EMS is great for:

Enabling people who aren't comfortable speaking out in meetings to
express their opinions.

Getting honest opinions (anonymously) on sensitive, highly political
issues.

Getting input in organizations where management has been largely
top-down and opinions of subordinates have not been valued.

Obtaining candid input from employees on morale and company
culture issues.

Identifying problems between departments or teams, and getting
them out on the table for discussion.

If you use EMS:

Rely on your technical people to make sure the system is up and working. Nothing kills a meeting like faulty support systems. Be sure you know how to operate the programs, especially if you are the meeting leader.

Give people a chance to get used to this form of meeting. Some will take time to adjust to technology. Give them the training they need.

Don't go overboard with EMS. Face-to-face discussions are still the way to solve problems and build consensus.

Videoconferences

A videoconference is just a regular old meeting with images bouncing off satellites, except that . . .

1. It starts on time. Because time is money in videoconferencing, there is a precise starting and ending time, and participants feel unusual pressure to move things along.

   Even if you normally straggle into a regular meeting fifteen minutes late, you're likely to show up on time for a videoconference, because if you don't you'll miss part of the meeting and others will miss part of *you*.

   If you normally digress and bring in extraneous agendas, you may hold back because you know time is limited.

2. Because at least some of the meeting takes place on the TV screen instead of in person, you have to use special techniques to come across professionally.

   - Opening introductions. Since participants will not have the opportunity to mill around and shake hands with everyone before the meeting, it is good to go around quickly and say who everyone is. The names will be on the agenda, but it is important to be able to associate a name with a face.

   - Visuals. Slides can be incorporated into the video transmission, and you should arrange this in advance with the conference technician. Desktop presentations can also be incorporated.

Flip charts or posters are all right; overheads don't work too well.

- Dress. White, red, and stripes don't act well on some video equipment. Check with your technician beforehand. Blue is safe.
- Notes and meeting materials. Bring these with you, of course, but learn to . . .

Go through materials without too much rustling and crackling. Paper makes distracting noises that will be picked up by the mike. Along the same line, don't bang or drum on the table.

Glance at your notes, but talk looking mostly at the camera. Try not to look down a lot, or side to side, which will make you look shifty and dangerous.

- Posture and expression. Sit up and lean forward. You'll look better and it will improve your energy. Practice animating your facial expressions to make yourself more appealing on video. Use a mirror at home, or better yet, practice with video close-ups. Keep doing it until you are happy with the way you look, or at least until you don't look like you've just been exhumed.

- Speaking voice. Today's microphones are very sensitive instruments and can pick up normal conversation just fine. There's no advantage in yelling, even though some of those in your meeting may be three thousand miles away.

When you are speaking, it helps to repeat your name, at least the first few times. "This is Fred, and here's what I think . . ." Keep your comments brief and to the point. Also, when you are not speaking, don't. If you carry on a side conversation, the mike will pick it up and confuse the people on the receiving end.

Keep it clear. Explain jargon and acronyms so everyone will know.

When you're talking, don't watch yourself on the monitor. You will only start thinking about how fat you look or how bad your hairstyle is, and you'll lose your concentration.

Big Meetings

Many companies have an annual convention when all the teams get together to compare notes and hear inspirational messages from company officers. Most professional and trade associations have conventions. At one time or another, you may be involved in putting on a big conference or convention. If you haven't yet, volunteer for this duty—it is quite an experience and can get you some valuable recognition. Here's how.

Meeting Design Considerations

1. **Focus.** Make sure your meeting is built around a single overriding theme—for instance, a major company direction, a big new product introduction, or an identified customer need. Try to make the theme specific. "Building Business in the Next Decade" is so broad it is weak. A better theme might be "Ten Ways to Beat Mass Merchants at the Value Game," "Adding 5% Market Share," "The Magic 12% [sales increase goal for next year]," or "The Beauty of Product X [new product]."

A problem with many big meetings is lack of focus, so dozens of presenters put on sessions that are unrelated to any theme or to each other, and participants go through a meeting that is disjointed and may send them home with a lot of ideas, but no specific mission to do anything better.

2. **Opening.** Once you have decided on the theme, design a dynamite opening that will grab everyone's attention and support the theme. For instance, "Ten Ways to Beat Mass Merchants at the Value Game" could open with video clips of your customers talking about what value means to them.

"Adding 5% Market Share" could open with a presentation of what 5 percent means, perhaps a sports figure talking about an added 5 percent in golf, tennis, football, or other sport.

"The Magic 12%" could begin with a magic show.

"The Beauty of Product X" could start with a dramatic presentation of the new product against beautiful artwork or scenery.

3. **Content.** If there are going to be breakout or concurrent workshops during the meeting, make sure each session supports the theme,

contributes to understanding the theme, and helps participants move toward its accomplishment. Each session should have its own written objectives, supporting the overall conference objectives.

Make content of the sessions entertaining (lively), informative, and meaningful to the audience.

Be sure session format is varied to keep the interest of the audience. Avoid a parade of speeches. After the opening sets the tone, each following session could have a slightly different format: panel discussion, problem-solving discussion group, tour, hands-on, and so forth.

Pay special attention to what happens after lunch. This is the toughest time to keep attention. Don't use slides in dark rooms. Get participants to do something. This is a great time for a problem-solving session.

Consider involving customers in making presentations and/or participating in panel discussions.

4. Invitation or meeting announcement. Think of the invitation as the first part of the convention. It should reflect the atmosphere you want to create—if it is to be a first-class affair, pay special attention to designing a classy announcement. Include something that will pique attention even before the meeting. For instance, going back to the "Magic" theme, you could include a small magic trick with each invitation.

The invitation should emphasize the benefits of the session to the attendees—even if they have to attend—so they will look forward to being there.

The invitation should include times, dates, a map of the location of the convention, the agenda—what will happen each day, transportation arrangements, dress—informal or business attire, and hotel arrangements.

5. Visuals. Big meetings live or die on their visuals. Even great presenters lose it if their visuals are mediocre. Yet time after time I go to conferences and see presenters who have worked hard to get their message right and have practiced so they are comfortable in front of the room, yet seem to have given little thought to their visuals.

6. Handouts. If you use handouts, be sure they are uniform (same typeface, margins, and so on) and that you hand out only material you are going to cover. Save reference pieces and articles for the end, or put them at the back of the room for people to pick up on the way out. If handouts are going into a notebook, three-hole-punch them.

Wait until the handouts get all the way around before you start talking about them.

7. Notebooks. If you can, forget handouts and use notebooks, so that the materials for the entire convention are in one place and nobody is distracted by passing stuff around. If you use notebooks, decide on a format (typeface, margins, and so on) and ask all presenters and session leaders to use that format so that the notebook has a look of uniformity about it. The use of preprinted color stripes or logos on the notebook pages can add interest. Illustrations, graphs, and charts also make material more exciting for your audience.

Make sure that pages in the notebook follow the material to be presented in each session exactly so that participants don't have to hunt around to find out where you are. Put reference materials at the end of each section or at the end of the notebook, not mixed in with materials to be covered in the session.

As I suggested in Part III, "Communication Skills," number the notebook pages. Nothing is less professional than for a session leader to say, "Turn to the page on marketing. It's the one that has the title 'Marketing Strategies.' It is right after the page listing major consumer groups, the one with the big chart showing consumer market size."

Instead, try: "Turn to page eight."

8. Room setup. Decide how you want the rooms for the conference to work. Large sessions, like the opening one, should probably be theater style, with aisles down the middle and at the sides. Smaller sessions can also be theater style or classroom style—people seated at tables facing the front. If you want group discussions, U shape is best, since participants face each other, and the leader can walk up and down in the middle of the group. For small group breakout discussions, just a room with some chairs and a flip chart are all that's needed.

Here are some other things you should think about:

- Tent cards: Does everyone know everyone else? At a large conference, maybe not. Have participants' names lettered on large tent cards and put in front of their places when they are in smaller discussion sessions. If participants move from session to session, they can take their tent cards with them.

- Name tags: Participants should have name tags. Be sure first names (nicknames) are printed in big letters, so people can glance down without bending over and squinting, catch the name, and begin talking like they knew it all along.
- Water: Most hotels and conference centers put out water. Be sure there is water for participants. Some also put out hard candy. It helps people get through the day.
- Coffee breaks: Coffee breaks have changed somewhat, reflecting changing habits of participants. While you should still arrange for coffee, don't forget decaf, tea, and designer water. Snacks can include pastries, but you should also provide fruit.
- Smoking areas: Find out where these are and tell people at the opening session. Since smoking annoys a lot of people, and most people don't do it anymore, tell the conference center to leave the ashtrays out of meeting rooms, or if they are in there, pick them up and get rid of them.
- Lunch, cocktails, dinner, hospitality room: These are all events to be planned. They are so participants can socialize, get to know each other, and have fun. If you have to have a speaker at lunch or dinner, make sure that speaker is entertaining and keeps the talk short. Nobody, not the world's most deviant masochist, wants to sit through an hour-long speech after dinner.
- Posters, flags, mementos, awards, prizes: You may want to have any or all of these, anything that will add excitement to your meeting and will help participants remember it. You also may want to have a photographer take group pictures, and a band for dancing or background music.
- Playtime: Most conferences have some, and you may want to carve out an afternoon for golf, tennis, fishing, or sitting by the pool. Find out who wants to do what ahead of time and make the necessary arrangements.
- Evaluation: If you plan to run future events like this, it helps to ask participants to evaluate the meeting. Your evaluation sheet should have questions on what participants felt was most helpful to them, what they would like to see improved, and an overall rating for the conference, to be used as a basis for comparison with future conferences.

Have participants fill out evaluations at the end of the last session and turn them in. Don't ask them to mail them, because most won't get around to it. Get them back right on the spot.

Keep in mind that participants are on a high at the end of the conference and the evaluations will be glowing. But, discounting that, you can get many good ideas on what you can do to make the next conference better.

SBI: Meetings are a great chance for you to show others your communication, leadership, team, and creativity skills. Do what you have to to make your best contribution to any meeting you attend.

17

REALLY STUPID IDEAS
Using Creativity to Solve Problems

> *"What we value most in this company is creativity. I want each of you to find new ways to manage your departments more efficiently without reorganizing them. I want creative ways to run the business that build on what we have done in the past. I want bold new ways to serve customers, at the same time maintaining our conservative image.*
>
> *In short, I want you to find ways to change while staying the same."*
>
> —Mark Zeman, CEO, Sub-Par Golf Equipment,
> in an address to the Management Committee

Creativity is a cat turned into a mountain lion. You start out wanting a little pet, and suddenly it gets out of hand and grows into a giant snarling monster. How could it have gotten so big and dangerous? What do you do with it now?

We have a love-hate relationship with creativity. We all want it, but when it produces new ideas (!), we're not so sure. We like the *idea* of new ideas, but when they appear, they threaten.

Executives and managers talk about the need to be innovative, then put up so many roadblocks and punishments for actually doing something new, most people retreat pretty quickly and go back to doing the same comfortable old thing. It is just safer and doesn't hurt as much.

A few companies have established climates in which creativity is actually encouraged—3M is a good example—but they have to work hard at it, because there are many conditions within organizations that hinder creativity:

1. **Company blubber.** It is usually harder to sell new ideas in big companies than in small ones, because big companies have so many departments and specialists reviewing everything, and so many levels of approval. New ideas going through that grinder come back looking very ordinary.
2. **Company whiskers.** The older the company, the more tradition it has established, and the harder it is to introduce change. "We've never done that before" flags fly all over.
3. **Company victories:** Oddly enough, success is a burden. The problem with it is that people want to keep doing what they did in 1965; it worked so well then. No matter that it is not cutting it today and the company is going down the chute. Just keep doing it better and better, and someday it will be 1965 again. (There is a point, though, usually just before the company goes belly-up, when management suddenly decides it will try anything.)
4. **Company thumbscrews.** Some organizations have all but eliminated risk by punishing mistakes quickly and fiercely. Some managers not only punish but never forget, and still talk about the employee who screwed up in 1980, even though that person has been outstanding ever since.

Still, companies like to see themselves as creative even if they are not. Just think about how popular the term "brainstorming" is. It originally meant an idea-generating session with set guidelines to open up creativity, but today it's used for almost any kind of get-together where thinking might be involved. Usually when people do get together to "brainstorm," they energetically and enthusiastically do everything possible to see that no creative ideas sneak in.

Why Bother with Creativity in the First Place?

Because there's no other answer today. You and your organization are dealing with problems that have no precedent: How do you produce more with half the people and budget dollars? How can you motivate people who are feeling rotten because all their friends got fired and they now have impossible workloads? How do you keep up with competition that is bringing out fantastic new products and services with the speed of light? How do you meet customer demands when customers themselves keep changing and sometimes don't even know what they want? How do you use technology to stay competitive?

There is no established way to deal with these challenges. You can't look in a book and see what someone did twenty years ago, because it isn't there—the issues are new and demand new ideas and approaches. Creativity is the key.

What Is Creativity Anyway?

Creativity has been so trampled many people have forgotten what it is. Recently someone said to me, "I would like to do what you do, but I don't have the creativity." As we talked a little further, I asked him about outside interests and he told me his hobby was doing cabinet-work. Not only did he build cabinets, he did his own designs. But he did not see that as creative, probably because he had repressed the notion of creativity after all his years in corporate.

When I run workshop sessions on creativity, I ask participants to name creative people. Often they cite Beethoven, Steinbeck, Michelangelo. Sometimes Edison. Almost never do they name anyone in business, or themselves.

Certainly, Beethoven was creative, writing symphonies for a hundred-piece orchestra in his head even after he was stone-deaf. John Steinbeck could think up characters that stay in your mind years after you have read about them. Michelangelo conceived exquisite murals, then painted them lying on his back.

That kind of creativity is overwhelming—but don't measure yourself against genius; few of us can aspire to that. Consider my definition of creativity:

> Creativity is the ability to free yourself from imaginary boundaries, to see new relationships and patterns, and in that way accomplish new things of value.

There is nothing in that definition that says you have to be a prodigy to be creative, or that you have to be specially gifted.

Team Creativity

Understanding creativity is especially important for organizations that are relying more and more on teams. Creativity helps teams do exceptionally good work rather than just everyday work—without it, teams spend hours coming up with plans anyone on the team could have developed in fifteen minutes alone.

But getting creativity to work in team situations is tricky because:

1. People have the feeling that creativity is flaky and has no place in the world of work: "It's okay for poets, but we're here to market deodorant, and that takes serious thinking."
2. People make assumptions about boundaries—what can be done and what can't. What is "appropriate." What management will tolerate and support and what it won't. These assumptions may be realistic, but often they are not. Nobody knows for sure until they are tested.
3. People are impatient and want answers now. The creative process keeps them from going for solutions the instant they hear the problem—stopping to come up with ideas can seem like a waste of time.
4. Team members feel they have to deal with every idea once it is expressed. It's hard to just let an idea hang there without doing something with it—usually finding something wrong with it.
5. There is always the fear of failure. Old, tired ideas that have been worked over a little are pretty safe. Team members know they work, if only marginally. At least they don't bomb completely. New ideas are untested, untried, and dangerous. They may fail.
6. Not everyone is on the team. There is always a good chance that if the team comes up with a new solution, other people in the organization will shoot at it: "Did you hear what the systems team came up with? Computer software that takes the place of sales reports! Salespeople don't understand the forms they have now, how are they going to learn to use the software? It will be chaos."
7. Teams use old traditional problem-solving methods because they are not familiar with the creative problem-solving process.

How Teams Normally Solve Problems

Here is an ordinary problem-solving system used by teams that don't know any better:

1. State the problem. Someone describes the problem, usually not in much detail, and before he or she is done, the team launches into step 2.
2. Go for solutions. Several team members offer opinions on what should be done to solve the problem. Some people state solutions with the attitude that the solution is so obvious it is a wonder they are discussing this at all. Even though some team members are already committed to solutions, the team leader asks for ideas.
3. Kill off ideas. As ideas are presented, people pounce on them, find things wrong with them, and once ideas are discredited, the team abandons them quickly.
4. Let assertive people dominate the meeting, and quieter people listen. Or drift off and dream. Talkers, listeners. It is the same people in every meeting.
5. End up with a solution. It is safe, uninspired, and usually very close to something that is already being done.

Applying Creativity to Problem Solving

Let's see what happens when we apply creative problem solving:

1. **Explore the problem.** In creative problem solving, the team spends more time examining the problem. Why is it a problem? What has been done before to resolve it? Also, the team decides who owns the problem—whose problem is it?

1A. **Generate beginning ideas.** Before going for solutions, the team generates *beginning* ideas. The term *beginning* is very important, because it allows people to come up with thoughts that don't have to be perfect or "final." They can experiment, play, and be outrageous and funny. This is central to creativity and is necessary to finding new solutions.

In this step, ideas are accepted and guarded. The rule is that no ideas are killed off or even criticized. All new ideas have things wrong with them; the team is told that at the outset and just lets ideas hang out even though their instinct is to slaughter them.

In this stage team members go for ideas that are illegal, immoral, and would get them fired—just to stimulate out-of-the-box thinking.

This step is also a lot of fun, and maybe that's why teams at first shy away from it: "Fun? You've got to be kidding. This is too important for fun." Later, they can't get enough of it.

1B. Build and connect for still more ideas. The team builds on the ideas generated but doesn't evaluate them, and still puts off going for solutions.

> Joe: *"Maybe we could use rhinos and elephants in our ads to show the power of our new product."*
> Annette: *"Yeah,* Animal House *with real animals."*
> Julie: *"Toga party."*
> Marty: *"How about Roman gladiators? They were powerful."*

The building process will produce some wild swings and will disturb people who are used to linear thinking (until they get used to it), but it will produce lots of ideas. Don't worry if most of them are ridiculous (the ideas, not the people). They may lead to that one great idea you are looking for.

2. Combine, modify, enhance. If 1A and 1B are successful, the team should have plenty of ideas, maybe hundreds of them. In this step, the team picks ideas that generate the most enthusiasm, like the one about the walrus flying from helium balloons, and begins to modify and change them with the goal of eventually coming up with something that is new, workable, solves the problem, and could be sold to management. See "Use creativity catalysts" on page 286 for ways to do this.

As the group works on ideas at this stage, the participants should be careful they don't revert back to some tired, overworked scheme that is pretty much in place now. There will be a pull to do this, because it is the safest way to go and the easiest to sell. Try to avoid that, and keep the newness in ideas as you bring them down to practicality.

3. Kill off ideas. There is no killing ideas in the creative process.

4. Everybody talks. Since in steps 1A and 1B there are no rights and wrongs, more people feel comfortable contributing. They know they are not going to be attacked. If they don't talk, team members ask them to.

5. The team comes up with a new solution. Usually, with the creative process, the solution is quite different from anything that has been done before.

6. Sell it to management. In some ways making the organization comfortable with something new is the toughest part of the process. The team has to devise ways to present the solution, gain acceptance, and introduce it so that it will not frighten people. Sometimes this is worthy of a creative problem-solving session all on its own.

Strategies could include:

Emphasizing benefits to management and the company.
Bringing in support, people management respect who like your idea.
Finding others who have used similar ideas and succeeded.
Having a cost-benefit analysis worked out. What will this cost and what can we expect to get back from it?
Taking on the burden of implementing the idea. Not leaving management with the impression that this will mean a whole new workload for them.
Showing enthusiasm for and confidence in this.

Here is an overview of the two processes side by side.

Normal Problem Solving	Creative Problem Solving
State the problem	Explore the problem
	Think of beginning ideas
	Build on ideas
Go for solutions	Combine, modify, enhance
Kill off ideas	
Some talk, some don't	Everyone contributes
Ordinary solutions	New solutions
	Sell to management

How to Get the Team Going

Let's say you have identified a problem or opportunity that needs your team's attention. You want to generate high-voltage creative energy in the group and come up with a new approach. Here's how:

Before the Meeting

1. **Recruit the right people.** Think about the composition of the creativity group. It might be the members of your existing team, but it might not. You may want to call on people outside the group. Include at least one person who doesn't know anything about the problem and won't be so close to it his or her thinking is restricted. Also, find someone who is offbeat, funny, or both. Keep the group small. Ten is too big. Five or six is about right.

2. **Find the right atmosphere**—a location that is conducive to new thoughts. Borrowing the boardroom, with its dark paneling and oil paintings of glowering past chairmen, is not good. Off-site is best, even a hotel conference room. It may look like a company conference room, but there is something stimulating about being in a new environment.

3. **Prepare the group.** Before your meeting, send out an agenda with a statement of the problem and what you hope to accomplish in the meeting. Attach a copy of the Creativity Checklist at the end of the chapter and ask the group to review it.

When You Meet

4. **Set the group free.** The first thing to do when you begin your session is to ask the participants to figure out how they will work together creatively and stay away from those actions that constrict creative thinking. Write their ideas on a chart, post it on the wall, and hold individual members of the group to their own guidelines. Here's an example from a group I worked with recently.

HOW WE WILL HELP OURSELVES
THINK CREATIVELY

We will:

Always say two good things about an idea before criticizing it.

Encourage quieter people to contribute.

Not let any one person dominate the meeting.

Encourage all sorts of bizarre off-the-wall ideas.

Relax and be playful. No one is going to see the original ideas.

Remember new ideas always have flaws.
That doesn't make them bad ideas.

Keep working till we find a new solution.

5. Use creativity catalysts. Here are a few that are sure to stimulate new ideas:

Analogies. Think of something your problem is like. Then think of what insights or solutions the analogy suggests.
Problem: One company division is losing customers at an alarming rate.
Analogy: It's like rats fleeing a sinking ship.

What does this suggest? Rats are leaving because they don't want to drown. Water is a hostile environment. Aha! Is there something in the way the division works with customers that makes it a hostile environment? Reengineering has cut the size of the technical staff, therefore service has suffered. Customers don't want to buy if they can't get product serviced. So they are going with other manufacturers. The rats.
Solution? Add more staff is the easy one. But it may not really be a new solution—or even possible. Hey! How about dealing with the hostile environment? It wouldn't be hostile if we could teach the rats to swim. How about teaching the customers to fix many of their own problems?

Problem: Getting the work done with reduced staff.
Analogy: It is like trying to push a boulder uphill.

What does that suggest? Boulders are heavy and hard to move. You can't move them by yourself. Get a bulldozer. Move it with a machine.

Are there machines that can do some of our work? Computers. What if we get a computer nerd to design some software for us?

Free association. Put the problem aside for the moment. Pick a word at random—from the dictionary, from a newspaper headline, or from names of objects inside or outside the building. Then ask the group, "What does this make you think of?" List any words they come up with. Anything, unrelated, pop-into-the-mind words are fine. Silly, raunchy, or shocking words are best, as in this real-life example.

Problem: The marketing and production people are at each others' throats all the time, and teamwork is nil. This is affecting the company's ability to get the right product to the customer on time.

Free association: From a list of newspaper headlines, team members decided to use "finger-pointing." The word association went like this:

Finger-pointing
Giving the finger
Fickle finger of fate
Karma
KamaSutra
Positions
Contortionist
Backache
Massage
Relaxation
Sleep
Dream
Nightmare

The group was asked to asked to go down the list and identify a word that grabbed it the most. After much discussion, kidding, and laughter, group members picked "contortionist," which they used as a spring-board to brainstorm ideas: "ties in a knot," "bent like a pretzel," and so on, until someone came up with "twist." This led to the idea of having marketing and production people twist to take each other's places. That was not possible on the job, but it was in the protected environment of a workshop.

And that's what was done. Marketing people became production people and were challenged to come up with production plans that would better meet marketing's needs, and a process for better teamwork with marketing. Production people did the same, playing marketing people. Each group had a reality checker from the department it was playing—but the RC could speak only if asked.

After the session, the groups got back together with senior management present and gave their reports. Again there was much laughter and kidding, but many good ideas came out. A cross-functional team was formed to put together action plans, and the teamwork between the two departments is much improved, and customers are happier. All from the finger.

A variation on this is:

Looking for clues everywhere. Suppose your team is working on how to rebuild loyalty in an organization that had been trashed with downsizing. How do you get the folks who survived the cut to recover?

Ask the team to go outside and wander around for five minutes and remember what they see out there.

"What did you see?"

"I saw a tree."

"How is a tree like this problem?"

"Well, the trunk is like the company with resources flowing up through it, and all the branches and leaves are like the departments and people."

"And how does the tree build loyalty?"

"Well, everybody is attached and they need the tree for food. But—wait—in the fall, the leaves change color and drop off."

"Are the leaves disloyal?"

"No, it's just part of the natural process. Maybe that tells us that employees aren't attached to the company forever. And it's not disloyalty, just part of the process. Maybe we shouldn't worry about loyalty. Maybe that isn't even the problem. Maybe we should just concentrate on keeping them 'well fed' when they are attached, and then let them go. Maybe we can't expect loyalty anymore."

"Let's think about ways to keep our people 'well fed.' "

This is an example of a long leap of imagination. But that's what creativity is all about, and outside clues help. There are clues everywhere. Steal ideas from any source—nature seems to be a rich one. Most "new" ideas are modifications/combinations/alterations of existing ideas. So feel free to grab one anyplace you can.

New perspective. Look at the ideas the team has generated. Can individual ideas be reversed, turned upside down, made bigger or smaller, painted a new color, looked at from inside out, raised, lowered, made of a new material, combined, eliminated, used for something else? Challenge the team to look at its ideas in new ways.

A competitor has just announced a new department to handle customer complaints. "Our goal is to eliminate complaints altogether" is what it advertises.

This is powerful stuff, and your team struggles with ideas on how to eliminate complaints until one member suggests, "What if we turned it around and increased complaints?"

That leads to ideas about the company wanting to hear about every problem, no matter how slight, and not letting any kind of dissatisfaction go unaddressed. The team hits on the following approach: "We love complaints! Chances are, you'll never have a problem with our product, but if you do, we want to hear about it, so we can fix it right away."

Into the molasses. Assemble all the information you can find about the problem or similar problems—memos, articles, books, ideas, past attempts to solve it, committee minutes, and so on, and have everyone review all of it. Then get them together and stack all the stuff up in front of them. Ask them to jump into the pile (mentally, of course) and start going through it as quickly as possible. Have large Post-it notepads handy, and as team members think of ideas or as trends become apparent, they should write key words, rip off the notes, and stick them on the wall. When everyone is done, look at the wall of notes. Move them around, combine them, build off them. Come up with a solution.

Take a vacation. Okay, you are stumped. Ideas are running dry and you aren't getting anywhere. Time for the team to take a vacation, even a half hour one. Stop work on the problem and get away. Not just a coffee break—try to immerse the team in some sort of stimulating environment. Turn on a soap opera, walk in the park, go to a good restaurant or to a museum. Read a short story. Later, when you come back to the problem, chances are you will have a creative new answer to it. Vacations work wonders—I don't know why, but they do.

Creativity Checklist

Here is a checklist you can give to team members to help them open up their own personal creativity. If each team member follows the checklist, the creativity of the team will increase dramatically.

CREATIVITY CHECKLIST

Team Members' Guide for Contributing to the Creativity of the Group

We are trying to find innovative new solutions. This checklist outlines your role as a team member in the creative problem-solving process.

☐ **Expect to be creative:** Before the session begins, tell yourself, "I will find new solutions." Make a commitment to thinking creatively. If you start out thinking you will be creative, you will have a much better chance of finding new ideas.

☐ **Help explore the problem.** When you see the problem, you may be tempted to go for solutions right away, but in this process you should hold off until the session leader tells you, so you and the team can learn more about the problem and come up with ideas.

☐ **Join in generating beginning ideas.** When you understand the problem, join your teammates in coming up with beginning ideas.

- Come out with any ideas that pop into your head at this point. They won't be perfect, but that doesn't matter.
- Still don't go for solutions. Have fun coming up with weird ideas.
- Go for quantity. Linus Pauling said, "The best way to have a good idea is to have lots of ideas." The more the better.
- Respect all your teammates' ideas: Don't evaluate any of them now. New ideas are flawed, but leave them alone. They will lead to better ideas as you go along. *Ideas are only ideas,* and you don't have to deal with each one as it comes up.
- Go for the outrageous. Wacko ideas are good because they stimulate energy and laughter in the group.
- Don't be limited by the present order of things. Think outside the box. Deliberately look for the unconventional and the untried.
- Expect uncertainty. New ideas create anxiety at first. "Suppose the boss walks in and sees these flip charts. He'd think we're nuts." As you become used to the process, your anxiety will disappear.

☐ **Play with ideas: build, combine, modify, enhance.** After the team has come up with a wide range of ideas, help the group pick the most exciting ones, then play with them to get more ideas and to make them stronger. Your team leader will show you how.

☐ **Find a solution.** End up with an idea that:

Is new.
Is workable.
Solves the problem.
Management will buy into.

☐ **Sell to management.** Work with the team to build strategies for getting buy-in.

> *"The gift of fantasy has meant more to me than my talent for absorbing positive knowledge."*   —Albert Einstein

---

SBI: Ideas are only ideas. You don't have to deal with each one as soon as it is expressed. New ideas have faults, but they often lead to better ideas—if they are allowed to hang around. Get your team used to that concept and you will be on the way to finding creative solutions.

CUSTOMER SKILLS

18

WIN-WIN FANTASIES

How to Get Things to Come Out the Way You Want

Tonya's Rule: If at first you don't succeed, whack 'em.

Every day you go to work hoping things will come out your way. You want projects to fall in line, obstacles and problems to disappear, and people to behave sensibly—just like you do.

It's not going to happen.

You just plain don't get everything you want in life. But every day you try.

Type A Influencing

There are two main ways to guide people and events. One is Type A Influencing, which is an adversarial, demanding, confrontational, winning-is-everything approach guaranteed to raise everyone's blood pressure—this is good old samurai-style negotiating.

It is also called "win-lose." It has dominated union-management negotiating over the years, creating such satisfying outcomes as the Homestead massacre and the baseball strike. It is also the accepted style in the courtroom today, where winning is everything and you must come out with the decision in your favor. The same is true in many political campaigns: "As your candidate, I'm headed for sainthood while my opponent is a stupid, lazy, sexual harassing thief."

We are raised to win. Winning is everything; coming in second sucks. What are the Buffalo Bills known for? Being so good they almost won it all four years in a row? No! They are known for losing the Super

Bowl four times. It is natural to carry this competitive, got-to-win attitude into any situation and turn it into Type A negotiation. Whether you are discussing a minor procedure change with someone from another department or the terms of a major sale with a customer, your first desire is to win, and you feel defeated if you don't get everything your way. At this level, when you and the other party are trying to get it all, your needs are opposite, there is little trust, and each of you is trying to exercise power over the other.

Type A Influencing may have its place, but it has many negative consequences: destroyed relationships, hardened no-give positions, and angry discussions that go on forever with nothing resolved. That's not the way Type A always works, but it does often.

Type B Influencing

Type B Influencing is gentler, less confrontational, and more cooperative. It involves trying to find a common objective and building on areas of agreement rather than concentrating on differences. It moves from wielding power to sharing power. It assumes there is something for everyone in any situation.

In Type B Influencing, the emphasis shifts from satisfying your own needs to finding ways to meet everyone's needs. This turns the discussion into more of a teamwork session than an adversarial one.

It is the type of influencing that builds and preserves long-term relationships while still achieving goals—or most of them.

Relations between retail buyers and suppliers are often built on Type A negotiating. But when JCPenney closed its automotive division, a billion-dollar business the company had built over twenty years, suppliers flew in to say "Thanks" and "Good-bye" to buyers. They did this because of good relationships, not because there was anything in it for them. There wasn't.

JCPenney was always demanding, always trying to wring out all unnecessary costs, but was always fair to deal with. Penney's understood that suppliers were its lifeblood, and that if they didn't succeed the company wouldn't, either—and it was careful to consider suppliers' needs.

Type B does not mean rolling over for anyone. It does not mean giving in or giving up. It means working together to find a solution that is satisfactory to both parties, making the pie bigger instead of squabbling over who gets the biggest piece. Everyone's needs are considered, trust is high, and power is shared.

Some call this "win-win." Sounds good; everybody loves a happy ending. You go in, talk it over in a civilized way, and everyone comes out with a prize. In actual practice there isn't a lot of win-win, because to be successful in influencing, you have to give up something. It's more like "win some–lose some."

You use your influencing skills every day: making a sale to a customer, reaching an agreement with a supplier, selling ideas to others in the company, getting support from your boss, and getting cooperation from your people. You use influencing in your private life, too: buying a car or a house, getting an upgrade on a plane, getting a credit card error corrected, or finding a new job. Let's see how Type B Influencing can help.

Ten Rules of Type B Influencing

1. **Think problem solving.** Every discussion is a chance for you and the other party to make things better for yourselves. Think of your discussion as a problem-solving session rather than one in which somebody gains and somebody loses, no matter that the other party doesn't see it this way. Type B Influencing is contagious, and once the other party finds you want to be reasonable, without being a patsy, they will move in your direction.

2. **Emphasize partnering and teamwork.** Identify, ahead of time, some common ground. You both may be after the same end result, whether it be making a profit, getting a fair deal, or building the business. It is just a matter of teaming up to agree on how to get there. When you take a longer view of what you both are trying to achieve, you have a better chance of being constructive rather than combative.

3. **Emphasize benefits.** The other party will be more influenced to buy your product, service, or idea if they see there is some benefit in it for them.

4. **Have a fallback.** Think of alternate options in every influencing situation. If you have only one option, you want it too much and may give away too much to get it.

Suppose you have your heart set on a trip to Wilmington, when the boss tells you she's taking you off that project and it won't be necessary to go. You can spell out all the reasons you should go, show how you can't do your other projects if you don't go to Wilmington, and if that fails, beg and plead. The boss will be very understanding but firm and tell you no. You have lost. Or you can quickly think of alternatives: You can ask to be put on another team that has business in Wilmington, or you can go to Topeka instead.

5. Line up your ducks. Support your position. Show that:

People the other party respects like your product, service, or idea and are willing to give testimonials.
You are expert in the area you are proposing, so the other party can have confidence in your opinion.
Similar proposals have turned out to be safe, without much risk.
Similar proposals have had major benefits for all involved.

6. Get the other party to invest time. The more time the other party spends in discussing and considering your proposal, the better chance you have of getting agreement. Time invested is commitment.

7. Keep emphasizing what you have in common. When things get tough, keep coming back to your common ground, and emphasize—for instance—your mutual need to serve the customer.

8. Don't issue ultimatums. An ultimatum has no place in Type B Influencing, so don't take a hard position as to what will happen if you don't get your way.

"If I don't get that Wilmington trip, I'll quit."
"Okay, fine."
"What I meant to say was . . ."

9. Watch the nuances—verbal and nonverbal clues. "I just thought of this" may precede something important the other person has had in mind all along. "To be very honest with you" may introduce something less than truthful, if not an outright lie. Leaning forward can indicate real interest; looking at a watch or out the window, not.

10. Protect everyone's self-esteem. There are no winners and losers. This is not the heavyweight championship, it is a business process. Also, this is not personal. It is about work. Or should be.

The Type B Influencing Process

Steps in the process are:

1. Plan and anticipate.
2. Open the discussion.
3. Problem solve.
4. Agree.
5. Strengthen the relationship.

1. Plan and anticipate. Always prepare before you sit down with the other party. Be sure you can state your proposal clearly and back it up with benefits for the other party. Practice out loud if you want to be extra confident.

Think of what the other party's overall needs are, how this issue relates to them and can help meet them. Then think of possible areas of agreement, how you can convince the other party that your needs and theirs are really the same.

Try to determine what the other party's demands and objections will be. Figure out how you will address them.

2. Open the discussion.

Set the tone. Always keep your end of the discussion on a high plane. Tell the other party you want to problem solve so everybody comes out better.

State your proposal. Tell the other party what it is you would like, backed up by why it will benefit both of you.

State your reasons. Don't come out with a proposal without stating the reasons for it. These should include benefits to the other party. Give one or two strong reasons and let it go at that. If you state a whole laundry list, the other party may attack the weakest.

Hold off the attack. When the other party makes a counterproposal, or flat-out rejects your proposal, use jujitsu. Go in the direction of the force. Acknowledge the other party's demands, showing you understand (but don't necessarily agree), restate what the other party said, and ask questions about it to clarify. Probe for the outcome behind it. Don't immediately go on the attack with another counterproposal.

If you feel disappointed by the counterproposal or denial, or if you are confused by it, say so. Then ask the other party to help you understand why he or she has taken that position.

Often the first response the other party makes is not the whole story, and you have to use digging questions to find out what is real.

"I can't work with that. Five days is too slow. I need twenty-four-hour delivery."

"You don't want to keep inventory on hand. You'd like us to get it to you as you need it?"

"Yes."

"We could promise you that, but it might add to the cost of the product. Is there any leeway in that twenty-four hours?"

"Well, I could stretch it to forty-eight in some cases."

"So forty-eight hours is your absolute limit?"

"With my present supplier, sometimes I don't get product for two weeks. I have to keep a warehouse full to cover myself."

"So you want it faster than two weeks."

"Much faster."

"Suppose I was able to guarantee you product in four days, at no extra cost?"

"That would be all right, as long as you could guarantee it."

3. Problem solve.

Ask lots of questions. The more you can get the other party to talk, the more you will find out about their needs, the more you will gain their respect by being interested in their viewpoint, and the more involved they will become.

Use silence. Give the other party a chance. Ask a question and shut up. After the other party offers an answer, sit there and stare like a spotted owl. He or she may come up with even more information, some of it revealing.

Come back to common ground. Take every opportunity to show that your needs are the same, even if they seem to be wildly different. Find as many areas of agreement as you can, and get them decided.

For instance, you and a customer are far apart on price and technical support. But still your overall needs complement each other: "You need components to build your products; we have to sell components to stay in business. Somewhere in there is a way we can work together to accomplish what we need to do."

Generate alternatives. Your two initial positions are just two of many possible ways to get to a common goal. In the example above, alternatives might be to:

- Redesign components at a lower price.
- Implement compatible systems so the customer can reduce inventory.
- Provide training for the customer in new inventory-management methods.

Get the other party involved in the spirit of brainstorming and coming up with new solutions.

Avoid raising red flags. When the going gets tough, keep a lid on and don't say things like "That's crazy," "You aren't being reasonable," or "You're dumb as a dinosaur." None of those is going to help you much. Instead of accusing, show what the situation is doing to you: "I'm having trouble understanding this" rather than "You aren't making this clear." Nobody can argue with the way you feel.

4. **Agree.** Defer any areas that are impossible to agree on, and agree on those that you can. Finding even a few areas of agreement sets a positive tone and helps keep the discussion on a Type B level. If you feel you are getting into a Type A situation, say so. It is okay to share your feelings and perceptions: "My sense of it is you aren't happy with this direction" or "I'm concerned because we're getting out of the problem-solving mode."

When the other party makes concessions, support them by saying that it is the right thing to do.

Sum up. Test your understanding and summarize now and then: "What I hear you saying is . . ." or "So far we have agreed to . . ." Take notes and write them up right away, especially those that deal with what was agreed on.

Reach overall agreement. Summarize the final agreement and ask the other party if you have stated it correctly.

5. Strengthen the relationship.

End on a positive note. Always leave the discussion on a high, even if you have drawn blood. Acknowledge your points of agreement, and that you made progress. If you didn't, tell the other party, "You know how to stand up for what you need, and I respect that. I hope we can build on this to work together as a team in the future."

Caveat Influencer

All right, let's say you are sitting down to talk about a sale. You may be trying to use Type B, while the other party is going for Type A. Here are some hardball tactics and what they mean.

1. Outrageous counteroffer. You have quoted a unit price of $10 to your customer. Your customer pretends to be very upset or disappointed, and says, "We couldn't possibly pay more than five."

What the outrageous offer means. The customer is testing to see how elastic your offer is. Both of you know there is no chance you will sell at $5, but the customer wants to see if there is room between $5 and $10 to talk. And how much room there is.

How to handle. Say you understand what the customer wants. Explain you can't sell product at below cost. Hold firm with $10 (at least for now), and try to move the discussion away from price. Explain the high quality of the product, the service that goes with it, terms, delivery—all the parts of value involved.

2. The big concession. After much discussion, the customer says, "Okay, okay, we might be able to go seven-fifty."

What the big concession means. This isn't anywhere near the price you want to get, but it is a concession of *half the difference* in your offers. That is a lot. It means that the customer has a lot of flexibility in what they will pay and might be willing to concede more.

How to handle: Tell the customer that $7.50 is much more realistic, but that you still are packing too much value into your product to sell it at that price. Ask the customer how the product will be used, resold, promoted, and so on, listening for common needs that you can reinforce. "I know you are concerned about service. Let me tell you about our warranty."

Incidentally, it helps if you can stall around until the other party makes the first concession. This gives you important information as to how flexible the other party is.

3. Apples and oranges. Your customer says, "Capitulation Corporation is selling these at seven dollars."

What apples and oranges means. The customer has gotten a price quote on something, but it may not be at all the same product you are selling. Capitulation Corporation might have quoted a price on a lower-grade item, or may not provide the support (service, warrantee) that you do.

How to handle: Ask the customer to show you the specs on the other product and explain why you are talking apples and oranges. Restate your customer's need for quality and service and how you can provide that.

4. Time is up. The customer says, "I have to have an answer by tomorrow or I am going with Capitulation Corporation."

What time is up means: The customer is setting a tight deadline in the hope that you will make a big concession at the last minute to get the sale. Maybe the customer has no intention of going with Capitulation Corporation, but hopes to get you to knock off some bucks.

How to handle: Try again to move the customer off price, then wait until the eleventh hour. You may want to make some price concession, but if you do, make it small. "I'll tell you what we will do, we'll sell for nine-fifty and give you some co-op money for advertising."

5. I'll ask the boss. The customer says, "I'll have to ask the boss for approval."

What ask the boss means: The customer is not negotiating for himself or herself—or at least is making it seem that way. It's much easier to negotiate if someone else is the decision maker: "The boss would feel a lot better about this if I can tell him he is saving a little more money. If you could come down another dollar, I think he'd go for it."

How to handle: Reemphasize your customer's need for the kind of quality and service you can provide. Offer to make a presentation directly to the boss.

6. **This is ridiculous** and there's no sense talking anymore. The customer seems very angry and impatient with the whole thing.

What "this is ridiculous" means: The customer may be putting on some dramatics to see if you can be shaken or intimidated into giving concessions. On the other hand, the customer may really be angry and impatient.

How to handle: Ask the customer why he or she feels that way. Give the customer a chance to vent. Then ask, "Where do you think we should go from here?"

> **SBI:** Always look for mutual needs so you and the other party can concentrate on areas of agreement rather than on differences.

INFLUENCING CHECKLIST

1. Plan and Anticipate

- ❑ Prepare and practice.
- ❑ Determine what the other party's needs may be.
- ❑ Think of areas of possible agreement.
- ❑ Anticipate demands and objections and how to handle.
- ❑ Think of benefits to the other party.

2. Open the Discussion

- ❑ Set a Type B tone.
- ❑ State your proposal.
- ❑ State your reasons, benefits to the other party.
- ❑ Hold off the attack.

3. Problem Solve

- ❑ Ask lots of questions.
- ❑ Use silence.
- ❑ Come back to common ground.
- ❑ Generate alternatives.
- ❑ Avoid raising red flags.

4. Agree

- ❑ Agree on what you can.
- ❑ Sum up.
- ❑ Reach overall agreement.

5. Strengthen the Relationship

- ❑ End on a positive note.

19

THE CUSTOMER IS *ALMOST* RIGHT

How to Win by Focusing on the Customer

"Management squawks about service all the time, but you wouldn't catch a real manager anywhere near a customer if his or her life depended on it. Some top executives don't even talk with the people in their organizations, much less the rabble out there that buys from them."

—Mary Chandler, VP of Customer Service
Programs, Imperial Imports International

Why Customers Suddenly Became Important

Everybody is nuts about customers today, but it wasn't always that way. For most of our business history, customers were seen as minor annoyances who had to be persuaded to buy what the company was producing.

But in the 1970s and 1980s global competition heated up at the same time customers were becoming more sophisticated and demanding, and suddenly everyone discovered customers. It's as if one day an executive came out of an office, looked around (note the eyebrows shooting up), and ran back in shouting, "There are customers out there! There are customers out there!" Word got around pretty fast, and people began to think that if there *are* customers, they must be important to business. Consultants made millions telling companies to pay attention to customers, and the money is still rolling in because— even after all the books, the speeches, and the training programs— companies are still struggling to get it right.

A sign of that struggle is that terms for customer service have risen in grandeur much faster than service itself has. "Customer service" became "customer satisfaction," which in turn evolved into "customer delight." Today, even delight isn't enough. Your company must be "customer intimate."

After putting customers under the microscope for a couple of decades, we have learned some things about them. One is that it is important to keep customers. It is so costly to get new customers that decreasing customer defections by 5 percent, according to studies by Bain & Company, can increase profits by 25 to 95 percent! An important byproduct: Keeping old customers increases job satisfaction among employees.

On the flip side, companies are learning that keeping their own employees helps them keep customers. Long-term employees give customers a stable base of contact with the company, allies who know them and recognize their special needs.

The Seven *Deadly* Sins of Customer Service

A few years ago, Jim Nordstrom of the Nordstrom Department Store family was the keynote speaker at a major convention. His topic was customer service—which is a natural, since Nordstrom's is widely regarded as the best in the business. They really know how to delight their customers.

He began his talk with this opening grabber: "Most of retailing," he said, "is pretty simple. The suppliers are out there, and we can get exciting merchandise. The financing is there, and we can build beautiful stores. But customer service . . . that's a son of a bitch!"

If you doubt that it is, try this. Next time you are with some friends, tell a story about some lousy customer service you experienced lately. They will be sitting on the edges of their chairs, not because they are enchanted with your tale but because they can't wait to tell their own customer service horror stories!

It is amazing that we can still talk about lousy service. Almost everyone recognizes that good customer service is the key to gaining a competitive edge, and a company that provides just a little better service than its competitors has a big advantage.

Companies work hard to improve service: CEOs talk about it endlessly, there are training classes, awards, and articles in the company newsletter—and yet, excellent customer service remains elusive. Why is customer service so tough, and why, after all the attention we have paid to it for twenty years, does it still leave a lot to be desired? Why did the American Customer Satisfaction Index, calculated by the University of Michigan and the American Society for Quality Control, actually decline from 1994 to 1995?

The problem is, even with all the honest efforts to improve service, many companies are neglecting key actions necessary to make customer service work, and worse yet, are unwittingly doing other things that actually *prevent* them from giving top-notch service. They are committing the Seven Deadly Sins of Customer Service:

1. Putting customer-contact people in the cellar. Paying them the lowest rate and putting them at the lowest level in the organization.
2. Not having standards for customer-contact people. ("Oh, you want me to get off the phone and wait on the customers?")
3. Not empowering them to make decisions for customers, and not training them in problem solving and other customer service skills.
4. Not insisting that management get involved with customers and lead by example.
5. Not asking customers what they want.
6. Allowing company procedures to get in the way of good service.
7. Measuring service levels against competitors rather than against what they could be, thereby settling for "good enough."

How many of these is your company guilty of? Maybe a lot of them; most companies are.

Not too long ago I was working with a customer service team charged with corporatewide service improvement. At our first meeting we decided the best way to start was to list those companies that give great service, then go out and visit them to find out what they do. Everyone thought that was a great idea. Then we sat and stared at each other.

No one could think of any!

Finally, we came up with three: Disney World, Nordstrom's, and Ritz Carlton. The fact that all but a handful of companies, despite herculean efforts, can't fix service, shows what a difficult job it is.

Connecting with Customers

As you go through the list below, keep in mind that everyone has customers. Even if you don't work directly with outside customers, you have customers within the organization. In fact, every time I use the word *customer*, I am talking about your internal as well as external customers.

Here are nine ways to build relationships with customers and increase your value to your employer.

1. Talk with Your Customers

Whether they are internal or external customers, you should talk with them. Set aside a time each week to sit down with a customer and talk about your relationship—ask the customer how well you are meeting his or her needs now, and how you could do it better. You don't need permission to do this. It doesn't cost anything except a little time. Do it.

Face-to-face is the best way to find out what is going on. Written surveys help some, but they are limited because there's no chance to dig into specific responses and find out what is really on the customer's mind. Focus groups are also of some value, but they are influenced by all the group dynamics of meetings and by the fact that they are focus groups to begin with.

But if you sit down one-on-one with a customer, set a positive we-are-in-this-together tone, ask the right questions, and accept criticism gracefully, you can find out a lot.

Some of it may be surprising. In a major study done for the retailing industry a few years ago, customers were asked what they wanted most. Number one turned out to be "Somebody to say hello." When customers come into a busy store, they want a salesperson to acknowledge they are there so they have some hope of being waited on.

In the meantime, retailers were busy developing sophisticated training programs on how to overcome objections and how to close the sale. They should have been training salespeople to say hello.

Now that almost everyone believes listening to customers is a good thing, a few people are advocating doing just the opposite. A handful of consultants and companies are saying customers don't know what they want, and if you listen to them you'll only make minor changes to what now exists and not come through with major innovative breakthroughs. If you do listen, you may get answers that are misleading. Most customers who stop buying from a company say they were satisfied or very satisfied with the company they bagged. If they were so satisfied, why did they leave? Maybe simple surveys get simple answers. What did you say the last time a waiter asked, "How is everything?"

You will have to decide what works best for you, but I'll tell you one thing, customers can tell you a lot if you ask the right questions. And that includes using digging questions to explore deeper than the first answer.

> *"We left to go with Amalgamated Assault Corporation because they gave us a better price."*
> *"That was the only reason?"*
> *"That's about it."*
> *"Did you talk with our sales rep about pricing?"*
> *"Many times."*
> *"And?"*
> *"Well, I think he was coming up with a new arrangement, but he was pretty arrogant about it."*
> *"Arrogant? How so?"*
> *"Well, he always made it seem like we were pretty stupid not buying your products."*
> *"So, you didn't get along well with that rep?"*
> *"Not at all. I really didn't like him."*

2. Treat Customers as They Want to Be Treated

You have to know your customers pretty well in today's diverse world. They are all different from one another and have a variety of needs. You can't assume that what you think of as good service is what your customers are looking for; nor can you be sure, just because one group of customers is happy with your service, that all of them are. As was outlined in number 1 above, you have to talk with them to find out.

3. Think of Your Customers and Yourself as a Team

Customers can be annoying, unreasonable, and balky. They want things faster, better, and cheaper, and make impossible demands—no wonder you sometimes think of them as adversaries. But they are still customers. They are part of a continuous flow that involves your suppliers, your company, and them—part of a team working to get products and services moving through the pipeline to the end user. When you think of customers as part of your team, you can think of ways to work together to lower costs, speed delivery, target precise needs, and much more.

Some companies are now partnering on cost-reduction projects with customers and sharing savings and overrun expenses. Others are teaming their service people with those of the customer to reduce downtime on equipment. Still others are putting their people on assignment with a customer to get a better understanding of that customer. Many are now developing and linking compatible computer systems.

Some are including customers on company teams, which makes a lot of sense. They spend a lot of team energy finding ways to serve the customer better—why not involve the customers, who are directly affected?

A good place to start is with the Customer Teamwork Questionnaire. Sit down with one customer at a time and use the questionnaire to see how well you are doing as a team. Each of you should fill out a copy of the questionnaire beforehand, and then discuss each question, concentrating on those questions where there is a wide difference in ratings and those where ratings are low. This should open up a candid discussion about your relationship and ways to improve it. (This works best if you have a limited number of customers, or major customers that warrant lots of attention.)

CUSTOMER TEAMWORK QUESTIONNAIRE

1. Overall, how well do you understand each other's business?

5	4	3	2	1
Very Well		Fairly Well		Not Well

2. How openly can you discuss problems together?

5	4	3	2	1
Very Openly		Fairly Openly		Not Openly

3. How well do you work together to find solutions to problems?

5	4	3	2	1
Very Well		Fairly Well		Not Well

4. To what extent do you feel a spirit of cooperation and teamwork in working together?

5	4	3	2	1
To a Great Extent		Somewhat		Not Much at All

5. How good are you at bringing disagreement out in the open and discussing it together constructively?

5	4	3	2	1
Very Good		Fairly Good		Not Good

6. How well do you listen to each other?

5	4	3	2	1
Carefully		Pretty Well		Don't Listen

7. What is your attitude toward each other?

5	4	3	2	1
Like Working Together		So-so		Hard to Do Business With

8. How well do you exchange product and other information?

5	4	3	2	1
Very Well		Fairly Well		Not Very Well

9. How much empathy do you feel toward each other?

5	4	3	2	1
A Great Deal		Some		Not Much

10. How well do you solve problems together?

5	4	3	2	1
Very Well		Reasonably Well		We Don't

11. How well do you come up with new ideas together?

5	4	3	2	1
Come Up with Many		Find Some		Kill Ideas Off Fast

12. How often do you find ways to improve teamwork?

5	4	3	2	1
Very Often		Fairly Often		Not Often

13. How well does the company satisfy needs for quality?

5	4	3	2	1
Very Well		Pretty Well		Could Be a Lot Better

14. How well does the company satisfy needs for service?

5	4	3	2	1
Very Well		Reasonably Well		Not Well

15. How well does the company satisfy needs for value?

5	4	3	2	1
Very Well		Fairly Well		A Long Way to Go

16. Overall, how well do you work together as a team?

5	4	3	2	1
Very Well		Fairly Well		Not Well

Scoring:

16–32	Mud wrestling.
33–48	You'll have to struggle to become a team.
49–64	On the right track. Chance to become a great team.
65–80	Model of great customer teamwork.

Questions to answer together:

Where do we work together the best? What is our greatest strength as a team?

_____

_____

_____

_____

What is our greatest opportunity to improve our teamwork?

_____

_____

_____

_____

What specifically should we do?

_____

_____

_____

_____

4. Problem Solve

Every customer has problems. These may be problems with you or within the customer's own company. Your highest service to customers can be helping them solve problems, and doing that can give you an extra edge over competitors, helping you build a long-term relationship with customers.

Maybe there is some expertise in your company you can offer the customer. For instance, if you have advanced systems capabilities, and your customer is just starting to automate, get your MIS people to assist the customer.

There are times when, in spite of your best efforts, you won't be able to address the customer's need at all. Take yourself out of the action and try to steer the customer to someone who can meet the need. You will leave the customer with a high opinion of you.

Involve your customers in your own problem-solving sessions.

5. Set the Example

A major department store, in the middle of a customer service improvement campaign, held early-morning training sessions for its salespeople. Management put on a good show and ran the sessions with energy and charm, and salespeople clearly were impressed with them. It was a key day to run these, because it was the kickoff of a big sale, when the store would be very busy.

Sure enough, right after the session, the store opened and customers poured in. They filled the departments, and salesclerks were frantically trying to greet them, help them with merchandise, and generally do all those things they had been reminded of in the training session.

Then the management team, still carrying the training materials, walked onto the floor, excused its way through mobs of customers, and disappeared into the office area without so much as offering to help one customer!

What message did that give to the salesclerks? It was very clear: Customer service might be important, but it wasn't important enough for management to waste its time on, so it couldn't be *very* important. Any inspiration that might have come from the training session was completely lost by management's failure to set the example.

Another "I Can't Believe It" award goes to managers who tell employees to use "please" and "thank you" when they talk to customers, but then never say "please" and "thank you" to the employees. Nancy Friedman of the Telephone Doctor says she hears that frequently from employees.

These are clearly situations in which management feels it is somehow exempt from the gritty work of doing what it asks employees to do.

And when management leads by going in the opposite direction . . . well, it's not too hard to figure out what happens.

You may not even manage a group of people, but that doesn't mean you can't lead by example. The way you work with customers will be noticed by everyone around you and can serve as a model for everyone in your area.

6. Get Rid of Roadblocks

Sometimes, in working hard to make your own area run as well as possible, you may inadvertently establish policies or procedures that hinder good customer service. Here's an example:

I was working with a client company on improving customer service. We looked at every aspect of service, and one source of customer irritation we found was the company check-cashing policy. The company cashed personal checks for customers at its branches but put them through a third-degree grilling before they would do it. We asked the accounting department about this procedure, and they told us they had to have it to protect the company against customers who bounced checks.

"How many customers bounce checks?"

"We don't know, but it happens, and it costs the company money."

"Can you find out how many?"

Well, the accounting department did some research and found the bad checks amounted to .5 percent of checks cashed. Half of 1 percent. So the company was alienating 99.5 percent of its check-cashing customers to protect itself from .5 percent.

The point is, the accountants were doing exactly what they were supposed to do—they were protecting the company's assets. But they hadn't thought that through to the effect it had on customers.

The moral of all this is for you to think of every decision you make and every action you take in terms of what it will do to the customer and the way that customer perceives the company as a place to do business.

Another client, a hotel and conference center, had a major roadblock to good service. Before any maintenance person could do repairs, he or she had to have a work order signed by the supervisor. The reason was so that work could be scheduled so that priority jobs could be done first. That makes sense, but what it did to customers didn't. A maintenance man would go to a room, for example, to fix a leaky faucet and the guest might say:

"Oh, the TV is acting up, too. Would you look at it?"

"I'm sorry, ma'am. I have to get a work order before I can do that."

"But you are right here. Why not just adjust it?"

"I'm sorry . . ."

The work-order procedure was never looked at with the customer in mind.

Go on a roadblock hunt to find out what you are doing to hinder customer service. At first you will probably think there are no roadblocks, but keep at it. You'll probably find plenty.

A few years ago I brought a bunch of regional executives from around the country together to do just that. They weren't happy about it: "We live and breathe customer service; we don't put up roadblocks." "Why would we shoot ourselves in the foot?"

"Well," I said, "as long as we're here, let's try to think of one or two roadblocks anyhow."

There was a little grumbling for a while. Then one fellow offered, "There might be one I can think of." I wrote his on a flip chart, and then another person volunteered a roadblock. Pretty soon things heated up, and by coffee break there were charts all over the room. In all, we thought of seventy roadblocks—this from a group who insisted there weren't any.

Once you have identified roadblocks, get to work and brainstorm ways to overcome them. This may take people from many departments—and maybe some customers—in a team effort, and it will take time. But your customers will value your work—and you.

7. Be Sure Your People Are Prepared and Empowered

Take a hard look at the people on your staff who deal directly with customers. Do they know what is expected? If not, get them together and develop standards, your own customer service guide. Do your people think answering the phone before the third ring is good service? Put it on the list. How about getting orders out the door in twenty-four hours? List that, too.

Are your people trained in customer service and problem-solving skills? Do they know how to deal with irate customers? If not, train them. Are they the lowest-level, lowest-ranking (lowest-esteem) people in the organization?

Maybe you can't change the organization or the pay, but you can help them understand the importance of their jobs to the company.

Here's an exercise that will help you and your people decide what the standards should be. Get them together and ask them to answer the questions below.

Describe a *good* customer service experience you had recently.

_____

_____

_____

_____

Now, list those things you liked about the experience. What made it a good customer service experience for you?

_____

_____

_____

_____

Ask your people to tell about their good customer service experiences and what they liked. Make a list of what they tell you. You should be able to come up with standards right from that list.

As a guide for you, here's a list that I compiled from participants who did the above exercise in dozens of customer service workshops.

I was greeted in a friendly way.
The salesperson smiled. I felt welcome.
They tried to solve my problem.
I returned merchandise with no hassle.
They seemed interested.
I felt they respected me.
They asked questions and listened.
They went the extra mile to do something for me.
I was surprised by getting much better service than I thought I
    would.
They couldn't help me, but actually found someone in another com-
    pany who could!

They followed up a couple of days later to see if everything was all right.
They tried to help, even though I knew it wasn't their job.
They dropped what they were doing to help me.
They knew their products and could answer my questions.

Once people agree on what customer service should be, and are trained in the skills needed to provide it, you can turn them loose to remedy customer problems and handle special requests on their own, without the delay of going up the line to get approval.

8. Follow Up and Take Action

Do what you say you will do. How many times have you been disappointed by someone who said he or she would do something for you and then did not?

A neighbor tells me in the past six months he has talked with a handyman, an electrician, and a building contractor about jobs around his house, some of them high-cost work. Each of the service people seemed eager for the work and told him they would get back with estimates. He has not heard from any of them!

Reliability is a precious commodity today, and customers value it—because they are surprised by it.

9. Never Quit

No matter how hard you work to understand customers, no matter how good you get at teaming up with them and removing roadblocks, no matter how much you improve service, you are never done. Competition keeps getting better, finding new ways to delight customers—and you'd better, too.

Again, this applies to internal as well as external customers. You may think you have no competition for internal customers, but with the amount of outsourcing going on today, everyone is vulnerable. If you are not a low-cost, quality producer with great concern for your customers, the company may just decide to go outside for your service, and if you lose your own company as a customer, there's not much left.

Continuous improvement should be your way of life. If things don't improve right away, stay with it. If they do, try harder to make them even better.

Part of not quitting is not settling. Tom Peters, in his book A *Passion for Excellence,* writes of a company president who commented on service by saying, "We're no worse than the rest of them."

There is some comfort for all of us in looking around and seeing that others have the same problems. Customer service meetings, if left to wander, often turn into anecdotal discussions of bad service. After a half hour or so of talking about customer service disasters, you can sit back and say, "See, we're not so bad after all." The problem is, comparing your service to the worst makes you comfortable with the mediocre.

You should be looking at the best and thinking of what you can do to be even better than they are.

As you work on continuous improvement, measure progress. Not in terms of number of hours of training provided, or number of new service ideas implemented, but in terms of results: customer retention loyalty, increase in sales per customer, and decrease in complaints.

One-on-One with Your Customer

Okay, now you are face-to-face with your customer, determined to give great service. There are a few common customer situations you should be able to handle—because chances are you will run across them at one point or another.

Your customer is irate. Something has gone really wrong. An important shipment hasn't arrived, a product has failed, or a promise hasn't been kept and your customer is steaming. Or maybe your customer just likes to beat up on people and you are handy. At any rate, you now have to deal with someone who is red-faced, with bulging neck veins and eyes of death. Not a pretty sight.

How to handle an irate customer:

1. Let the customer vent. In fact, encourage it—"Tell me what the problem is." The average angry person will start to run out of insults about your ancestry in a minute or two and calm down a bit. If you let him or her talk (or yell, as the case may be).
2. Ask questions. This shows that you are interested and that you are listening. What the customer wants is not so much to yell at you but to get the problem fixed. By asking about it, you give the customer hope that you might do something about it.

3. Show empathy: "I know how you feel. That happened to me last week." Empathy is a great healer.
4. Disarm the customer. Ask, "What would you like us to do?" "What would make this right for you?" When you ask the customer to give his or her solution to the problem, you are giving the customer some control, and the customer, surprisingly, may just come up with something more modest than what you had in mind. Remember, the customer expects you to be defensive and hard to deal with, and the customer is pumped for a fight. Ask this kind of question and watch the customer deflate right before your eyes.
5. Agree on a solution. Then make sure it is carried out.

You have to give your customer bad news. The order won't be ready on time, the product is back-ordered, the credit department has cut the customer off, a problem you thought was fixed has reoccurred. You come in, the customer smiles, you shake hands. Now, how do you drop the bomb and still keep the customer?

How to give bad news:

1. Be direct. State the bad news, clearly, up front.
2. Apologize. Tell the customer you are sorry, and mean it.
3. Emphasize the relationship: "Things have been going so well with us . . ."
4. Give the customer hope. Have a remedy in mind and suggest it to the customer. (Since the customer may be in a state of shock over the news, this is not a good situation in which to ask the customer to suggest a remedy.)

"John, I'm sorry to have to tell you this, but the credit department has put a hold on your last order, and we won't be able to ship it. I really feel bad about it, we've done so much business together, but you are way overdue on past invoices.

"I want to get this fixed as much as you do, and here's what I'd suggest. I'd like to have Fred from credit spend some time with you to work out a payment arrangement so that we can get back on track. When you show good faith in meeting the new payment schedule, I'm sure they will release your order. How does that sound?"

The customer asks for help, but the request is not something you have the skill to handle, and you have to refer the customer somewhere else inside (or outside) your organization.

How to help the customer:

1. Once a customer comes to you with a problem, take ownership of it, even though you can't fix it yourself.

   Tell the customer what you will do, *not* what he or she should do:

Don't say	Say Instead
I don't know.	I'll find out for you.
We can't do that.	Let's find a way to accomplish what you want.
You'll have to . . .	Here's what I'm going to do.
It's against policy.	Let's see if there's a way to do this.

2. Take positive action to move the problem along. Take on the burden of doing that yourself.
3. Find out who can help the customer, and put them in contact with each other.
4. Follow up to see that the problem is fixed to the customer's satisfaction.

The customer is unreasonable, annoying, and generally making your life miserable.

How to deal with a difficult customer:

1. Own the problem. You won't solve much by accusing the customer of bad behavior, so assume the problem is with you.
2. Tell the customer how you feel, avoiding any finger pointing: "Janet, I sense you aren't happy with our relationship, and that bothers me, because I want to work well with you and give you the kind of service you want. I must be doing something wrong, so I want you to tell me what I can do to correct it."
3. Listen to what the customer says. Janet may not even feel there is a problem, and may be surprised. Making life miserable may just be her way of being friendly. When she finds out how you feel, she may even adjust her behavior in the future.
4. Agree on a course of action, then follow it. It may not improve

the situation, but at least you have tried. If you can't improve the situation, live with it, or consider trading accounts with someone else who may be able to deal with her.

You've made a promise to the customer:

What to do about a promise:
1. Keep it. No excuses. Do what you say you will do.

Getting Yours: Your Responsibility as a Customer

What? Customers have a responsibility for good service, too?

Yes, you have a responsibility.

To yourself.

As a customer, you are an expert on customer service. You are also half of the service equation—the missing half if you aren't helping yourself get better service. Don't assume that if service is good, the company has the sole responsibility to maintain it, or if service is bad, the company has the sole responsibility to fix it. You should take an active role in the process to make sure you get the service you want. Consider this . . .

The best service is no service. Tired of unresponsive tellers, brokers who lose your money in the market, or travel agents who don't want to be bothered? If you can't change them, you can do without them. ATMs allow you to get cash without dealing with another person. With computer software, you can buy mutual funds and lose money all by yourself. With an on-line service you can hunt for reduced airfares, book your flight to Peoria, and set up your dream vacation on your own.

The nice thing about technology is that it pays attention, it doesn't close just when you are getting off work, and it doesn't tell you "That's not my job."

If you have to deal with actual people . . .

Don't make things worse. Remember, many frontline people are low paid, poorly trained, not motivated, and have little latitude or incentive to give good service.

And they have to deal with *you*. Dealing with people is not always the most fun thing to do. People can be unreasonable, illogical, impatient, and annoying. Some are neurotic or riddled with the pain of personal failure, and, having no one else to take it out on, use customer service people. Maybe there are just a few, but those are the ones customer-contact people remember, the ones who cause them to wake up screaming at three A.M.

Don't be one of the loonies who makes life a horror for people. Speak up when there's a problem or when you don't get what you want, but be careful to distinguish between what the customer service person can control and what he or she cannot.

State what you want, tell the service person if you are upset, but keep it on a businesslike basis and don't make it a personal issue. Sometimes a little kindness or empathy can work wonders. Recently I arrived at a hotel after a long flight feeling as if I needed a transfusion. The clerk at the counter informed me the hotel was overbooked, but since I had a confirmed reservation, they were going to put me in another hotel—maybe Ma and Pa's Cabins, ten miles out of town, for all I knew.

I told the clerk, "I'm not happy about this. I've been traveling all day, and I have meetings tomorrow morning here in this hotel." Then I stopped, smiled, and said, "Hey, I know it's not your fault. You've prob-ably been yelled at all evening for this. But I wish there was something you could do to help me." The clerk said, "Just a moment, sir," and marched into the back room where hotel clerks go to hide. A minute later she came out and said, "We are going to put you in a junior suite at the same rate." Was it something I said? I don't know, but I didn't have to go to Ma and Pa's.

Let your needs be known at the outset. State them early on so the seller knows. If you don't like airline food, don't complain—do some-thing. Call ahead and order a special meal. Most airlines have them. If you reserve a room with an ocean view, get the hotel to state that on the confirmation slip; when you get there and are given a room that faces a brick wall, you can show the desk what you were promised and demand it.

Be persistent. If you have a refund or adjustment coming, don't get shoved off. Be relentless in going after what is rightfully yours. Some-times it takes many letters and calls to get the job done. Each month *Condé Nast Traveler* prints tales of travelers who succeed in getting re-funds and exchanges from cruise lines, overseas merchants, rental car companies, and resorts—but only after many tries and much frustration. Keep at it.

Give praise for good service. Here's where you can encourage and recognize good service. Everyone likes recognition, and none of us get a whole lot of it. "Thanks for your help—you did more than I thought you could, and I appreciate it." "It's always fun doing business with you—I always look forward to it." "Thanks for the quick turnaround. It really helps." How many opportunities are there to give recognition? Probably more than you think. Look for chances and do it. Even write a letter once in a while.

Treat suppliers with special care.

- Suppliers are not second-class citizens just because they are the sellers and you are the buyer. You need them.
- Always return phone calls, as you would expect others to. Keep appointments and be on time.
- Try to be fair and use Type B Influencing.
- Build relationships. The better you work together, the more chance the vendor will respond to your special needs. When you begin working as a team you may be able to find ways, for instance, to bring costs down.
- Provide help and advice to suppliers whenever asked or when you see a need.
- Think about this, in case you get in trouble where you are. Suppliers are an important part of your network—do you know how many people go to work for suppliers? A lot.

SBI: Think through every decision and every action to determine what effect it will have on the customer.

Success in the Reengineered World

We have come a long way together. We've covered the seven key skill areas essential for your survival and success in today's reengineered world: career skills, endurance skills, communication skills, follower skills, leadership skills, team skills, and customer skills.

Now it is up to you. As I suggested at the outset, don't try to do everything at once. Set your priorities and get to work, starting with the area that will do the most for your career. Practice using the methods you learn, and reward yourself for small improvements. When you feel you have made significant progress in one skill, move on to another, and so on until you have taken yourself through all seven skills: a total personal development program.

As you progress, you will gain confidence and the respect of others. You may even find, as many have, that learning and skill development are addictive, and will become lifelong habits.

I have enjoyed sharing my thoughts and ideas with you, and I hope this book will enrich your life, both materially and in terms of the satisfaction and joy you will receive from learning and doing better on the job.

The best of success.

Bibliography

Books, Articles, and Sources of Additional Information

Chapter 1.

Bongiorno, Lori, and Byrne, John A. "The Best B Schools." *Business Week*, October 24, 1994. pp. 62–72.

Bridges, William. *JobShift*. Reading, Mass.: Addison-Wesley, 1994.
A new look at jobs.

Champy, James. *Reengineering Management*. New York: HarperBusiness, 1995.
How to *really* do it. Co-author of *Reengineering the Corporation* takes another look at reengineering and why it hasn't lived up to expectations.

Drucker, Peter F. *Managing in a Time of Great Change*. New York: Truman Talley Books/Dutton, 1995.
It all begins and ends with Drucker. Still giving great insights after all these years.

Hamel, Gary, and Parhalad, C. K. *Competing for the Future*. Cambridge: Harvard Business School Press, 1994.
How to anticipate the future and dominate it.

Chapter 2.

Kiechel, Walter. "Preparing for Your Outplacement." *Fortune*, November 30, 1992, pp. 153–54.

McDermott, Linda. *Caught in the Middle: How to Survive and Thrive in Today's Management Squeeze*. Englewood Cliffs, N.J.: Prentice-Hall/Simon and Schuster, 1992.
Practical advice for today's middle manager. If you are one, you should have this book.

Sheehy, Gail. *New Passages: Mapping Your Life Across Time*. New York: Random House, 1995.
Help for going through life in uncertain times.

Tichy, Noel, and Sherman, Stratford. *Control Your Destiny or Someone Else Will*. New York: Doubleday, 1993.
How Jack Welsh wins allegiance at GE.

Tyson, Eric. *Personal Finance for Dummies.* San Mateo, Calif.: IDG Books, 1994.
 Fun to read, good advice.

Chapter 3.

Gatto, Rex. *Controlling Stress in the Workplace.* San Diego: Pfeiffer and Co., 1993.
 A small, easy-to-read book with many good ideas.
Leatz, Christine. *Career Success/Personal Stress.* New York: McGraw-Hill, 1993.
 Some good suggestions on coping techniques.
Miller, Lyle, et al. *The Stress Solution.* New York: Pocket Books, 1993.
 By three Ph.D. therapists. Good sections on auditing your stress and cop-
 ing techniques.

Chapter 4.

Carnevale, Anthony, and Stone, Susan. "Diversity: Beyond the Golden Rule."
 Training and Development, October 1994, pp. 22–39.
Hammer, Michael, and Champy, James. *Reengineering the Corporation.* New
 York: HarperCollins, 1993.
 A classic on this subject. This is the way it should be done—whether it
 can be done or not is another story.
Jacob, Rahul. "TQM: More Than a Dying Fad?" *Fortune*, October 18, 1993.
Jamieson, David, and O'Mara, Julie. *Managing Workforce 2000: Gaining the
 Diversity Advantage.* San Francisco: Jossey-Bass, 1991.
 A complete guide to managing diversity.
Lewis, Jordan D. *The Connected Corporation: How Leading Companies Win
 Through Customer-Supplier Alliances.* New York: Free Press, 1995.
Main, Jeremy. *Quality Wars: The Triumphs and Defeats of American Business.*
 New York: Free Press, 1994.
 A readable book by a respected journalist. Contains anecdotes on compa-
 nies that have succeeded or failed and lessons to be learned.
Sherman, Stratford. "The Voice Within." *Fortune*, August 22, 1994, pp. 92–100.

Chapter 5.

Covey, Stephen, and Merrill, Roger. *First Things First.* New York: Simon and
 Schuster, 1994.
 350 pages on time management, and much more. If you have time to
 wade through it all, it's good stuff.
Lakein, Alan. *How to Get Control of Your Time and Your Life.* New York:
 Signet, 1973.
 A classic in the time-management field.
McGee-Cooper, Ann. *Time Management for Unmanageable People.* New York:
 Bantam Books, 1993.
 An entertaining book for right-brained people. Good advice; fun to read.

Smith, Hyrum. *The 10 Natural Laws of Successful Time and Life Management*. New York: Warner, 1994.
> More on time and life.

Chapter 6.

Friedman, Joel; Boumil, Marcia; and Taylor, Barbara. *Sexual Harassment: What It Is, What It Isn't, and What You Can Do About It*. Deerfield Beach, Fla.: Health Communications, 1992.
> Many cases and examples.

Garner, James. *Policically Correct Bedtime Stories*. New York: Macmillan, 1994.
> A good read when it all gets too serious.

Petrocelli, William, and Repa, Barbara Katz. *Sexual Harassment on the Job*. Berkeley, Calif.: Nolo Press, 1992.

Chapter 7.

Kotter, John. *The New Rules: How to Survive and Thrive in Today's Post Corporate World*. New York: Free Press, 1995.
> By a Harvard professor. Good information on nontraditional careers. Many pages of homilies.

Nussbaum, Bruce. "Corporate Refugees." *Business Week*, April 12, 1993, pp. 58–65.

Chapter 8.

Bedrosian, Margaret. *Speak Like a Pro*. New York: John Wiley and Sons, 1987.
> Full of good advice. This book will help you.

Blake, Gary, and Bly, Robert. *The Elements of Business Writing*. New York: Macmillan, 1993.
> A short guide to business writing. Clear and direct.

Harris, Richard. "Practically Perfect Presentations." *Training & Development*. July 1994, pp. 55–57.

Strunk, William, and White, E. B. *The Elements of Style*. New York: Macmillan, 1979.
> The classic book on this subject.

Workshop: "Put It in Writing." Widely used and effective. For information, contact the International Writing Institute, 1-800-CLARITY.

Chapter 9.

Kiechel, Walter III. "Learn How to Listen." *Fortune*, August 17, 1987, p. 107.

"Listening to Learn, Learning to Listen." *Info-Line*, published by the American Society for Training and Development, issue 806, 1988.

Merker, Hannah. *Listening*. New York: HarperCollins, 1994.

Nichols, Michael. *The Lost Art of Listening*. New York: Guilford, 1994.

Steil, L. K.; Summerfield, J.; and deMare, G. *Listening: It Can Change Your Life*. New York: John Wiley and Sons, 1983.
> An informative book. Steil was a pioneer in listening training.

Chapter 10.

Bing, Stanley. *Crazy Bosses*. New York: Morrow, 1991.

Bramson, Robert. *Coping with Different Bosses*. New York: Carol Publishing Group, 1992.

Fritz, Roger. *How to Manage Your Boss*. Hawthorne, N.J.: Career Press, 1994.

Hochheiser, Robert. *How to Work for a Jerk*. New York: Vintage, 1987.
> Humor and good advice on managing upward.

Chapter 11.

McLagan, Patricia, and Krembs, Peter. *On-the-Level: Performance Communication That Works*. St. Paul: McLagan International, 1988.
> Feedback methods that make sense, by the expert in the field. Available through McLagan International, (612) 631-2034.

Chapter 12.

Bennis, Warren. *On Becoming a Leader*. Reading, Mass.: Addison-Wesley, 1989.
> Must reading. By a USC professor who has spent years studying leadership.

Covey, Stephen R. *Principle-Centered Leadership*. New York: Fireside, 1990.
> Built on *The 7 Habits of Highly Effective People* (also by Covey) and inspiration from the Bible, this book has insights into management and leadership that will make you think.

de Waal, Frans. *Chimpanzee Politics*. New York: Harper & Row, 1982.
> Lessons from the apes.

Dumaine, Brian. "The New Non-Manager Managers." *Fortune*, February 22, 1993, pp. 80–84.

Hallstein, Richard. *Memoirs of a Recovering Autocrat*. San Francisco: Berrett-Koehler, 1993.
> A personal transition from manager to leader. Useful examples and anecdotes.

Kantor, Rosabeth Moss. *When Giants Learn to Dance: Mastering the Challenge of Strategy, Management, and Careers in the 1990s*. New York: Simon and Schuster, 1989.

Kouzes, James, and Posner, Barry. *Credibility: How Leaders Gain and Lose It, Why People Demand It*. San Francisco: Jossey-Bass, 1993.

Merrill, David, and Reid, Roger. *Personal Styles and Effective Performance*. Radnor, Pa.: Chilton, 1981.
> A good primer on working with the various behavior styles.

Seibert, Donald V. *The Ethical Executive.* New York: Cornerstone Library, 1984.
Written by a former CEO (JCPenney), this book has some good
thoughts on personal values and the importance of moral commitment
to success.

Tannen, Deborah. *How Women's and Men's Conversational Styles Affect Who
Gets Heard, Who Gets Credit, and What Gets Done at Work.* New York:
William Morrow, 1994.

Tichy, Noel, and Sherman, Stratford. "Walking the Talk at GE." *Training &
Development,* June 1993, pp. 25–35.

Wheatley, Margaret. *Leadership and the New Science.* San Francisco: Berrett-
Koehler, 1992.
Lessons in leadership and organization from the world of quantum
physics. Will make you think.

Chapter 13.

Arnold, William. *The Human Touch.* New York: Wiley, 1993.

Klubnik, Joan. *Rewarding and Recognizing Employees.* Burr Ridge, Ill.: Irwin, 1995.
Ideas for individuals, teams, and managers.

Kuczmarski, Susan. *Values-Based Leadership.* Englewood Cliffs, N.J.: Prentice-
Hall, 1994.

LeBoeuf, Michael. *The Greatest Management Principle in the World.* New
York: G. P. Putnam's Sons, 1985.
Short, entertaining book on making people and organizations more
productive.

Chapter 14.

McLagan, Patricia, and Krembs, Peter. *On-the-Level: Performance Communication That Works.* St. Paul: McLagan International, 1988.
Feedback methods that make sense, by the expert in the field. Available
through McLagan International, (612) 631-2034.

Chapter 15.

Goleman, Daniel. *Emotional Intelligence.* New York: Bantam, 1995.
It's not all IQ. Being smart helps, but how you relate to others on the job
today is all-important.

Parker, Glenn. *Cross-Functional Teams: Working with Allies, Enemies and
Other Strangers.* San Francisco: Jossey-Bass, 1994.

Shonk, James. *Team-Based Organizations.* Homewood, Ill.: Business One Irwin, 1992.

Chapter 16.

Doyle, Michael. *How to Make Meetings Work*. New York: Wyden, 1976.
  All-time great book on meetings. Read it.
Frank, Milo. *How to Run a Successful Meeting—In Half the Time*. New York:
  Simon and Schuster, 1989.
  Thoughts and anecdotes on meetings. Fun to read.
Silva, Karen. *Meetings That Work*. Burr Ridge, Ill.: Business One Irwin, 1994.

Chapter 17.

Edwards, Betty. *Drawing on the Right Side of the Brain*. Los Angeles: J. P.
  Tarcher, Inc., 1979.
  It's about drawing, but the lessons in creativity apply anywhere.
Goleman, Daniel; Kaufman, Paul; and Ray, Michael. *The Creative Spirit*. New
  York: Dutton, 1992.
  A beautiful book, colorful, exciting to read, and informative.
Higgins, James. *101 Creative Problem-Solving Techniques*. Winter Park, Fla.:
  New Management Publishing Co., 1994.
Parnes, Sidney J. *Source Book for Creative Problem Solving*. New York: Scrib-
  ner's, 1962.
  An old book, still makes sense.
Prince, George M. *The Practice of Creativity*. New York: Collier Books, 1970.
  A classic in the field, with ideas and methods that are still valid.
Von Oech, Roger. A *Whack on the Side of the Head*. New York: Warner, 1990.
  A creative look at creativity.

Chapter 18.

Albrecht, Karl. *Added Value Negotiating*. Homewood, Ill.: Business One
  Irwin, 1993.
  Albrecht has good advice, as usual.
Anderson, Kare. *Getting What You Want*. New York: Dutton, 1993.
Ury, William. *Getting Past No*. New York: Bantam, 1991.
  From confrontation to cooperation.

Chapter 19.

Bell, Chip. *Customers as Partners*. San Francisco: Berrett-Koehler, 1994.
Blanchard, Kenneth. *Raving Fans*. New York: Morrow, 1993.
Whiteley, Richard. *The Customer Driven Company*. Reading, Mass.: Addison-
  Wesley, 1991.

Index

About the Author

William N. Yeomans is founder and president of The Yeomans Group, Inc., a management consulting firm providing services to large- and medium-sized companies in a wide variety of industries.

Prior to forming the Yeomans Group in 1988, he had many years of experience as a senior executive, including serving as Director of Human Resource Development for JCPenney, where he was responsible for all training and development activities for 200,000 employees at every level in the organization and played a major role in Penney's corporate repositioning.

He was elected the 1988 National President of the American Society for Training and Development, a 50,000-member association of training professionals, and in that capacity worked on many national and global issues.

Yeomans is a recognized authority on management and careers. He has written several books on this subject, including the bestselling *1,000 Things You Never Learned in Business School* (Dutton) and the *JOBS* series. His work has also appeared in the *New York Times, Glamour, Mademoiselle, Training & Development Journal,* and *The Journal of General Psychology.*

He is a frequent speaker at national conventions and at colleges and universities, and has appeared on network television.

Yeomans has an MBA from Cornell University and graduated with honors from Hamilton College. He lives with his family in a 200-year-old converted gristmill in New Jersey.